Need, Risk and Protection in Social Work Practice

Need, Risk and Protection in Social Work Practice

**EDITED BY
STEVE HOTHERSALL
AND
MIKE MAAS-LOWIT**

Series Editors: Jonathan Parker and Greta Bradley

LearningMatters

First published in 2010 by Learning Matters Ltd.
Reprinted in 2011 (twice).

© 2010 George Allan (chapter 10), Amy Clark (chapter 7), Steve J Hothersall (Introduction, chapters 1, 2, 3, 5 and Conclusion), Jackie Loxton (chapter 2), Mike Maas-Lowit (Introduction, chapters 3, 4, 6, 9 and Conclusion), Rory Lynch (chapter 7) and Anne Shirran (chapters 2 and 8).

British Library Cataloguing in Publication Data
A CIP record for this book is available from the British Library.

ISBN: 978 1 84445 252 1

The right of George Allan (chapter 10), Amy Clark (chapter 7), Steve J Hothersall (Introduction, chapters 1, 2, 3, 5 and Conclusion), Jackie Loxton (chapter 2), Mike Maas-Lowit (Introduction, chapters 3, 4, 6, 9 and Conclusion), Rory Lynch (chapter 7) and Anne Shirran (chapters 2 and 8) to be identified as the Authors of this Work has been asserted by them in accordance with the Copyright, Designs and Patents Act 1988.

Cover and text design by Code 5 Design Associates Ltd
Project management by Deer Park Productions, Tavistock, Devon
Typeset by Pantek Arts Ltd, Maidstone, Kent
Printed and bound in Great Britain by the MPG Books Group

Learning Matters Ltd
20 Cathedral Yard
Exeter EX1 1HB
Tel: 01392 215560
info@learningmatters.co.uk
www.learningmatters.co.uk

Dedication

We would like to dedicate this book to our friend and colleague *Amy Clark*, with all best wishes for a long and happy retirement.

Steve, Mike, Jackie, Rory, Anne and George.

Contents

Notes on contributors

Steve J Hothersall is a Senior Lecturer in Social Work at the Robert Gordon University, Aberdeen. He is the author, co-author and co-editor of a number of publications including: *Social work with children, young people and their families in Scotland* (Learning Matters); *Social work and mental health in Scotland* (with Mike Maas-Lowit and Malcolm Golightley: Learning Matters). His main interests are in law, social policy and child care with a special emphasis on attachment theory. He is a founding member of the *International Association for the Study of Attachment* (http://www.iasa-dmm.org/index. php/contact/) and also sits on the Editorial Board of the *British Journal of Social Work*. Steve maintains a practice base as a children's safeguarder and a curator *ad litem*, and in his spare time he indulges his passion for the music of Ludwig van Beethoven.

Mike Maas-Lowit embarked on an initial career in residential childcare in the early 1970s and then in mental health social work. He worked as an Approved Social Worker in the South of England and then as a Mental Health Officer in Scotland, where he still lives and works. He has been involved in the development of MHO training since the mid 1980s and has written material for and advised the Scottish Government on matters in relation to social work, mental health and law. Since 1993, Mike has also been closely involved as a voluntary chair of *Pillar* Aberdeen, a small cutting-edge voluntary agency which offers social support to people whose lives are challenged by poor mental health. He is also co-author (with Steve J Hothersall and Malcolm Golightley) of *Social work and mental health in Scotland*.

George Allan qualified as a social worker in 1976 and has worked primarily with adults. He has held front-line practitioner, planning and management posts in the substance problems field in both the statutory and voluntary sectors. He currently lectures on substance problems issues at The Robert Gordon University. George has a particular interest in the effective implementation of the 'Hidden Harm' agenda.

Amy Clark was a lecturer on the postgraduate Masters Course in social work at the Robert Gordon University for eighteen years and now works part-time as a practice teacher. She trained as a generic social worker and completed her MSc in social gerontology. She worked as a senior social worker responsible for training and education and practice developments and managed several residential establishments and was a registration and inspection officer. Amy has a particular interest in life history assessments, older people's resilience and all aspects of residential care.

Jackie Loxton has been a Lecturer in Social Work at The Robert Gordon University, Aberdeen for the past 13 years. Her practice experience is in the field of mental health and children and families. She is currently Course Leader for the Postgraduate Certificate Mental Health Officer Award. Her particular interests are in the field of mental health, adult support and protection and the involvement of service users in social work education.

Rory Lynch comes from Donegal in Ireland and has been living and working in Scotland for 35 years. He has worked primarily within the fields of single homelessness and mental health where he has carried out international work in the area of the self-evaluation of well-being. He is currently a member of the Distance Learning Programme for Social Work at RGU and has a special interest in Human Growth and Behaviour and Social Work with Older People.

Anne Shirran is a Lecturer in Social Work. Since qualifying as a social worker, Anne has worked in criminal justice both as a field officer and as a prison based social worker and team manager at HMP Peterhead. Prior to taking up her current post, Anne was a Practice Learning Facilitator. Her interests include practice learning and research into effective interventions with offenders.

Introduction

In this book we look at a number of issues central to social work and social care practice in all its manifestations: need, risk and protection. This trinity has a particular focus in twenty-first century social work and social care; so much so that we wrote a book about it, and current practice is replete with references to meeting need, assessing risk and providing protection.

The book is in two parts: in Part One we look at the issues of need, risk and protection from a conceptual perspective: what are these things? What do they mean? What do they look like? We add more depth to this by adding a discussion of the related issues of capacity and incapacity, themes that have been around for centuries but ones that have taken on new life in the last few years as we have developed more sophisticated mechanisms to recognise, assess and respond to their presence and effects.

These interrelated themes and their growth in the world of social work and social care are considered by reference to changes in society, in particular the advent of 'risk' as something of a defining force in all our lives, but particularly in relation to vulnerable people and groups and the nascent sense of 'risk aversion' within professional practice.

Part One offers a tour through these concepts with a range of activities for the reader to undertake in order to help them to start thinking clearly and critically about these issues in an informed way before we look at these in detail within the context of particular areas of social work and social care practice.

Part Two looks at the issues of need, risk and protection in relation to children, young people and their families (Chapter 5), mental health (Chapter 6), older people (Chapter 7), criminal justice social work and probation (Chapter 8), disability (Chapter 9) and substance use (Chapter 10). Each of these chapters provides a range of activities for you to undertake with a focus on particular elements within a specific area of practice. Together, these provide a thorough introduction to the significance of need, risk and protection in social work and social care in the twenty-first century.

Part One

Chapter 1
Need and vulnerability

Steve J Hothersall

ACHIEVING A SOCIAL WORK DEGREE

In this book, both the National Occupational Standards in Social Work and the Scottish Standards in Social Work Education will be referred to.

National Occupational Standards
Key Role 1: Prepare for, and work with, individuals, families, carers, groups and communities to assess their needs and circumstances.
- Work with individuals, families, carers, groups and communities to enable them to analyse, identify, clarify and express their strengths, expectations and limitations.
- Work with individuals, families, carers, groups and communities to enable them to assess and make informed decisions about their needs, circumstances, risks, preferred options and resources.
- Assess and review the preferred options of individuals, families, carers, groups and communities.
- Assess needs, risks and options taking into account legal and other requirements.
- Assess and recommend an appropriate course of action for individuals, families, carers, groups and communities.

Key Role 2: Plan, carry out, review and evaluate social work practice, with individuals, families, carers, groups, communities and other professionals.
- Identify the need for legal and procedural intervention.
- Plan and implement action to meet the immediate needs and circumstances.
- Regularly monitor, review and evaluate changes in needs and circumstances.

Key Role 3: Support individuals to represent their needs, views and circumstances.
- Advocate for, and with, individuals, families, carers, groups and communities.

Key Role 4: Manage risk to individuals, families, carers, groups, communities, self and colleagues.
- Identify and assess the nature of the risk.
- Balance the rights and responsibilities of individuals, families, carers, groups and communities with associated risk.
- Regularly monitor, re-assess, and manage risk to individuals, families, carers, groups and communities.

Key Role 5: Manage and be accountable, with supervision and support, for your own social work practice within your organisation.
- Carry out duties using accountable professional judgement and knowledge-based social work practice.
- Monitor and evaluate the effectiveness of your programme of work in meeting the organisational requirements and the needs of individuals, families, carers, groups and communities.

Key Role 6: Demonstrate professional competence in social work practice.
- Identify and assess issues, dilemmas and conflicts that might affect your practice.
- Devise strategies to deal with ethical issues, dilemmas and conflicts.
- Reflect on outcomes.

continued

3

Achieving A Social Work Degree continued

Scottish Standards in Social Work Education
Key Role 1: Prepare for, and work with, individuals, families, carers, groups and communities to assess their needs and circumstances.
• Assessing needs and options in order to recommend a course of action.

Key Role 2: Plan, carry out, review and evaluate social work practice with individuals, families, carers, groups, communities and other professionals.
• Identifying and responding to crisis situations.
• Working with individuals, families, carers, groups and communities to achieve change, promote dignity, realise potential and improve life opportunities.
• Producing, implementing and evaluating plans with individuals, families, carers, groups, communities and colleagues.
• Developing networks to meet assessed needs and planned outcomes.
• Working with groups to promote choice and independent living.

Key Role 3: Assess and manage risk to individuals, families, carers, groups, communities, self and colleagues.
• Assessing and managing risks to individuals, families, carers, groups and communities.

Key Role 4: Demonstrate professional competence in social work practice.
• Working within agreed standards of social work practice.
• Understanding and managing complex ethical issues, dilemmas and conflicts.

Key Role 5: Manage and be accountable, with supervision and support, for your own social work practice within your organisation.
• Contributing to the management of resources and services.
• Working effectively with professionals within integrated, multi-disciplinary and other service settings.

Key Role 6: Support individuals to represent and manage their needs, views and circumstances.
• Representing, in partnership with, and on behalf of, individuals, families, carers, groups and communities to help them achieve and maintain greater independence.

Introduction

This chapter introduces you to the central concept of *need* in its many guises and helps you to think about these in relation to social work and social care. We shall also consider how need is often treated as a somewhat relativistic concept and one having connections to other themes, including *vulnerability*, *risk* and *protection*.

The chapter draws on a range of ideas from different and sometimes disparate disciplines so that we can begin to think about need more creatively and understand why, within the context of late modern societies, need is very much at the forefront of discussions around welfare, social work and social care practice and how, within human services, the derivations of *vulnerability*, *risk* and *protection* manifest as specific policy and practice-related issues and what relevance and influence these have in terms of your day-to-day practice as a social/care worker.

First, when we talk about 'need(s)', what is it we are in fact referring to? What is a 'need'? What sorts of 'needs' do we have? Do we all have the same needs? Are some needs more important than others and if so, which ones and why these? Who should meet them?

Should we be responsible for ourselves, or does the state have a responsibility towards us, or should it be someone else entirely, such as a family member or a friend who carries that responsibility? If the state is seen as having a role, which it clearly does in the UK, how should it do this? And does this mean that we have a *right* to such provision? Furthermore, any discussion about need presupposes some awareness of what it is we mean when we talk about 'welfare', as need and welfare are inextricably connected and we also have to consider the issue of fairness or social justice (Newman and Yeats, 2008) in terms of how need ought to be responded to.

Definitions, theories and interpretations of need

When beginning to think about any idea, concept or issue, it is often useful to go to the dictionary as a starting point. The *Shorter Oxford English Dictionary* (*SOED*) (OUP, 2007) offers us the following in relation to 'need':

Need:

1 Necessity for a course of action arising from facts or circumstances.

2 Necessity or demand for the presence, possession, etc., of something.

3 A condition or time of difficulty, distress, or trouble; exigency, emergency, crisis.

4 A condition of lacking or requiring some necessary thing, either physically or (now) psychologically; destitution, lack of the means of subsistence or of necessaries, poverty. Now also a condition of requiring or being motivated to do, a necessity to do.

Some of these definitions, especially number 4, will be quite useful to us in understanding what we mean by the term 'need'. So what is a need? In a broad sense it is generally taken to refer to the state that pertains in the absence of something that is deemed to be necessary, usually for the continued and often basic functioning of the organism; it is something which, if not adequately met, is likely to compromise the capacity of the organism to meet other needs and therefore promote and maintain wellbeing and at the extreme, an unmet need may actually threaten survival.

What types of need are there?

We have to think about how we *define* and *describe* need and how and why we *categorise* and *prioritise* it as we do.

Below we look at a number of different interpretations and theories of need and try to establish how meaningful these are in relation to social work/care practice. For example, one way of thinking broadly about this is to list these as *physical* needs, *psychological* needs, *emotional* needs and *social* needs. We could also add *spiritual* needs to this.

Using the categories above, draw up a list of needs that all human beings would share.

Comment

What did you come up with? Your list could potentially be endless, such is the span of human need. However, here is a short, basic, but by no means comprehensive list for you to compare yours with.

Physical = Water, food, shelter, warmth, reproduction.
Psychological = Stimulation, cognitive activity.
Emotional = Love, affection, trust, understanding.
Social = Contact with others, friends.
Spiritual = Communion with others and with one's beliefs

Would you say then that these are some of our *basic* or *primary* needs? In order to claim that this is so, we have to be sure that these are generalisable to *all of us* and that a failure to have these needs met would result in our capacity to function being impaired to the extent that it might result in us being unable to meet other needs and, taken to extremes threaten our very existence. If this is indeed so, this appears to suggest some kind of essential criterion or *hierarchy* regarding (basic) needs and you might also have recognised connections between these differing types of need.

We should also think about whether the distinction between physical, psychological, emotional, social and spiritual needs is 'real' or whether it is too artificial. Could all of the needs to which we have referred be seen as essentially *social*? We could use this sense of the term *social* on the basis that all these needs affect our capacity to be *social beings*, so they are essentially *social* needs. This brings in another dimension: to what extent are our (basic) needs able to be met without reference to society (i.e. other people and structures)? Can an individual meet his or her needs alone or do we need the structure of a society around us to facilitate this? For example, how would you ensure a clean supply of water? Would you have the knowledge and skills necessary to find water (in the absence of taps and bottled water in the shops, which are clearly developments resulting from a long human history of social cooperation)? Would you have the ability to ensure that the water was disease free? How would you guarantee the source? The same would apply to food sources and, particularly, to those needs seen as *psychological* and *emotional,* which depend almost *entirely* for their satisfaction on the availability of others (that is, they are socially oriented).

Some writers would in fact argue that all our realities are socially constructed and socially mediated (Berger and Luckman, 1979; Searle, 1995) including our sense of who we are (Cooley, 1904/1998; Mead, 1934) and how we develop psychologically (Vygotsky, 1978).

Doyal and Gough, citing Nevitt, make the following point:

> *Social needs are demands which have been defined by society as sufficiently important to qualify for social recognition as goods or services, which should be met by government intervention.*

(Nevitt, 1977, p115 in Doyal and Gough, 1991, p10)

We shall consider this point below when we look at the history of need. We shall see that society has generally and for a long, long time deemed that some needs are so important and all encompassing that the most effective way to meet them is to do so *collectively*, via the creation and implementation of *law* and *policy*. However, this is not to imply that such an orientation on the part of the state is necessarily and uniquely driven by benevolence and concern for the masses *per se*. On the contrary, state intervention in relation to social need is one that is often influenced by reference to wider agendas, including those of social control. The history of public policy development in Scotland (Hothersall and Bolger, 2010) and across the UK generally (Fraser, 2009) can clearly be seen to represent state responses to unmet need at particular times and often to reflect the prevailing *zeitgeist* in terms of the particular *form* a policy response to need might take.

Theories and interpretations of need

A hierarchy of human need

This is one theory of human need, developed by the American psychologist Abraham Maslow (1970). Maslow actually spoke of motivation in the sense that it is need that motivates us to do anything and everything. He argued that there are essentially five categories of need, subdivided into two sub-sets (*deficiency* motives or needs and *being* motives or needs), which he saw as being ranked *hierarchically*, as in the 'famous' triangle below (Figure 1.1) with the paramount internal drive being the motivation to achieve one's fullest potential. This ultimate goal was that of 'Self Actualisation' and refers to the satisfaction of the need to understand, to give and to 'grow' as a person. This however can only be achieved if all other lower-order needs have been met.

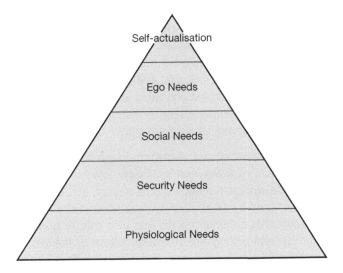

Figure 1.1 Maslow's hierarchy of need

Maslow said that each level of need must be sufficiently satisfied before one can 'progress' upwards to meet the needs on the next level. So, our need for oxygen, food and water, sex (for reproductive purposes only in this regard), sleep and the elimination of waste takes priority over other needs when these arise. We then concern ourselves with ensuring that our 'safety' needs are attended to: being safe, feeling safe. Thereafter, the other needs within each of the levels in turn are attended to. However, we don't consciously think 'I need to meet all my physiological needs this morning, then I can look at the others after lunch'. We simply 'get on with it' until a certain 'need' effectively tells us that it must be met. For example, when you feel tired, you reach a point where you have to *sleep* otherwise your body begins to shut down and the need for sleep cuts across anything else you might be doing at the time, which might be addressing other needs higher up the hierarchy. This base-level need is so crucial to our well-being that it just has to be met and, when that point arises, *nothing else matters*. In relation to level two, the safety needs, these can even be compromised if level one needs are not met. If, for example, you are starving, you will be prepared to compromise your own safety needs by facing considerable danger to obtain food. This is because the need for food is paramount.

You might however be experiencing self-actualisation by listening to the *Arietta* of Beethoven's piano sonata in C minor opus 111, when you learn that the date you had for tonight has been called off. This jeopardises need at the level of 'love and belongingness' and your priority will be to find out why it has been cancelled. Your capacity to concentrate on higher activities to the same extent will be compromised until you have more information.

References to 'lower-levels' of need should not be taken to imply that they are less important. In fact, it could be argued that the contrary is the case and the idea of 'higher-order' and 'lower-order' needs only represents their depiction within a hierarchical structure. As such, they may be (diagrammatically) accurate while actually belying the higher-level *significance* in the broad scheme of things of those needs at lower levels.

In reality, however, there are many people across the world that never get beyond meeting those needs at level one. For example, think about some of the war-torn places we hear about on the news, or some countries where poverty appears to be endemic. In the UK, where absolute poverty is rare, there are many who do not get much beyond the second level. Many people in receipt of social work and social care fall into this group; perhaps homeless, isolated and excluded and there are many people who cannot attend to their own level one needs without assistance: think of someone with motor neurone disease or someone who has a severe learning difficulty.

In the field of social work and social care, many individuals are dependent upon others to help them to meet a number of lower-level needs. For example, someone may not have enough income to provide sufficient food, warmth, shelter, etc. for their family; a young child, exposed to sexual abuse by an adult, may need someone to help them meet safety needs and someone who has experienced the loss of a spouse may need assistance in addressing needs for love and belongingness brought about by the loss. These issues raise the question of *who* should provide this help and *how*? Should it be the state via social work/social care services and if so, what form should this support take? Who should pay for it, and ought it to be a priority for the social work/social services department *relative to their other operational priorities*? The various theories of need and approaches to it described below should help you to think a little more clearly about these things.

A theory of (universal?) human need

Doyal and Gough (1984; 1991) offer two main arguments regarding the issue of need. First, that the concept of need is central to any discussion regarding the role of welfare in contemporary society and second, that as a concept it should be reformulated to ensure that it can be applied to a broad range of contemporary problems. They argue that these activities are essential to act as a counter to New Right Individualism and what they see as a shift away from a *collective* approach to the meeting of human need. For them, there should be agreement on what constitutes *universal needs;* the things that we *all* require in order to be able to function adequately, like adequate water, food and clothing, appropriate shelter and adequate levels of health. Note here though that they do not (or cannot) specify *how much* or the *form* such a requirement should take, as this would be culturally and historically *specific* and therefore *relative*. It is important to think about this because there is a danger of seeing this argument as one based around a certain degree of *absolutism* concerning need. For example, you may be familiar with the work of Townsend (1979) in relation to poverty and his notions of *absolute* and *relative* poverty. The former categorisation was an attempt to identify and fix a rock-bottom level of goods and services which all of us required in order to function; below this level, life is difficult to sustain. Current social security levels (subsistence) are based close to this thinking, as are eligibility criteria for access to services, which we shall consider later. At the broader universal level, it is important to distinguish between *what* is needed and *how much* of it is needed. We can come to some level of agreement regarding the former, but would need to be more relativistic with regards to the latter because of the 'elastic' nature of relative poverty.

Doyal and Gough suggest that basic individual needs relate to those primary goals that must be achieved if an individual is to attain any subsequent goal. In this conception, *survival/health* and *autonomy/learning* are pivotal elements. However, these fundamental needs can only be met if four *social* pre-conditions are present: *production, reproduction, culture/communication* and *political authority*. *Production* refers to the view that any society must make available enough 'need-satisfiers' (for example, water, food, shelter) to ensure minimal levels of health and survival. *Reproduction* is essential to ensure that there are enough people to maintain society. The skills and values regarded as being necessary for production and cultural reproduction must be *communicated* to people, while adherence to the basic rules aimed at promoting and supporting structures designed to uphold well-being and survival are given legitimacy and force via *political authority*. These approaches to thinking about need make it quite clear that both the individual *and* the collective (in the form of society) are necessary components in the satisfaction of need and that this 'duality' is inevitable (Giddens, 1984).

Having the means to identify *what* needs we have, the issue then becomes how these are *satisfied* or met, by whom, in what form and for how long.

A taxonomy of social need

In his seminal paper, Bradshaw (1972) proposed that human need manifests and is defined in certain ways depending upon a number of factors. He does not discuss whether there are universal needs or whether some needs are more important than others *per se*. Instead, he suggests that the ways in which need is dealt with *as a concept* can vary according to who is *experiencing* it and who is *defining* it. Implicit here are *subjective* determinations of what need *is, who* has a need and *how* it should be responded to.

In his opening to the paper, Bradshaw states that:

> *The concept of social need is inherent in the idea of social service. The history of the social services is the story of the recognition of social needs and the organisation of society to meet them.*

(Bradshaw, 1972, p640)

He then goes on to quote from the Seebohm Report (HMSO, 1968) which said that '... the personal social services are large-scale experiments in ways of helping those in need'. This is echoed by TH Marshall (1976) who said that 'Welfare ... is a compound of material means and immaterial ends' (in Timms and Watson, 1976, pp51–2). These comments help us to appreciate that need is ever-present and that as a society we are committed to deal with it *collectively* where we can, assuming that there is some level of agreement on the nature of it. Bradshaw provides us with the following arrangement or *taxonomy*, in which he highlights four conceptions of need.

Normative need: This is what the professional or other person with expertise in an area or subject defines as need in any given situation. This definition would usually be supported by reference to some generally agreed upon standard regarding the need in question. For example, you might be said to be depressed when you reach a particular score on the Beck Depression Inventory (Beck et al., 1961), or you might be said to be in need of nourishment when your weight falls below a set standard. Nowadays, most social work and social services departments have sets of 'eligibility criteria' that are used to determine who is in need such as to merit the delivery of a service. This assessment is usually based on the outcomes of a point-scoring system. For example, if you are 90 years old, live alone, have no family or other social supports and have limited mobility, you are likely to be deemed to be more needy than a 90-year-old living alone with good mobility and good family supports.

Such classifications of need are open to claims of paternalism. The standards to which people refer (and perhaps *defer*) in order to make a judgement may conflict with other normative measures and may also change over time. Eligibility criteria are reviewed regularly and may appear to the recipient to be either more or less generous or facilitative depending on whether the person gets what they think they need. Which leads us on to consider the next category, that of *felt need*.

Felt need In this classification, need is equated with *want*. A person is simply in felt need if they feel themselves to be in need. It is argued that this is usually inadequate as a 'true' measure of need because of the element of subjectivity inherent within the individual. For example, if a person feels a need to own a Rolls Royce car, they are in felt need, regardless of any lack of objective merit of that need.

Expressed need This is felt need turned into action. Here, unmet need is determined by reference to those who are requesting the service. This raises issues about those people who, by themselves are perhaps unable to express their felt need. Therefore, as a measure, it is unreliable unless taken in conjunction with other criteria. For example, an individual with a profound learning disability is unlikely to be able to recognise their need for 24-hour support. Therefore it would be up to professionals to make this claim on the person's behalf.

Comparative need Here, the measure of need is taken by reference to the character-istics of a particular group *who are in receipt of a service* for which they already have an identified need. This measure is then applied to other groups with similar characteristics *who are not in receipt of a service*. These latter groups are then said to be in need, based on this comparison.

A history of need

The issue of need is wrapped up in notions of well-being and *welfare*; in order to be well, in the broad sense, certain needs have to be met consistently. If some needs are not met, we will fail to achieve that standard of well-being that allows us to function effectively as a human being within our particular milieu. As we have seen, there are some individ-uals and groups who for many reasons are unable to meet certain of their own needs without help from others. These 'others' might be the family or friends of those fortunate enough to have them. For those who have no such naturally occurring supports, it has to be the comfort of strangers that they rely upon. Often this reliance takes the form of vari-ous institutions of the state specifically set up and designed to address such situations of unmet need.

Over the course of history, it has been acknowledged that there are certain commodities to which everyone requires access. One of the most efficient and effective ways of ena-bling this has been via a collective and centralised effort, organised in a democracy by those elected to govern; in essence, the state. As such, any discussion of how the state responds collectively to need involves us thinking about the role of *law* and *social policy* (*see* Hothersall and Bolger, 2010 and Fraser, 2009).

The Poor Laws implemented across the UK from *circa* the sixteenth century can be seen as early attempts by the state to regulate social life as a response to the potential for social unrest. History tells us that state intervention, in whatever historical form, has frequently arisen as a response to the threat of social disorder, often because of disquiet in the popu-lace generated by unmet need. In this instance, state involvement, as a means of meeting social need while simultaneously minimising the likelihood of social unrest, manifested itself as the provision of *poor relief* to those who could not work.

From a Scottish perspective, the Act of 1579 remained the basis of Scots Poor Law, with minor amendments in 1597 and 1672, until the passing of the Poor Law (Scotland) Act 1845. These early arrangements were essentially church-based, drawing funds from Kirk donations (Cage, 1981). However, as secularisation increased and committed churchgoers decreased, this compromised the capacity of the Kirk to finance the system.

In England, the Poor Law Act of 1601 (referred to as 'The 43rd of Elizabeth') legitimised a distinction between three groups of poor. The *impotent poor* (the elderly, the sick, the disa-bled, etc.) were those to be housed in the poorhouses or almshouses and given relief (or support), because it was acknowledged that they were *unable* (not *unwilling*) to meet their own needs. The *able-bodied poor* were to be forced to work, and later allowed to reside in the workhouses. The *idle poor*, who were seen as those who could work but refused to, were placed in 'corrective' sections of the workhouses and punished. This is perhaps one of the first publicly and officially articulated descriptions of different categories of people who, according to the state, had different needs and therefore had different types of *eligibility* for assistance or services from the state.

Modern social policy is invariably aligned to the *Industrial Revolution* (a phrase coined by one of the great nineteenth century reformers, Arnold Toynbee), where vast numbers of people began living and working together in close proximity to each other in the developing industrial centres of production. This generated a number of challenges for the governments of the day, who had to respond to the changing needs of the population. This included increasing concerns over poor public health and sanitation, squalor, disease (especially cholera), ignorance, air pollution, industrial injury and deaths and the increasing use of children for labour. Control of the situation was needed. A series of rules was required within which social life could operate to the benefit of the economy of industrial production.

For many commentators, the new Poor Law of 1834 is seen as the starting point for the modern history of social policy, although any discussion of such issues must acknowledge that similar centralised responses had been evident in earlier epochs, because (as we have seen) the effects of industrialisation were no different to those of earlier social phenomena in Elizabethan times: the effects of enclosures and other agrarian-based issues caused similar difficulties in their time and had themselves necessitated collectively centralised responses. Any contemporary discussion of social policy has to have some reference to history. This is necessary because modern social life is clearly a product of the past.

> *History is not a recipe book; past events are never replicated in the present in quite the same way ... [However] ... We can learn from history how past generations thought and acted, how they responded to the demands of their time and how they solved their problems. We can learn by analogy, not by example, for our circumstances will always be different than theirs were. The main thing history can teach us is that human actions have consequences and that certain choices, once made, cannot be undone. They foreclose the possibility of making other choices and thus they determine future events.*
>
> (Lerner, 1997, pp199–213 quoted in Hendrick, 2005, p11)

To the above we can also add that human *inaction* can have much the same effect.

By the turn of the twentieth century, a number of laws and policy initiatives had emerged, all of which sought to address many of the ills of late Victorian society resulting from the expansion of labour under capitalism. These included improvements in arrangements concerning child labour, the development of a hospital system, which grew from the earlier introduction, and subsequent expansion of poor-law hospitals and improvements to public health (legislated for from 1848). The Liberal reforms (1905–1914) were the beginnings of growing social awareness.

The inter-war years, a period of massive social change, saw further developments in relation to policy, particularly with regard to unemployment and national health insurance. The Second World War, as a *total war*, tended to reduce social distinctions and increase social mobility and the persistence of child poverty and widespread poor nutrition served as a wake-up call for the nation. The coalition government during the war years introduced a range of measures including the Determination of Needs Act 1941, which abolished the dreaded Household Means Test. Other measures introduced from

1940 included free school meals and milk for all school children, free milk for mothers and babies and a wide-ranging programme of free immunisations (especially against diphtheria, which actually killed more children than bombs). The post-war reconstruction was central to the thoughts of most people at the time and, in some respects, the cessation of World War II provided a platform for a number of important social reforms.

The *Beveridge Report* (Beveridge, 1942) was published in December 1942. It was this that identified 'the five giant ills' of society (want, disease, ignorance, squalor and idleness). Want was targeted by national schemes and systems of social insurance and social security. Disease was to be targeted by a national health service offering free health care to all. Compulsory education for children targeted ignorance while squalor was to be addressed through a national programme of house building by local authorities, with particular attention to public health matters. Finally, a system of labour exchanges and allowances to deal with unemployment was intended to address idleness.

The period from 1951 to the advent of the tenure of Margaret Thatcher as Prime Minister in 1979 is seen as the last great period of welfare consensus. From an ideological perspective, all political parties during this time tended to agree that state intervention in certain areas of private life, along with the public regulation of large sectors of the economy should be the norm. Many previously privately-run amenity services were brought into state ownership by nationalisation. Such a position tended to eclipse the usual ideological positions adopted by the respective political parties. However, this tradition of liberal ideas came to a halt when Mrs Thatcher came to power and adopted a neo-liberal approach to policymaking and welfare, which emphasised the role of the free market, the value of individualism and a minimal role for state intervention.

The history of need is also the history of welfare, which is not a modern idea even if the term itself is. What the above illustrates is that for thousands of years there has been a role for *collective action* in meeting human need. As society has become more complex, it has become more sophisticated in terms of how this is done. Social work and social care practices are fundamentally designed to assist in the identification and meeting of need within a broad socio-political and organisational context.

Perspectives on welfare

What should be the role and purpose of welfare? In the welfare literature, we can identify five interrelated perspectives that offer different understandings of human nature and the relationship between individuals and the state. Deacon (2002) summarises these as follows.

Welfare as an expression of altruism This perspective sees one of the primary functions of welfare as being to *redistribute* resources and opportunities in order that this might create a sense of mutual obligation and help, thus providing a broad framework for the expression of altruism. This perspective is focused upon the issues of *inequality* and is more concerned than the other perspectives (below) with the identification and measurement of social need.

Some of the key elements of this perspective on welfare include the view that state benefits should be seen as being no different from other forms of benefits such as occupational benefits or tax relief and that all benefits should be non-means tested, offered without prejudice and perceived as being but one route to utilising the resources of the state to assist individuals in fulfilling their own potential.

This approach to welfare is to effectively overlook any attempt to explain poverty by reference to the behaviour of the poor themselves. In its rejection of an individualistic account of poverty, where the question of whether people's own behaviour represents some meaningful choice in relation to explaining why they may be poor, it becomes focused upon broad structural factors, perhaps at the expense of considering any role of and for human agency.

In some respects the avoidance of these issues left this perspective open to criticism and to subsequent challenges from conservative and neo-liberal welfare ideologies, in which a strong individualist approach took hold. This was particularly the case when welfare spending continued to increase. In its wake, critics of altruism promoted the development of the notion of 'welfare dependency' and the alternative perspectives below have all developed as a critique of this one.

Welfare as a channel for the pursuit of self-interest In this approach, the baseline assumption is that the majority of people will act rationally to further their own self-interest and that of their dependents, the objective of any welfare system being to channel such behaviours in ways that promote the common good. In order for such an approach to be effective, entitlements to common resources should *reward* those behaviours and attributes that promote the common good and *penalise* those that do not. A simple example might be a system where those actively seeking work are rewarded by a higher benefit payment that those who refuse to seek work. As Deacon comments:

> [W]elfare policies cannot attain their ends by coercion; nor can they rely on appeals to altruism. All they can do is create a framework that channels the individual pursuit of self-interest (p48).

Welfare as the exercise of authority In this approach, the baseline assumption is that the poor are poor because they do not/cannot respond to opportunities for improvement or advancement because of inherent flaws in their own characters. Therefore, the solutions are to be found in the exercise of authority, not in the development of progressive frameworks that encourage self-motivation. In order to do this, any entitlement to welfare should be conditional upon people behaving in certain, prescribed ways. This approach aims to force the poor to discharge their obligations towards the common good by getting paid work and contributing to the economy which generates more resources for all. This addresses their obligations as citizens. The perspective has little in the way of sympathy for the potentially stigmatising effects of welfare programmes as stigma would be seen as a form of perverse incentive.

Welfare as a transition to work This perspective argues that welfare, in the form of cash benefits, should not be overly generous, as generosity was seen to undermine incentives to work. In many respects, this perspective adopts the principle of *less eligibility,* very common in the era of the Poor Laws, whereby the rate of state benefit was never to be greater than that of the lowest paid worker. Benefit and state assistance should be seen as temporary and as a bridge between unemployment and paid work.

Welfare as a mechanism for moral regeneration This view would similarly see welfare as temporary and as something to be avoided because the ultimate aim of everyone is to *contribute* to the common good, rather than just drawing from the common pool of resources. There is a strong moral stance here, which assumes that the receipt of welfare is something to be avoided, because of the stigma attached to it and assumptions made about those in receipt of it (Deacon, 2002, pp1–2).

The above perspectives have different ways of viewing the role that welfare should have in relation to meeting particular needs. They offer differing accounts of, and differing emphases upon, the role of the individual and the role of society in relation to the creation of need. They also differ in approaching how the state ought to respond to need: by reference to the role of the collective or by reference to the role of the individual. They present differing views as to *what should be,* rather than offering an analysis of *what is.*

Need and social work

As a social worker the issue of need is something you will be dealing with every day. It is related to issues such as vulnerability, risk and protection, which we cover elsewhere in this chapter and other parts of the book. So, what is the connection between need and social work? Essentially, social work (and other forms of social care) is about meeting people's needs on behalf of the state. This might be in the form of statutory social work services delivered to children and their families, including child care and protection services (Hothersall, 2008; Frost and Parton, 2009), services to those with mental illness and those who may be vulnerable and in need because of incapacity (Hothersall, Mass-Lowit and Golightley, 2008; Gould, 2009; Johns, 2007) and those people with other forms of disability or impairment (Bigby and Frawley, 2009; Oliver, 2009; Kristiansen, Vehmas and Shakespeare, 2008). These services would be seen as being focused upon addressing individual need, whereas other services have a focus on the needs of the wider community and the general populace, such as criminal justice services. Social workers who work for a local authority (a statutory agency) will also be involved in delivering non-statutory social work services, as will those social workers employed by private or voluntary organisations. There is no essential difference in relation to the issues they are trying to address in meeting need, but some services are *statutory* in that they are mandated by statute (law). Often those are the services that are given priority, usually because they have as their focus the most vulnerable people in society, or because the consequences to individuals, groups, communities and society at large of not addressing certain needs via the delivery of these services could be severe.

ACTIVITY 1.2

Look at the list below and make a note of any needs you feel which might arise because of the particular situation or condition. How might these impair or otherwise affect a person's well-being and/or their functioning? Then consider who should be responsible for meeting the needs you identify.

Schizophrenia	*Type 1 Diabetes*	*Racist abuse*
Poor housing	*Severe learning disability*	*Child sexual abuse*
Heroin addiction	*Alzheimer's disease*	*Homelessness*
Stroke	*Unemployment*	*Poverty*
Alcoholism	*Migration to the UK*	

You may have thought that some of these needs have different causes *and, where the cause is seen to lie with the individual concerned, this may have influenced how you responded to the questions above. Was that the case?*

Comment

Within social work and social services generally, the aim is to respond to unmet need as it arises. This aspirational goal is enshrined in legislation. However, we have to consider first whether it is in fact possible to meet *all* unmet needs and second whether it is the responsibility of the *state* to do this.

In response, we have to consider which needs have priority over others and whether these needs are primary to the goal of allowing people to meet other, less essential needs themselves. Such is the issue of primary needs, secondary needs and wants, as discussed above. In terms of whether the state should be the prime agent of meeting need, consideration has to be given here to the role and influence of *ideology* and *economics*.

Ideology refers to a set of underpinning ideas and values that inform thought, language and subsequent action. In relation to social policy, these *ideologies of welfare* are indicative of the role the state should play in relation to public and private life (Taylor, 2007). They therefore represent manifestations of political ideologies which, broadly speaking, run along a continuum from the *left* to the *right*. According to Heywood (2003):

> *An ideology is a more or less coherent set of ideas that provides the basis for organised political action, whether this is intended to preserve, modify or overthrow the existing system of power. All ideologies therefore ... offer an account of the existing order, usually in the form of a 'world view' (and) advance a model of a desired future, a vision of the 'good society'... and explain how political change can and should be brought about ... (p12).*

Classifying ideology

There are many ways in which ideology can be classified, but the two below should help to clarify matters.

Left ─────────────────➤ Centre ──────────────────➤ Right
(Collectivists ──────────➤ Reluctant Collectivists ──────────➤ Anti-Collectivists)

This simplistic arrangement shows those on the left as being pro-welfare and in favour of the public provision of services. The left also prefer a collectivist model of provision that applies to all, as well as viewing welfare as having an institutional base (i.e. that welfare provision is the business of the state).

Those on the right of the spectrum are generally opposed to state welfare provision and favour an individualistic (or anti-collectivist) approach and a free-market economy. Welfare provision for times of need is seen as something for which individuals make their own arrangements (for example private pension schemes).

These positions have many variants, from strong to weak. Those positions occupying the centre ground are those that see a mixed economy as being viable and permissible within certain limitations: see Figure 1.2.

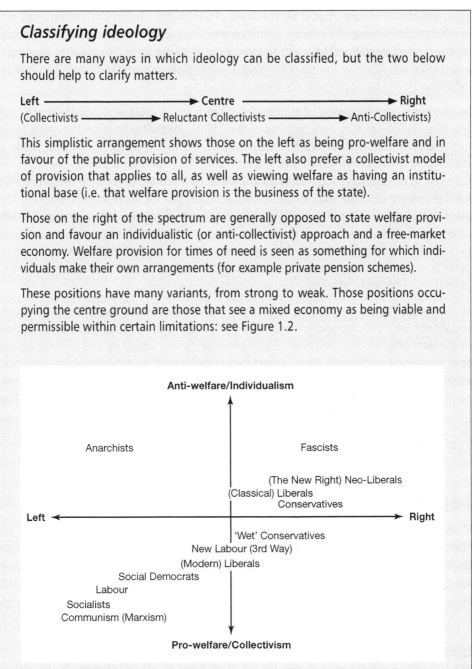

Figure 1.2 Typologies of welfare

These typologies work because of 'ideal types'. Within the extreme positions, we can see what appear to be inconsistencies. For example, fascism would see no place for outright dependence and the claims by Russia for the adoption of communism based upon Marx would by some be seen to be untrue. Perhaps however we should think about the need for a clear *ideology of welfare* rather than welfare as a concept and as a practice based simply upon the prevailing ideology of the time?

Thus, whether the state should be the main player in the meeting of certain individual needs depends among other things upon the prevailing ideology; a more left-wing, social-ist government would probably aim to have a broad-based system in place to respond to and meet need, whereas a more right-wing, individualistic government might feel that the individual should be responsible for these things.

In relation to the relevance of *economics*, from a social work and social services per-spective, the community care reforms of the 1980s, following hard on the heels of the neo-liberal policies of the Thatcher Government, led to the introduction of a mode of social work provision which had economics at its forefront: *care management*. In this mode of service delivery, social workers and other care professionals were responsible not for the *delivery* of social work or social care services, but for assessing and devising care plans that were economically viable. This viability rests upon delivery by a provider who offers the best value and is seen as being more cost-effective. This heralded the introduc-tion of what many see as the 'social work business' (see Harris, 2002), with the emphasis upon business models as a means by which social work and social care services could be provided as effectively, efficiently and economically as possible.

While it would be folly to assume that money grows on trees and that the cost of services should not be a consideration, it could be argued that human need has been sacrificed at the altar of economics and that service providers (state, voluntary and private) have as their focus 'best (economic) value', sometimes at the cost of 'best human value'. It is inter-esting to note that over the last fifteen years or so, there has been a growth in both the number and the *complexity* of eligibility criteria devised by service providers which effec-tively ranks need from 'essential' to 'low' priority and accords services to those at the top of the list, usually determined by reference to conceptions of *normative* and *comparative* need which are clearly seen to be relative concepts.

Legislative and policy responses to need

If we take a look at a range of statutes, for example the Mental Health Acts of 1983 and 2007 (England and Wales), the Mental Health (Care & Treatment) (Scotland) Act 2003 and the Mental Health (Northern Ireland) Order 1986, the Adults with Incapacity (Scotland) Act 2000 and the Mental Capacity Act 2005 (England and Wales), the Adult Support & Protection (Scotland) Act 2007, the Children Acts of 1989 and 2006 (England and Wales), the Children (Scotland) Act 1995 and the Children (Northern Ireland) Order 1995 to high-light just several examples, we see that they make provision to deal with particular broad categories of need which are seen to arise as a result of mental disorder, incapacity, risk of harm arising out of a range of conditions in adulthood, such as infirmity of old age and immaturity in childhood. You have already completed an exercise where you have looked at the types of needs that might arise because of a particular situation or condition; these laws take as their starting point the collective wisdom in relation to a range of broad conditions and states of being and they create general frameworks within which specific needs can be located and the provisions of the law can then be applied proactively and more individualistically to afford care, treatment and/or protection. The chapters in Part 2 of this book look at law and policy in more detail.

ACTIVITY **1.3**

Think of the types of needs that might arise because:

(a) you are a child;
(b) you have a mental illness;
(c) you have some form of incapacity (for example, arising out of dementia or a physical disability which makes you completely unable to communicate);
(d) you are in extreme old age, with poor health, fading eyesight and hearing.

Do particular needs associated with these states of being bring with them an increased likelihood or risk of harm or vulnerability? If so, think about why this might be and what sort of harms might arise.

Comment

All humans are *vulnerable*. When we speak of vulnerability, what is it we are referring to and are there some individuals and groups in society that are more vulnerable than others? If so, who are they and what is it that makes them more vulnerable than the rest of us? If we again turn to the dictionary, we get the following definitions:

> *vulnerability (noun): the state or quality of being vulnerable.*
> *vulnerable (adjective): able to be wounded; (of a person) able to be physically or emotionally hurt; liable to damage or harm, especially from aggression or attack; assailable*

(SOED, 2007)

These definitions offer us a general sense of the notion of vulnerability, but it could well be argued that such definitions apply to all of us *all of the time* but, in a greater degree, only to some of us *most of the time*. This is an important distinction and one that we shall elaborate on to help us to understand the relevance and significance of special measures to protect those who may fall into the latter category. Kottow (2003) states that [*V*]*ulnerability is a human condition from which we all suffer, and because of its universality we all agree that equal protection is due to every member of society* (p461). He refers here of course to those actions by the state designed to afford all of us a level of basic security via social protection underpinned by reference to social justice, for example, public health, individual health care, protection from violence and other forms of aggression, etc. Kottow then goes on to say that there are people within society for whom such basic or standard measures are *not enough because many individuals suffer from some sort of deprivation that predisposes them to additional and compound forms of harm*, and this he refers to as 'a state of *susceptibility*' (p462–emphasis added). This notion of deprivation refers to disability, immaturity, illness or any other condition or state of being that increases the potential for suffering harm.

Hurst (2008) suggests a broader definition of vulnerability, referring to the *increased potential that one's interests cannot be protected* (Hurst citing Agrawal, 2003, pp194–5). Hurst proposes that vulnerability equates with *an identifiably increased likelihood of incurring additional or greater wrong* (p195). The particular reason for this increased likelihood or susceptibility is not specified, which is correct as to try to do so would lead to a very long list indeed. Rather, the issue would appear to hinge upon the use of professional judgement, moral character and professional assessment skills to determine, at an individual or group level, those factors likely to increase one's vulnerability beyond what might be expected to be normative and to apply judgement in the use of resources to minimise this increased susceptibility to harm. These resources may be external and material or may well be internal resources of the individual or group; for example an increased sense of self-efficacy and other resilience factors.

C H A P T E R   S U M M A R Y

This chapter has considered the issue of need in its many guises and taken you through a number of differing interpretations of this contested concept. We have also considered how the idea of need is tied to time, space, people and power in how it is defined and operationalised. These ideas form the basis of much welfare provision and we have also looked at how differing political ideologies can effect whether and how welfare in its various forms is delivered.

From the perspective of practice, we have seen how different conceptions of need can be affected by the use of certain and sometimes specific criteria to de-limit service provision, and we have also looked at how certain conditions and states-of-being can generate different sorts of need and what the role of the state is in relation to these and we have looked at some of the laws and policies that exist to help with this.

This chapter has offered an account of one of the three main themes in this book, need, risk and protection, and Chapters two and three will now focus on these other related areas.

FURTHER READING

Doyal, L and Gough, I (1991) *A theory of human need.* Basingstoke: The Macmillan Press.
This is an in-depth account of the issue of human need and how it might be addressed.

Lowe, R (2005): *The welfare state since 1945.* Basingstoke: Palgrave Macmillan.
This books looks at a number of key issues and has a useful focus on the effects of the market on welfare provision in the UK.

Rodger, JR (2000) *From a welfare state to a welfare economy.* Basingstoke: Palgrave Macmillan.
This useful text considers the apparent shift away from a collective approach to welfare and well being to one where the focus is more upon individuals to provide this.

Chapter 2
Risk

Jackie Loxton, Anne Shirran and Steve J Hothersall

A C H I E V I N G   A   S O C I A L   W O R K   D E G R E E

National Occupational Standards

Key Role 1: Prepare for, and work with, individuals, families, carers, groups and communities to assess their needs and circumstances.

- Review case notes and other relevant material.
- Liaise with others to access additional information that can inform initial contact and involvement.
- Evaluate all information to identify the best form of initial involvement.
- Work with individuals, families, carers, groups and communities to identify, gather, analyse and understand information.
- Work with individuals, families, carers, groups and communities to enable them to analyse, identify, clarify and express their strengths, expectations and limitations.
- Work with individuals, families, carers, groups and communities to enable them to assess and make informed decisions about their needs, circumstances, risks, preferred options and resources.
- Assess needs, risks and options taking into account legal and other requirements.
- Assess and recommend an appropriate course of action for individuals, families, carers, groups and communities.

Key Role 2: Plan, carry out, review and evaluate social work practice, with individuals, families, carers, groups, communities and other professionals.

- Plan and implement action to meet the immediate needs and circumstances.
- Work with individuals, families, carers, groups, communities and others to avoid crisis situations and address problems and conflict.
- Carry out your own responsibilities and monitor, co-ordinate and support the actions of others involved in implementing the plans.

Key Role 3: Support individuals to represent their needs, views and circumstances.

- Prepare reports and documents for decision-making forums.
- Present evidence to, and help individuals, families, carers, groups and communities to understand the procedures of and the outcomes from, decision-making forums.
- Enable individuals, families, carers, groups and communities to be involved in decision-making forums.

Key Role 4: Manage risk to individuals, families, carers, groups, communities, self and colleagues.

- Identify and assess the nature of the risk.
- Balance the rights and responsibilities of individuals, families, carers, groups and communities with associated risk.
- Regularly monitor, re-assess, and manage risk to individuals, families, carers, groups and communities.

continued

Achieving A Social Work Degree continued

- Assess potential risk to self and colleagues.
- Work within the risk assessment and management procedures of your own and other relevant organisations and professions.
- Plan, monitor and review outcomes and actions to minimise stress and risk.

Key Role 5: Manage and be accountable, with supervision and support, for your own social work practice within your organisation.

- Manage and prioritise your workload within organisational policies and priorities.
- Use professional and managerial supervision and support to improve your practice.

Key Role 6: Demonstrate professional competence in social work practice.

- Review and update your own knowledge of legal, policy and procedural frameworks.
- Use professional and organisational supervision and support to research, critically analyse, and review knowledge-based practice.
- Implement knowledge-based social work models and methods to develop and improve your own practice.
- Exercise and justify professional judgements.

Scottish Standards in Social Work Education

Key Role 1: Prepare for, and work with, individuals, families, carers, groups and communities to assess their needs and circumstances.

- Assessing needs and options in order to recommend a course of action.

Key Role 2: Plan, carry out, review and evaluate social work practice with individuals, families, carers, groups, communities and other professionals.

- Identifying and responding to crisis situations.
- Producing, implementing and evaluating plans with individuals, families, carers, groups, communities and colleagues.
- Tackling behaviour which presents a risk to individuals, families, carers, groups, communities and the wider public.

Key Role 3: Assess and manage risk to individuals, families, carers, groups, communities, self and colleagues.

- Assessing and managing risks to individuals, families, carers, groups and communities.
- Assessing and managing risk to self and colleagues.

Key Role 4: Demonstrate professional competence in social work practice.

- Evaluating and using up-to-date knowledge of, and research into, social work practice.
- Working within agreed standards of social work practice.
- Understanding and managing complex ethical issues, dilemmas and conflicts.
- Promoting best social work practice, adapting positively to change.

Key Role 5: Manage and be accountable, with supervision and support, for your own social work practice within your organisation.

- Working effectively with professionals within integrated, multi-disciplinary and other service settings.

Key Role 6: Support individuals to represent and manage their needs, views and circumstances.

- Representing, in partnership with, and on behalf of, individuals, families, carers, groups and communities to help them achieve and maintain greater independence.

Introduction

In this chapter we will explore what is meant by risk in relation to social work and social care practice. Generic aspects of risk assessment and risk management will also be discussed with the aim of enabling you to begin to think your way through this complex area.

In recent years, risk assessment and risk management have come to dominate the fields of social work and social care with the expectation being that social workers will meet need while ensuring that those deemed to be at risk, be they individuals or the public at large, are afforded protection (see Chapter 3). What this means is that social work continues to grapple with the issues of 'care' versus 'control' that lie at the heart of practice. This duality has almost always existed but has recently been brought into sharp relief as the demand for greater accountability in the public sector has increased and media scrutiny continues to surround the perceived 'failures' of social work (Scottish Executive, 2004; Laming, 2009).

What is risk?

Within social work and social care, a major component of the work undertaken with service users revolves around the assessment and management of risk and there are a number of definitions for the term depending upon the service user group being referred to. Much has been written about the concept of risk and how over time this has developed from thinking about vague notions of 'chance' to using a more scientific approach to predict the likelihood of a particular event or behaviour. This emphasis on the 'appliance of science' to calculate risk is based on a number of factors. But before we can measure risk, we have to define what it is and in what context it is being considered and measured. Ayto (2005) identifies the word risk as originating from the Italian word 'risco' which was associated with gambling during the seventeenth century. Blackburn (2000, p177) suggests *Risk generally refers to the possibility of loss or costs when an outcome is uncertain, but in clinical and criminal justice settings, it means the **chance of an adverse outcome*** (emphasis in original). Nowadays, risk tends to carry negative connotations and as such has perhaps led to the social work profession becoming more risk averse. Carson and Bain (2008) suggest that risk is:

> *an occasion when one or more consequences (events, outcomes and so on) could occur. Critically (a) those consequences may be harmful and/or beneficial and (b) either the number and/or the extent of those consequences, and/or their likelihood, is uncertain and/or unknown* (p242).

Generally, when we discuss risk, we are looking at two very different things at the same time. In the first instance we might talk of the chance or probability that something is going to happen, but then the outcome could be a bad or undesirable thing. The word 'chance' is relatively neutral whereas the word 'risk' tends to be more emotive and laden with connotations of harm, damage and unpleasantness. So if we go to cross a road, do we consider this to be 'risky' because there is a chance we might be knocked down?

ACTIVITY **2.1**

Risk in everyday life

Think about the term risk as referred to above and make a list of the 'risks' you take every day. For each example, make a note of the particular factors or elements of the situation that are the potential source of the risk. Were these elements generally positive things or were your thoughts mainly on the potentially bad things that could happen?

Comment

Daily living can be a risky business and much of our time is spent negotiating situations where there is a chance of something good or bad happening although most daily living activities such as making a cup of tea or crossing the road are well rehearsed situations where we anticipate little possibility of harm. Other types of activities, however, carry a higher risk of something negative happening – extreme sports or financial dealing on the stock market. The focus in these activities is on the chance or possibility of something *good* happening with the resulting rewards even though there may be serious consequences should something negative happen.

You will see from the above discussion that already we are in the realms of discussing how we calculate the probability of positive or negative outcomes and how we attempt to weigh up the possible or likely consequences, not only in relation to ourselves, but also in relation to other people, particularly family, friends and those closest to us. Essentially, the processes you have just engaged in are those of risk assessment.

The historical context of risk

Risk developed as a social construct during early modernity (*circa* nineteenth century) as probability, calculation and statistical evaluation became more prominent (Bernstein, 1997). This change in the construction of risk demonstrated the move away from previous notions of 'natural' dangers such as floods or other disasters, which were held during the Middle Ages to result not from human error or responsibility but from the laws of nature, to recognition of the role of human agency in terms of the potential for risk. The transition into modernity and our increasing knowledge about the world and how it operates clearly places the concept of risk within the broader context of human behaviour.

The term 'risk society' emerged during the 1990s to describe a society that is organised in response to risk. The term is closely associated with several key writers, in particular Anthony Giddens (1990) and Ulrich Beck (1992) who suggest that the advent of the risk society is conceptualised in a particular way by both politicians and social scientists and

> *designates a developmental phase of modern society in which social, political, economic and individual risks tend to escape the institutions for monitoring and protection in society.*
>
> (Beck, 1992, p5)

Our quest, according to Beck, has become to systematically strive to prevent or minimise all risks. This may be seen in relation to interventions regarding economics, health and the environment with policies reflecting the belief that through systems of regulation and accountability we can control and regulate it (Cooper, Hetherington and Katz, 2003), although an over-reliance on mechanised risk assessment procedures may lead to risk aversion. The emphasis on developing systems of regulation and accountability has become increasingly evident in organisational structures with an emphasis on procedures and audit. Hood, Rothstein and Baldwin (2001) suggest that these differing approaches to risk and risk taking are likely to be more evident in those policy areas that are more susceptible to influence by public outcries and media scrutiny while Furedi (2002) suggests that risk taking has lost its positive connotations and is now primarily associated with negative outcomes, hence the tendency to minimise and, where possible, avoid it. Furedi claims *cleansing the term accident from our cultural narrative inexorably leads to a relentless search for someone to blame* (2002, p11).

In the early twentieth century risk began to be constructed around and increasingly equated with danger and dangerousness. This conception was largely attributable to prevailing notions of the dangerous 'underclasses' within society (usually the poor and the working classes) rather than particular conceptions of dangerous individuals (Pratt, 2000) and as such led to a rise in the level of social controls put in place to reduce the perceived risks posed by this 'dangerous' underclass.

While the original meaning of risk therefore related to the calculation of the probability of outcomes both positive and negative, within social work the term has latterly come to be associated with negative consequences and dangerousness.

Contemporary views of risk

Risk is not a new phenomenon but the language used to refer to it and the way it is constructed *has* changed. Much of this has been in direct response to serious incidents where someone has been harmed and political and professional labelling, often influenced by media coverage, affects the way in which the concept is framed and subsequently articulated in policy. Words and phrases such as 'dangerousness', 'seriousness', 'harm', 'uncertainty' and 'likelihood of negative outcomes' are now synonymous with risk. Stalker (2003) considers that risk is likely to be referred to as different things in relation to different groups: as *vulnerability* in relation to older people and those with learning disabilities; as *dangerousness* in relation to offenders and some users of mental health services and as *significant harm* in relation to children (see Chapter 5), although the conceptualisation of risk in social work as being principally concerned with harm or adverse outcomes needs to be understood within the wider social context.

Risk can be characterised in different ways. According to Walker and Beckett (2004, p42) if it is seen within a 'risk control perspective', risk is framed as a negative thing constituting a threat or a danger. In this conception the emphasis is upon professional responsibility to identify the level of risk and to develop strategies to eliminate it. Alternatively, if risk can be located within a 'risk taking perspective', where risk is viewed positively with an emphasis on its role in relation to self-determination and empowerment, this can lead to very different outcomes. Central to each of these approaches is the capacity of the social worker to identify potential risk factors alongside those protective factors that might offset the risk of harm or provide opportunities for growth, all of which is predicated on the effective use of professional judgement, which becomes an essential ingredient in determining risk levels and how these might be reduced and/or managed.

How we view and understand risk is located within a broader social context that has become increasingly complex and uncertain. Carson and Bain (2008) refer to the issue of uncertainty and suggest that it *is a dimension, not an element of risk taking* (p19). At times it might be possible to exert some control over the degree of uncertainty; however this is likely to be determined by the overall context within which this is being calculated. An understanding of the role of uncertainty is necessary when working within complex situations as it may inform and influence the *margin of error* (p19). Uncertainty occurs as a result of the myriad of factors within a given situation including the behaviour of individuals, their personality traits and a wide range of other external influences all of which reduce the accuracy of any assessment being undertaken because uncertainty represents that which cannot necessarily be foreseen.

The 'risk society' and risk aversion

Definitions of risk are contested, indicative of its (social) construction within society (Berger and Luckman, 1979; Searle, 1995) as risk can be ambiguous, and variously defined dependent upon context, application and the perspective used, and it has to be acknowledged that we cannot eliminate risk entirely. It is an integral part of everyday life as the earlier parts of this chapter have indicated. The conceptualisation of risk in social work as principally concerned with harm or adverse outcomes needs to be understood within the wider societal context and given these factors, an undue emphasis on formal procedures to guide practice can lead to defensive practice.

The 21st Century Review of Social Work in Scotland Changing Lives (Scottish Executive, 2006a) highlighted the need to review approaches to risk assessment but it also suggested that social workers lacked confidence and had become increasingly risk averse, suggesting that this was indicative of an *aversion to risk in society, leading to restriction of practice and limiting life opportunities for people who use services* (p9). Similar views are echoed by Beresford (2007) while Barry (2007) takes a much broader view of the situation and concludes that:

- *most of social work's current accountability systems are reactive, adversarial and stifle professional autonomy;*

- *there is not a culture of learning from mistakes that enables confidential reporting and discussion of near misses; likewise, there is no culture of corporate responsibility;*

- *there is little confidence in the predictability of risk assessment tools and yet they are becoming the priority and the focus of much worker–client contact; tools thus tend to replace rather than inform professional judgement;*

- *social workers' views of risk are largely absent from the literature and yet they actively engage with risk on a daily basis;*

- *differing organisational cultures, differing definitions of risk and a hierarchy of professional expertise may deter the development of a common understanding and language of risk;*

- *the relationship between worker and client is paramount to effective working and yet is being eroded by the language and politics of risk.*

(Barry, 2007, piv)

These comments suggest that risk aversion is very much to the fore in professional social work practice at this time. Why is this? Furedi (2002) suggests that risk aversion is a consequence of the depiction of harms and dangers portrayed by both the media and politicians and the significance of organisational response to complaints and litigation resulting in the emergence of a 'blame culture' that may leave workers feeling apprehensive and self-protective which can result in shifting blame on to others:

> *A culture of blame has developed in response to systemic failures to protect individuals and the wider community, which is forcing social workers into monitoring behaviour rather than actually helping people to make changes.*

(Scottish Executive, 2006a, p1)

This view of a particular emergent form of practice has been evident for some time. Howe (1992; 1996) observes that there has been a shift in terms of the nature of assessment away from using information to help understand and *explain* behaviour (to discern *why*) to a concern upon recounting *what* happened and *who* was responsible for it, so that:

> *coherent causal accounts which attempted to provide a picture of the subject within their social context was of declining importance, for the key purpose of the social worker was to gather information in order to classify clients for the purpose of judging the nature and level of risk and for allocating resources.*

(Parton, 2008, p260)

In many instances it will be the level of *risk* rather than the presence of *need* (see Chapter 1) that will determine whether someone meets the criteria for a service. More recently, with the advent of nascent ICTs (Information and Communication Technologies), how professionals use information is changing and the knowledge that such 'byte-sized' information yields is being increasingly seen as not being amenable to the application of critical skills for the purposes of effective assessment and ultimately, interventions (Parton, 2008; Frost and Parton, 2009). Arguably, such technologies are in danger of yielding information that is not 'fit for purpose' and the same could be said about the (over-) reliance upon formalised and actuarially based risk assessment tools (RATs) whether these be paper or electronically based. The issue here is one that brings to mind the notion of what Duncker (1945) identifies as 'functional fixedness', the propensity of people to see an object (in this example, a particular (risk) assessment format) in its original form that prevents them from adapting its function to suit novel circumstances. Nationally the findings of both *Changing Lives: Report of the 21st Century Review of Social Work in Scotland* and the GSCC report *Social Work at its Best: A Statement of Social Work Roles and Tasks for the 21st Century* (2008) express concern over the apparent 'de-skilling' of the social work profession.

So why as a profession is there concern over risk aversion and what are the drivers influencing this? Maintaining a focus on user-led services can be difficult at a time when resources are scarce and often 'kept in reserve' for those cases deemed to be at the most risk. The impact of media involvement when there are failures 'within the system', as in the cases of Caleb Ness (O'Brien, Hammond and McKinnon, 2003) Victoria Climbié (Laming, 2003) and 'Baby Peter' (Laming, 2009; OFSTED et al., 2008) can result in social workers taking fewer positive and calculated risks and becoming *risk averse*. At times this becomes an organisational feature where the agency as a whole can become risk averse following a significant event. For example, figures released to the press subsequent to the tragic death of Baby Peter have resulted in the 'Baby Peter effect': the number of care orders increased by 70% between November 2007 and November 2008 (*Daily Telegraph*, 6 December 2008).

The current context of practice in relation to risk, how to assess it and how to manage it, is complex and demanding. What is clear is that an over emphasis on procedural approaches to risk assessment and its management does not enable workers to develop the necessary skills and confidence in their professional judgement. We shall consider these elements below.

Risk assessment

A risk assessment can only identify the probability of harm, assess the impact of it on key individuals and pose intervention strategies which may diminish the risk or reduce the harm. Assessments cannot prevent risk.

(Hope and Sparks, 2000, p137)

Risk assessment is the purposeful gathering of relevant information, which is then analysed and interpreted by reference to knowledge, values and skills and the application of professional judgement. An assessment of risk has a number of functions: to identify those factors likely to lead to risk, danger, hazard or threats to well-being, and those protective factors which might reduce or offset these and minimise any risk and it also seeks to inform how a situation might best be managed through a risk management plan.

In spite of what you might think, there is no definitive or infallible way of predicting with 100 per cent accuracy the likely outcomes of any given situation. Risk assessment relies on the availability of an extensive repertoire of skills, knowledge and abilities on the part of those professionals concerned and perhaps, more importantly, upon the use of their professional judgement to make sense of what are often confused and confusing situations. Professional judgement, informed as it is by reference to knowledge, values and skills can act as the 'glue' that can bind the many differing factors together and help to make the unintelligible intelligible and the unmanageable more manageable. The assessment of risk is best understood as forming a part of every assessment undertaken, although some situations will have the potential for much higher risk than others but in the process of any assessment, the presence of risk *must always be considered*.

Titterton (2005) sees risk assessment as:

the process of estimating and evaluating risk, understood as the possibility of beneficial and harmful outcomes and the likelihood of their occurrence in a stated timescale (p83).

This definition retains the notion of risk as having positive *and* negative elements and introduces the time-bound nature of the assessment of risk. Risks in a given situation are not static but will change over time, as they are *dynamic*. This mirrors earlier work by Brearley (1982) whose generic framework for risk assessment takes into account both the positive and negative aspects of risk.

ACTIVITY 2.2

Identifying risk

Helen is 19 years old and has a moderate learning disability. She lives with her parents and currently attends a day centre three times a week. She has expressed a wish to move to supported accommodation.

Helen has been very protected in her upbringing, her parents tending to do everything for her. They are very concerned about this situation and feel that the risks are too great. They are worried that she will not be able to manage daily living tasks and that she may be taken advantage of.

Using Titterton's definition of risk assessment, outline the areas where risk exists in relation to Helen moving into supported accommodation.

Comment

In assessing Helen in her current situation you will want to gather a information on a range of things, including her ability to manage daily living tasks such as cooking, cleaning and shopping, her ability to budget, her understanding of sexual matters and how she manages relationships. You will also need to consider what support networks she has.

Clearly the potential for harm exists in all of these areas but there is also the possibility of benefit. For Helen the potential benefits exist in developing skills, confidence and independence. Your mindset is important here; if you concentrate only on possible harm, the benefits of adopting a risk-taking perspective will be lost.

It is useful at this point to consider the relationship between risks and need.

In Chapter 1 we saw how social work and social care responded to people's needs on behalf of the state. In this chapter we have considered how notions of risk should form part of every assessment, as there is a complex relationship between need, risk and available resources.

ACTIVITY 2.3

Turning need into risk?

Let us return to Helen's situation. It may be that you identify that Helen would need the services of a support worker on a daily basis once she moves in to supported accommodation. However, budgetary constraints within the agency mean that this level of support will not be possible. In not being able to meet this particular need, how might this impact on your assessment of risk in relation to Helen? Are the risks increased for her and if so, what are they?

Comment
It may be that a move to supported accommodation without the level of support identified is not possible. You will see from this example that thresholds and criteria for intervention within agencies may limit abilities to meet needs and will influence whether a risk-taking approach is adopted. Within the current context of limited resources it may be argued that the emphasis upon the assessment of *need* has moved to that of an assessment of *risk* and that this reflects a move towards more protection-focused services (Corby, 2003 and see Chapter 5), and that it is largely predicated on the availability of resources.

Risk assessment tools, professional judgement and the decision-making process

There is an increasing emphasis on the *proceduralisation* of risk and an expansion in the development of formalised risk assessment tools. The belief is that the use of standardised and formalised measures will enable workers to more accurately measure the risks and therefore be in a better position to effectively manage it. However, while such tools should serve to assist in the process of assessment, concerns have been expressed that the tools themselves have become the priority and have tended to *replace* rather than *inform* professional judgement (Barry, 2007).

There are two basic approaches to risk assessment – actuarial (statistical) and clinical methods (professional judgement). In recent years the development and use of actuarial tools has increased. Actuarial tools involve a statistical calculation of risk and rely on a comparison of key factors about an individual with the statistical frequency of these within a matched sample (base-rates). The use of statistical methods is prevalent within criminal justice and probation, relating to the prediction of the risk/likelihood of re-offending. In England and Wales the National Offender Management Service (NOMS) plays a central role in public protection through the management of offenders during sentence.

Professional judgements rely on the knowledge, skills and experience of individual practitioners. As social workers we need to be able to state clearly the rationale for our decision-making and the use of actuarial tools in conjunction with professional judgement (referred to as *consensual approaches*) can increase the *defensibility* of risk decisions and most risk assessment instruments now combine both these elements.

Kemshall (2003) identifies the following criteria regarding the 'defensible decision'.

- All reasonable steps have been taken.
- Reliable assessment methods have been employed using information gathered and methodically analysed.
- Decisions have been recorded and acted upon.
- Adherence to agency policy and procedures is evident.
- Practitioners and managers have been analytical and proactive.

Sources of error in the prediction of risk

	Prediction Yes	Prediction No
Outcome Yes	**(a)** True Positive ++	**(b)** False Negative -+
Outcome No	**(c)** False Positive +-	**(d)** True Negative --

Figure 2.1 Sources of error in the prediction of risk

Decision–making is not an innate skill, but something that we learn. Much of this revolves around the experience we have of problem-solving and the methods we use. Being able to recognise sources of error assists effective decision-making. Macdonald and Macdonald (1999) state that:

> If a decision involves risk, then even when one can demonstrate that one has chosen the unarguably optimal course of action, some proportion of the time the outcome will be suboptimal. It follows that a bad outcome in and of itself does not constitute evidence that the decision was mistaken. The hindsight fallacy is to assume that it does (p22).

Human error can occur at any stage during the risk assessment process through inadequate gathering or analysis of the relevant information and identification of risk factors. It can also occur as a result of bias on the part of the worker. An example could be when a worker becomes too closely aligned with a case and fails to 'see' the risk factors or over-emphasises the protective factors. These sorts of factors can be seen to have been in operation in the cases of Victoria Climbié (Laming, 2003) and Baby Peter (Laming, 2009). However, no risk assessment can predict every eventual outcome and situations will continue to occur where false negatives arise (see Figure 2:1 above).

Research into decision-making has highlighted how too much information can result in 'information overload' (Simon, 1956). Where this occurs the worker becomes unable to synthesise the accumulated data, particularly in situations involving complex and multiple needs and a combination of risk factors. This, coupled with uncertainty and the probability of negative outcomes can impact significantly upon critical processing skills and affect the decision-making process resulting in errors of prediction and judgement.

In some instances, errors arising from organisational factors can occur. Such organisational error can result from pressures within the agency, often associated with budgetary constraint and resourcing which may be directly linked to raising the thresholds of need and effectively turning this into a threshold of risk. A good example of this is 'eligibility criteria'.

In such instances workers might be tempted to over-emphasise the risk factors, thus raising the risk classification level in order that the service user receives a service. Conversely, in some situations, particularly when there has been significant media coverage and or societal disquiet, agencies might in turn lower the risk/need threshold to avoid negative outcomes and associated media coverage. An example of this can be seen in relation to the actions of several local authorities and their employees consequent on the publication of reports into the management of the Baby Peter case (OFSTED et al., 2008; Laming, 2009). Following critical comments and media concerns about procedural and agency roles within this case, several local authorities were seen to increase the number of care applications being made (Johnston, 2008).

RESEARCH SUMMARY

Summarising risk assessment

Brearley (1982) provides a generic framework to help us think about risk, although it is framed in terms of negatives. He identifies the following elements:

Risk: *this is identified (somewhat cumbersomely) as the relative variation in possible outcomes, based on degrees of probability, all of which is influenced by the following.*

Hazards: *these are the factors likely to increase the likelihood of undesirable outcomes and can be sub-divided into two categories:*

Predisposing hazards, *which we can also consider as being similar to static risk factors often referred to in actuarial risk assessment tools. These include known factors in a person's background that may increase the likelihood of a negative outcome based on their significance when compared across populations. These would include a history of past offending, previous occasions of the behaviour(s) under assessment, living in a poor neighbourhood, low educational achievement, etc. These are often seen as 'facts' in relation to the situation as they will not change.*

Situational hazards *include those factors which, if present, are likely to increase the possibility of a feared outcome and could include substance misuse and increased stress levels and a range of other things which inhere in the environment of the individual concerned. These are also referred to as* dynamic factors *in many risk assessment frameworks and tools.*

Dangers: *these are the feared outcomes of the hazards, for example re-offending, harming oneself or someone else, falling ill.*

Strengths: *these are those factors within any situation that are likely to reduce the impact of the hazards and therefore theoretically reduce the likelihood of the danger occurring. In the same way that hazards can be split into predisposing/static and situational/dynamic, strengths can likewise be categorised in this way.*

Moore (1996) offers a similar generic approach to risk assessment and management and focuses upon the need to attend to context, individual factors, *and* applied factors *in relation to the risk. She provides an accessible commentary on the importance of the timing of assessments, the characteristics of a good risk assessment framework, how to plan key*

continued

interventions, sources of error and the ethical issues such things can generate, base rates and bias and a host of relevant information relating to the role of motivation and the agency responses to risk and its management.

In all of these descriptions of risk and how to approach it, remember that while the language and terminology may differ, the essential ingredients remain the same: identify the individual, get to know them, get to know all you can about their situation, previous risks, the potential hazards and the potential strengths. Risk is something to be worked with; it is dynamic, fluid and at times messy, but it needs to be addressed in a systematic and coordinated fashion.

Risk management

In contrast to a wide-ranging literature on and the emphasis given to the *assessment* of risk, much less has been written in relation to the *management* of risk. Assessment by itself will not reduce the risks, so risk *assessment* and risk *management* should be viewed as inseparable.

Davis (1996) defines two approaches to risk management: risk minimisation and risk taking. He contends:

> *the risk minimisation approach locates risk in a deficient and potentially dangerous minority of individuals who need to be identified, registered and managed by medication and surveillance (1996, p113).*

Such a narrow definition of risk, she argues:

> *fails to engage adequately with issues of risk as they affect the majority of service users (1996, p113).*

In contrast, the risk-taking approach is

> *one developed by practitioners working with an explicit agenda to involve and empower ... service users (1996, p114).*

Within this approach, risk is viewed as positive and normalising and one where the starting point is

> *not a service framework or set of practice procedures but a set of shared values, which inform practice (1996, p114).*

Although Davis writes with the area of mental health in mind, we would argue that such views are equally applicable across all areas of practice.

Titterton (2005) discusses risk management as focusing on trying to *increase benefits, as well as minimising harms* (p92). He sees risk management as a *process for ensuring that potential benefits identified by the risk assessment are increased and that the likelihood of harms occurring as a result of taking a risk is reduced* (p92). Core to these ideas is a systematic approach that includes active monitoring and review.

Wherever possible the inclusion of the service user within the risk management process should be encouraged, as establishing a working partnership can be a positive feature of managing the risks posed. This is consistent with positive social work values and best practice to minimise risk, develop strengths and harness protective factors.

Practitioners will be involved in developing risk management plans that more frequently now evolve through multi-agency and inter-professional agendas (for example, in Criminal Justice the MAPPA arrangements: see Chapter 8). Therefore good communication is essential and this includes a common understanding of the language used to identify and prioritise risk factors as well as an understanding of the role and remit of other professionals and regard for their particular areas of expertise as well as an awareness of the dynamics involved in establishing and maintaining effective collaborative arrangements (Hothersall, 2008; McLean, 2007). Within the risk management process, there must be a clear understanding of who is to do what, when, where and how, with these details being recorded. It is usual for a professional to be identified to take the lead role, and this often falls to the social worker holding the case.

Risk management begins from the premise that risk cannot be eliminated, but if the risk is appropriately managed it can reduce the impact of any harm. The management plan will identify risk behaviours and identify measures to be taken to reduce their occurrence, which in some instances might involve restrictions on the individual's rights and freedoms. This is an important point, which can have serious ethical implications as restrictions on individual personal freedoms may be imposed based not necessarily on what a person may already have done, but on *what they have not yet done*.

When managing risk, interventions must be proportionate to the degree of perceived risk and the resources required to manage it; it should be robust but not overly defensive, with measures adopted to reduce the climate of risk aversion. Risk management should be reasonable, balancing the dichotomy of possible issues of discrimination and infringement of rights with responsibilities to protect individuals and the general public (Kemshall in Lishman, 2007). Risk management plans should contain strategies to address specific aspects of risky behaviour that might include attendance on various programmes to address issues like substance misuse or offending behaviour and might also include other education-focused programmes on parenting or therapy sessions involving a range of 'talking treatments', etc.

The management of risk necessarily involves a monitoring role particularly in relation to the degree of compliance with those measures being implemented. If the person is actively engaged with the process, this can be seen as a factor that might reduce risks, whereas non-compliance might suggest that there are in fact more risks to worry about.

Risk management will also need to consider what strategies should be put in place to protect the public or individuals identified as being at risk. This might require the use of specific court orders to restrict the individual if deemed appropriate such as exclusion orders. Risk management plans also need to consider the safety of practitioners. Due to the nature of the work, home visits are a necessary requirement, and often practitioners are required to challenge behaviours that can result in anger and hostility. Practitioners must remain alert to the potential risk to themselves by checking all available information to establish if there have been any previous incidents of violence or risk of harm. Agencies as employers have a responsibility to ensure the safety of their employees and many organisations have adopted 'lone working' policies.

Under the Health and Safety at Work Act 1974 and the Management of Health and Safety at Work Regulations 1999 both employers and employees have a responsibility in terms of taking all reasonable steps to ensure the safety of staff; this includes completing a risk assessment and identifying a risk management plan.

C H A P T E R   S U M M A R Y

This chapter has looked at the issue of risk, locating it in both its historical and contemporary context. We have considered how the concept came to be attached to notions of dangerousness, in some respects losing any positive connotation it ought perhaps to have. We have looked at how risk is all around us and how it operates on a day-to-day basis in all our lives. The chapter has also looked at how risk is defined within the area of social work and social care and considered how and why risk is assessed and managed, both in relation to individuals and, briefly, in relation to groups (although this is considered in more detail in Chapter 3).

What is crucial to your understanding of risk is that it is ever-present and guarantees can never be given that it has been or can be eliminated entirely; it *can* be reduced and it *can* be managed. Theoretically, it could be eliminated, but as the discussion around sources of error and bias above highlighted, in this respect *we can never be certain*. Professional practice therefore must engage with risk in a dynamic way and practitioners have to be supported in their assessments and judgements around these difficult areas and, where it is appropriate, take calculated risks to enhance well-being.

FURTHER READING

Moore, B (1996) *Risk assessment: A practitioner's guide to predicting harmful behaviour.* London: Whiting and Birch Ltd.
This is a classic text and one deserving of a much wider readership. It offers a clear, well laid out account of risk, what it is, what it isn't and what sorts of things practitioners might usefully do to make it more intelligible and more manageable, recognising that it will always be unpredictable to some extent.

Brearley, PC (1982): *Risk in social work.* London: Routledge and Kegan Paul.
This book offers a generic framework for conceptualising and understanding risk. Again, a useful text.

Chapter 3
Protection

Mike Maas-Lowit and Steve J Hothersall

National Occupational Standards

Key Role 1: Prepare for, and work with, individuals, families, carers, groups and communities to assess their needs and circumstances.

- Liaise with others to access additional information that can inform initial contact and involvement.
- Evaluate all information to identify the best form of initial involvement.
- Work with individuals, families, carers, groups and communities to identify, gather, analyse and understand information.
- Work with individuals, families, carers, groups and communities to enable them to analyse, identify, clarify and express their strengths, expectations and limitations.
- Work with individuals, families, carers, groups and communities to enable them to assess and make informed decisions about their needs, circumstances, risks, preferred options and resources.

Key Role 2: Plan, carry out, review and evaluate social work practice, with individuals, families, carers, groups, communities and other professionals.

- Assess the urgency of requests for action.
- Identify the need for legal and procedural intervention.
- Plan and implement action to meet the immediate needs and circumstances.

Key Role 3: Support individuals to represent their needs, views and circumstances.

- Assess whether you should act as the advocate for the individual, family, carer, group or community.
- Assist individuals, families, carers, groups and communities to access independent advocacy.
- Advocate for, and with, individuals, families, carers, groups and communities.

Key Role 4: Manage risk to individuals, families, carers, groups, communities, self and colleagues.

- Identify and assess the nature of the risk.
- Balance the rights and responsibilities of individuals, families, carers, groups and communities with associated risk.
- Regularly monitor, re-assess, and manage risk to individuals, families, carers, groups and communities.

Key Role 5: Manage and be accountable, with supervision and support, for your own social work practice within your organisation.

- Carry out duties using accountable professional judgement and knowledge-based social work practice.
- Monitor and evaluate the effectiveness of your programme of work in meeting the organisational requirements and the needs of individuals, families, carers, groups and communities.
- Use professional and managerial supervision and support to improve your practice.

continued

Achieving A Social Work Degree continued

Key Role 6: Demonstrate professional competence in social work practice.
- Review and update your own knowledge of legal, policy and procedural frameworks.
- Use professional and organisational supervision and support to research, critically analyse, and review knowledge-based practice.
- Implement knowledge-based social work models and methods to develop and improve your own practice.

Scottish Standards in Social Work Education
Key Role 1: Prepare for, and work with, individuals, families, carers, groups and communities to assess their needs and circumstances.
- Assessing needs and options in order to recommend a course of action.

Key Role 2: Plan, carry out, review and evaluate social work practice with individuals, families, carers, groups, communities and other professionals.
- Identifying and responding to crisis situations.
- Working with individuals, families, carers, groups and communities to achieve change, promote dignity, realise potential and improve life opportunities.
- Producing, implementing and evaluating plans with individuals, families, carers, groups, communities and colleagues.
- Developing networks to meet assessed needs and planned outcomes.
- Working with groups to promote choice and independent living.
- Tackling behaviour which presents a risk to individuals, families, carers, groups, communities and the wider public.

Key Role 3: Assess and manage risk to individuals, families, carers, groups, communities, self and colleagues.
- Assessing and managing risks to individuals, families, carers, groups and communities.

Key Role 4: Demonstrate professional competence in social work practice.
- Evaluating and using up-to-date knowledge of, and research into, social work practice.
- Working within agreed standards of social work practice.
- Understanding and managing complex ethical issues, dilemmas and conflicts.
- Promoting best social work practice, adapting positively to change.

Key Role 5: Manage and be accountable, with supervision and support, for your own social work practice within your organisation.
- Managing one's own work in an accountable way.
- Contributing to the management of resources and services.
- Managing, presenting and sharing records and reports.
- Preparing for, and taking part in, decision-making forums.
- Working effectively with professionals within integrated, multi-disciplinary and other service settings.

Introduction

This chapter deals with the growth and development of legislation and policy in relation to personal and public protection and is therefore closely aligned to our earlier discussions on need and risk in Chapters 1 and 2 and it will inform some of the discussions you will encounter in Chapter 4 regarding *capacity* and *incapacity*.

Governments generally have two levels of responsibility: the general protection of all citizens by way of broad policies to meet their health, welfare and general safety needs and secondly, a responsibility to afford special protection to those who experience greater levels of vulnerability and who are also more *susceptible to harm* (Kottow, 2003). To illustrate this point, consider the issue of road safety. If the government fails to properly manage the risks posed by road transport, the general public is at heightened risk and government has failed to protect. Consequently it makes laws and regulations in relation to things like speed limits, wearing safety belts and so on. Within this general vulnerability in relation to road transport, there are specific groups who are more susceptible to the vulnerabilities of road traffic than the norm: children, for example. With this awareness, the government has extra duties to put in place special protective measures such as regulation of special seats for babies in cars, reduced speed-limits near schools and play parks, etc.

There are other groups who are at heightened risk of harm for a multitude of reasons (such as chronic illness, poor mental health, disability, poverty, childhood or old age, etc.), which especially preoccupy us in this chapter. The close relationship with risk arises because people are in need of protection to the degree to which they are at risk of harm: a toddler playing with a ball on a busy street, or an older person who is disorientated because of dementia is at greater risk of harm than a healthy adult walking down that same street. Consequently they are in need of greater levels of protection.

In this chapter we will examine the growing public and governmental preoccupation with risk and the need to protect certain groups and individuals who are considered to be extraordinarily vulnerable. We will look at the broad culture in which policy has developed around this subject and we will examine it from both sides (the beneficial and the detrimental) and we will consider how and why it is that governments, professionals, society and all of us increasingly attempt to devise structures in which to manage risk and afford protection to certain groups. We will then look at examples of specific law and policy devised as a means of protecting those most susceptible to harm, the most relevant to this book lying generally very close to various pieces of legislation in areas of childcare, mental health, adult support and protection and criminal justice which are covered in detail elsewhere in this volume.

The socio-historical context for state involvement in the protection of vulnerable citizens

Any discussion regarding protection must include reference to the notion of 'parens patriae', which is Latin for 'parent of the country' where the monarch or any other authority (the state, generally), is regarded as the legal protector of those unable to protect themselves (*SOED*, 2007). This legal concept is the basis for all protective legislation, policy, procedure and ultimately practice, including that which has regulation as its main aim.

The use of the concept was first recorded in the UK in the seventeenth century in relation to adults who were deemed to be *non compos mentis* (not of sound mind) and who required the protection of the state to safeguard and protect their welfare. Subsequently, the doctrine was extended and applied to children

continued

> *The socio-historical context for state involvement in the protection of vulnerable citizens continued*
>
> and it has subsequently evolved through time because of the implementation of the Magna Carta in 1215, the introduction of the *Writ of Habeas Corpus* and the growth of common law, all of which have delimited the power of the sovereign and transferred this to the institutions of the state in the form of rights and obligations towards its citizens. These ideas have a long, long history and are enshrined deep within our constitution and now find renewed applicability in the various adult protection measures on the statute books across the UK, including incapacity legislation, mental health legislation and nascent vulnerable adult legislation. The ECHR and the UNCRC also reflect these principles.
>
> The notion of someone being *in loco parentis* differs from but is in essence an extension of *parens patriae* and refers to situations where the state, its representative agencies or an individual has the temporary care of someone who lacks legal capacity (see Hothersall, 2008; Hothersall, Maas-Lowit and Golightley, 2008 and Chapter 4). This doctrine effectively operationalises that of *parens patriae* where formal proceedings have been implemented, although if you as an individual are spending some time with an individual who lacks legal capacity, you would be deemed to be acting *in loco parentis* under common law and would have certain obligations towards them, notably a *duty of care*.

The particular focus here will be upon that which is good or beneficial and that which is bad or problematic in the unavoidable and incremental growth of protective and regulatory law and policy relating to the promotion of welfare. We ask the reader to carry all three elements (the good, the bad and the unavoidable) in mind, so as not to misunderstand our message: there are people living in any large and complex society who are less able to protect their interests than the majority; their armour is perhaps thinner than that of others. Such people are therefore more likely to be susceptible to abuse, neglect, exploitation and harm. This likelihood is what we generally call *vulnerability* and is inherently connected to the notion of *risk*. As such, it is a *good* thing that risk has become a standard part of the furniture of modern policy and practice, and nothing said that is critical of our growing preoccupation with risk and protection should detract from this perspective.

The growth of risk and the need for protection: Good, bad or unavoidable?

The minute risk is conceived as the chance occurrence of something detrimental happening, there is a danger that a person or body will be identified as having a responsibility to prevent it or to protect those who may be at risk from it. It can then become an exercise in apportioning blame when bad things do occur. This is because the resulting harm may be perceived as *a failure to protect*. Turn this idea out into the public domain, in close proximity to the political arena, and it will grow exponentially. We are all too familiar with the results being paraded across the media: see, for example *Who is to blame for Britain's knife-crime?* (*Daily Telegraph*, 26 May 2008) and *Binge Britain: Under 21s now face ban on buying alcohol* (*Daily Mail*, 14 August 2008) to mention but two contemporary preoccupations of UK politics in relation to risks to health and public order. Another example of the linkage between risk, protection and blame is found in the now well publicised case of Baby Peter (or Baby P), who was killed by his mother's partner and subsequently featured in a long-running *trial by media* of various parties in Haringey Council in London (see for example Pascoe-Watson, 2008; Garrett, 2009).

ACTIVITY **3.1**

Consider some of the differences between the 2009 response to the global swine flu pandemic and the responses to the Black Death (the plague) when it arrived on British shores in 1348 (Kelly, 2005). Try and think about how and whether the plague might have been predicted in the fourteenth century and how it might have been (should have been?) responded to by the government of the day. Did they have the knowledge and the technology then? How and why might the responses then have differed from those we could expect today?

Comment

In 2009, the UK government faced criticism from its opponents and critics that it ought to have done more to anticipate the risk of swine flu and that it had a responsibility to manage the risk of catching it once the spread of the illness was pandemic. On the other hand, while governments did make some response in the 1340s and 1350s, there would have been no consideration that the plague, which killed at least 1 in 3 people across Europe, was anyone's responsibility to anticipate, prevent or minimise. The problem that confronts us in the change of perception from 1348 to 2009 is the growing idea that everything ought to be predictable in a basically unpredictable world and that, where it remains unpredicted, it is someone's fault. This results in growing attempts to create policy structures that meet every possible contingency from global financial crises to the prediction of who is likely to commit crimes of violence against whom, where and when. This in its turn increasingly erodes civil liberties (for example in moves to make everyone carry identity cards or in the growth of CCTV cameras in public places) and it tends to standardise and bureaucratise the systems in which professionals work.

Many of these ideas are synthesised in the thinking of Ulrich Beck (1992), whose work postulated the *risk society*, in which post-modern society is increasingly organised and motivated by its responses to the perceived dangers that it faces. Beck, among others, suggested that this preoccupation permeates all aspects of society. For our purposes, it is evident in the world of politics, in the influence of media, in the process of government and policy making and in the design and delivery of services. Aspects of this are closely linked to the work of a sociologist of an earlier generation: Max Weber was interested in the growth of bureaucracy (1947), which he saw as being characterised by regulation, standardisation and hierarchical organisation, and we can see much of Weber's early nineteenth century observations in the structures of modern government and its agents. The link between

Weber and Beck for our purposes is that Weber foresaw that rational bureaucracy is a form of organisation that will multiply and grow into all corners of civil life. In the same way, Beck saw that the concept of risk would pervade all aspects of society, from concern about the environment to the regulation of sexual and other forms of behaviour.

In this discussion it is not disputed that the case of Baby Peter, for example, was an instance where there were systemic and systematic failings that contributed to his death, and that these ought to have been addressed in order to detect the risks he faced and to prevent his awful death. However, living life in this world involves constant engagement with unpredictable forces, and we meet these forces by taking risks in order to address our needs. For the purposes of policy formation, governments seem to be trapped into a situation in which there is a risk to them of not having identified and managed all potential risks. *The Sun*'s coverage of the Baby Peter case demonstrates very clearly what the potential dangers are for any government or its agents (in this case, Haringey Council) of apparently failing to manage a significant risk. It seems disrespectful to reduce a small child's tragic death to this equation, but a major driving force in modern policy making must be the awareness of the power of media-amplified public outrage about failure to identify and manage a particular risk and to afford appropriate levels of protection (Munro, 1996, 2008a).

However, what the above argument fails to capture is that we know far more about the world and human beings now than we ever have. For example, in 1348 the ravages of the Black Death were upon this country but it was not understood that disease is caused by microbiological infections, invisible to the naked eye. It was not evident, as it is now, that we can find out how diseases like the plague or, to use a contemporary example, H1N1 (swine flu) come into being, how the transmission may be minimised and how it may be treated. Once these things are known, the world still remains an unpredictable place, but the growth of knowledge, largely mirrored by the growth of technology, increases the *expectations* on governments to assume a fuller responsibility to protect its citizens and means that it then becomes *reasonable* to ask the state to minimise what are *known* risks. If the risks are known or predictable, then the issue becomes one of apportioning blame if the bad things happen, even if their occurrence was in fact *unavoidable*.

The protection of vulnerable groups and individuals in the UK

As the term *risk society* implies, risk is such a diverse and widespread preoccupation of the state that it would not be possible to cover all the bases of even social work and social care's narrow corner of the field. Besides, the subject-specific chapters that follow will provide much of the detail relating to risk and protection in those areas. Here though we will highlight a few key issues regarding risk and protection followed by some illustrative examples to advance our thesis that:

- risk is unavoidable;

- a preoccupation with it is ever growing and it has therefore to be managed;

- an awareness of risk is essential to good practice;

- it has both beneficial and detrimental aspects, which if properly managed can enhance practice outcomes for all and, importantly for the purposes of this chapter,

- the need for protection is crucial for some people and that how this is done depends upon the availability of relevant frameworks (including law and policy), effective assessment, proactive intervention, good communication and critical awareness.

Using these themes, let us now look at the main areas within practice where issues of risk and the need for protection are more likely to be evident and why this might be so. Before we do this though, we need to remind ourselves that we are in fact talking about those situations where need is equated with the negative connotation of risk and it is *the state and its agents* who have a responsibility to protect the general public or an individual *where there is no-one else to do this*. We have already considered some of these issues around need in Chapter 1 and you might want to revisit these now.

Protection of vulnerable groups legislation (PVG legislation)

This type of law and policy aims to operate within the broader *structural* elements of society regarding the need to afford protection to vulnerable groups. Through its implementation there now exists a range of statutory vetting and barring schemes that provide filters through which those people who apply to work with children, young people and other vulnerable groups have to pass. The catalysts for much of this were the murders of Holly Wells and Jessica Chapman in Soham by Ian Huntley in August 2002. The public inquiry that followed, chaired by Sir Michael Bichard (Bichard, 2004) led among other things to the introduction of the Safeguarding Vulnerable Groups Act 2006 (SVGA) and the Safeguarding Vulnerable Groups (Northern Ireland) Order 2007 (SVGO) and the creation of the Independent Safeguarding Authority in England, Wales and Northern Ireland and with the introduction of the Protection of Vulnerable Groups (Scotland) Act 2007 (PVG), the Protection of Vulnerable Groups Scheme in Scotland, overseen by the Scottish Government. These comparable arrangements across the four countries aim to ensure that people who have regular contact with vulnerable groups through any form of work (paid or voluntary) do not have a known history of harmful behaviour and if they do, they will be barred from working with such groups. In this situation, anyone who has been barred and is found to be working in any capacity will be prosecuted. Employers have a legal obligation to process all employees through the relevant scheme, and a failure to do so can lead to prosecution (HM Government, 2009; Scottish Government, 2009a; 2009b).

All of these arrangements are designed to extend a range of protective measures to a wide range of vulnerable groups, and they also impose a degree of *regulation* upon the professional workforce. These are important developments, but they should not allow us to slip into complacency. These regulations, like any other, are only as effective as the people implementing them. The checks that are undertaken are likely to only reveal *known* harmful behaviours, although for all social work and social care workers, enhanced disclosures include reference to *intelligence* sources and also take account of non-criminal convictions (cautions, etc.) that may, collectively or otherwise, be an *indicator* that an individual might be unsuitable to work with vulnerable people. This was what happened in the case of Ian Huntley; he had no relevant convictions, but he did have a considerable number of cautions and other incidents that had brought him to the attention of the police and the authorities over a number of years, which, if taken together, would have indicated a cause for concern. This does not mean, however, that the tragedies in Soham could have been prevented even if Huntley's past had been 'visible' to potential employers. What it could have done though is to have prevented him from obtaining employment as a school caretaker, which gave him easy access to children. In much the same way Vanessa George, the nursery worker in Plymouth who was convicted of abusing children and taking and distributing indecent images of them, had been working there for three years before the abuse was discovered. At the time of her employment she would have been subjected to vetting procedures under the Protection of Children Act 1999 (E&W) as was Huntley. This notwithstanding, murders and abuse were still perpetrated, so the existence of rules and regulations should never be taken as a *guarantee of protection*.

The direct protection of vulnerable populations

Children and young people

As you will see in Chapter 5, there is a range of fairly complex arrangements in place across the UK that aim to offer care and protection to those children and young people deemed to be at risk of harm (Broadhurst, Grover and Jamieson, 2009; Hothersall, 2008; Munro, 2008b). Although the terminology might be slightly different across the UK, the issue here is whether the level of need of protection for a child constitutes an unacceptable or negative risk and crosses a certain threshold, and the test is whether the child is likely to suffer *significant harm*. This concept has generated enormous debate over the years and will continue to do so because what might be significant in relation to one child may not be so for another. The use of such a phrase is, however, essential as it allows for the active consideration of a range of other factors that may or may not mediate the level of harm to the child and these will be different for everyone and every situation. We might think that there will always be some situations that are clearly dangerous and unacceptable for all children and young people although as society evolves, what we perceive as unacceptable is subject to change.

Whether a child or young person is deemed to be in need of protection is predicated on a thorough *assessment* and *analysis* of the situation. Risk assessment protocols vary across the UK in terms of their detail although the underlying principles tend to be the same. The formalised arrangements to protect children and young people have evolved over time and their effectiveness is as much about the action or inaction of individuals as it is about the structure of systems and this is commented upon in Chapter 5.

Adults at risk of harm/vulnerable adults

Across the UK there is a range of statutes in place that provides the mechanisms to afford protection to vulnerable adults or adults deemed to be at risk of harm. These differences in terminology across the four countries should not detract from the central objectives of these provisions and neither should semantics interfere with decisions to act on the basis of concerns about the well-being of someone who is, for whatever reason, at a heightened risk of harm.

In broad terms, the provisions that now exist fall into two categories: those that relate to people with a mental disorder, 'however caused or manifest' and those individuals for whom the capacity to make decisions and act autonomously has in some way been compromised and as a result they would likely benefit from intervention by either the state or a private (trusted) individual through relevant legislation (Brown, 2009; Gould, 2009; Hothersall, Maas-Lowit and Golightley, 2008; Ward, 2008). Strictly speaking, legislation relating to matters of capacity and incapacity can be relevant where an individual has problems with this as a result of a mental disorder, so there is a clear overlap.

In relation to those individuals who are suffering from a mental disorder there are the provisions of the Mental Health Acts 2007, 2003 and 1983 (England and Wales; see Dow, 2008), the Mental Health (Care and Treatment) (Scotland) Act 2003 and the Mental Health (Northern Ireland) Order 1986 (currently under review: see DHSSPSNI, 2009). Modern welfare legislation is increasingly characterised by the inclusion of over-arching *principles* through which all actions under that law must be mediated. Setting binding principles in law is a way of ensuring that people's human rights are preserved and, of course, since the introduction of the Human Rights Act 1998, all UK law must conform to our rights as set out in the *Articles of the European Convention of Human Rights* (Convention for the Protection of Human Rights and Fundamental Freedoms as amended by Protocol No. 11, Rome, 4.xi.1950).

These various Acts have detailed sets of *principles* that make it a binding duty for anyone who has formal powers under the Acts, to make decisions and commit actions only with regard to these principles. For example, in making a decision to detain a person in hospital for treatment, all the people involved in the process must have regard for the *wishes and feelings* of the person subject to the proposed detention and they can only invoke those powers that are the *least restrictive and necessary* in relation to the *freedom of the subject,* which must be *proportionate* and *take account of the views* of other significant people such as the person's carer.

The main principles can be summarised as follows:

- non-discrimination;

- equality;

- respect for diversity;

- reciprocity (where compulsory powers are imposed by law, a parallel obligation is imposed on providers of care and treatment services to provide appropriate services);

- informal care (should be considered before formal compulsion);

- participation (of service users as far as possible in the process);

- respect for carers;

- least restrictive alternative;

- benefit (any compulsory intervention should be of benefit to the person).

There is also a special set of principles that have a particular focus on the needs and rights of children who may be subject to provisions under the relevant statute (Hothersall, Maas-Lowit and Golightley, 2008).

The second category, of *incapacity*, is only considered in the eyes of the law to rest upon two factors:

- the existence of a mental disorder (mental illness, personality disorder or learning disability) of a nature or degree that warrants the removal of the ability to make a decision; or

- a physical disability of a nature or degree which makes the communication of any decision impossible.

To explore the first of these reasons, clearly not everyone with a mental disorder lacks capacity to make decisions. The step of taking decision-making powers away from one person and giving them to another is such a fundamentally serious step in terms of human rights that the degree of mental disorder must be serious enough to justify it. Regarding incapacity by virtue of physical disability, the clearest example would be that a person could not be considered able to make decisions if in a persistent vegetative state or a prolonged coma. However, there are other progressive conditions, such as motor neurone disease, Parkinson's disease and dementia, which can so impede a person's ability to communicate decisions as to render them incapable.

These statutes, the Mental Capacity Act 2005 (England and Wales), the Adults with Incapacity (Scotland) Act 2000 and, for the time being, the Mental Health (Northern Ireland) Order 1986 provide legal mechanisms for the protection of adults at risk of harm by virtue of a lack of capacity (see Chapter 4).

In Scotland, there is another unique piece of legislation that has a much broader definition of vulnerability. The Adult Support and Protection (Scotland) Act 2007 regards vulnerability as being caused by:

- disability;

- mental disorder;

- illness;

- infirmity.

In situations of extreme vulnerability, the 2007 Act offers a range of controversial powers including the power to take the adult into protective care, to exclude the perpetrator of harm from access to the adult and to offer continuing supervision and monitoring of any situation in which an adult may be at risk. These orders are made following application to the Sheriff Court and, while none of them may be made if the adult opposes them, the Sheriff will have powers to over-rule the adult's opposition, if they feel that the adult has been placed under *undue pressure*. It should be noted that some critics have objected that, by giving the Sheriff power to over-rule the adult's objection, the Act may discourage people from coming forward to seek its protection.

The core territory of *mental health* legislation is the care and treatment of anyone with a mental disorder who is so adversely affected by it that they cannot make critical treatment decisions and they are therefore a risk to either their own health, safety or welfare or to another person who may require protection from their actions. The purpose of the principle interventions under the various Acts is to secure care and treatment for the *patient* even in circumstances where they object to receiving such help and protection. The treatments enforceable under compulsion are limited to specific treatments for mental disorder. In other words, it could be used to force treatment for depression but not for appendicitis, angina or a broken leg.

The core territory of *incapacity* legislation is the wide-ranging protection of any adult who experiences incapacity because of mental disorder or inability to communicate because of physical disability. The various powers to protect are via the removal of the adult's authority to make decisions and determine choices by the transfer of those powers to another person (such as a welfare or financial attorney or guardian). The powers are not determined by a fixed list contained in the Acts, but are intended to be of as wide a scope as will be of help to the adult with incapacity. Powers of treatment under the Act are not just fixed upon treatments for mental disorder but may extend to dentistry and physical health treatments as well as issues of intervention in relation to the management of finances and property.

In Scotland, the Adult Support and Protection (Scotland) Act 2007 is intended to fill some specific gaps in the powers of the other acts. While the Adults with Incapacity (Scotland) Act 2000 is about transplanting the adult's authority to make choices and decisions on to another person, the 2007 Act is about preventing others from harming or exploiting them. It is intended to strengthen the powers of any vulnerable adult in order to protect him or her from harm and is not designed to replace decision-making powers with any proxy powers or necessarily to force a person into protective care or to receive protective treatment, and the legislation relating to capacity/incapacity and vulnerability in Scotland also has particular value in relation to people with physical disabilities (see Chapter 9).

All of these legal provisions are supported by a range of policy documentation in the form of *Codes of Practice*; these offer detailed guidance on the interpretation of statute and procedural matters which, when understood and aligned with sensitive practice, allow practitioners to engage with these difficult areas with more confidence (Department for Constitutional Affairs, 2007; Scottish Government, 2008a; 2008b; 2008c; 2008d; 2008e; 2008f; Scottish Government, 2009a; 2009b).

Criminal Justice

In its broadest sense, policy both steers practitioners into the use of specific tools of risk *assessment* and into specific structures for risk *management*. The *Multi-Agency Public Protection Arrangements* or MAPPA (Home Office, 2005; Scottish Executive, 2006;) and *Public Protection Arrangements: Northern Ireland (PPANI)* (Northern Ireland Office, 2008) are examples of policy-led structures for *risk management* with a particular focus on offenders and the criminal justice systems of the four UK countries.

In England and Wales, the Criminal Justice and Court Services Act (2000) established the MAPPA and placed them on a statutory basis, subsequently enhanced by the provisions of the Criminal Justice Act (2003). The legislation requires that the police, prison and probation services work collaboratively as a 'responsible authority' to ensure the implementation of the MAPPA (acting jointly as the 'responsible authority') across all 42 areas of England and Wales. In Scotland, the MAPPA are underpinned by the Management of Offenders (Scotland) Act 2005 and operate across the eight Criminal Justice Authorities there involving police, social work, the Scottish Prison Service (SPS) and the NHS as the 'responsible authority' (Scottish Executive, 2000) whilst in Northern Ireland, the Criminal Justice (NI) Order 2008 adopts a similar approach with its PPANI (Public Protection Arrangements: Northern Ireland). The aims of these arrangements are broadly similar across the four countries; namely, to establish multi-agency arrangements for the *identification of offenders to be supervised under MAPPA/PPA,* to provide a framework to facilitate the effective *sharing of information about offenders,* and to *assess* and *manage* the risks posed by them. There are three categories: Registered Sex Offenders; Violent and Other Sex Offenders and Other Offenders, each of which is assessed against a three-point scale, with three being the highest, although it is important to note that it is not the assessed/perceived degree of risk that determines the categorisation and the level of supervision, *but the degree and level of intervention and management required* and this fact is illustrated by the recent inclusion of offenders with a mental disorder into MAPPA (see Hothersall, Maas-Lowit and Golightley, 2008 and see Chapter 8).

From the discussions above, a fairly common process may be deduced: something harmful or undesirable happens in the public domain, and the ever-growing responsibilities of government, interested professionals and watch-dog bodies require them to make inquiry into what went wrong in order to learn lessons from it and to prevent the same thing happening again. The lessons learnt can result in changes to the law and policy to shift practice away from a recurrence of what is now perceived as a fault in the system. The reality in relation to 'lessons learnt' however appears somewhat different from this ideal. Of the many inquiries into the deaths and serious injuries of children for example (see chapter 5), the general consensus would appear to be that the same difficulties tend to arise time after time (Reder, Duncan and Grey, 1993; Reder and Duncan, 1999; 2003; 2004). Sometimes (as in the case of Baby Peter (Laming, 2009; Garrett, 2009)) the process is muddied by too much media-driven public interest, and predictably this occurs more around emotive issues, for example, where children are involved.

CASE STUDY

Caleb Ness *Caleb Ness was a baby who lived his short life in Edinburgh, Scotland. He died aged 11 weeks at the hands of his father in 2001. While the tragedy of Caleb's death took place around the time that the Borders situation was uncovered (see below), there are other similarities in the short-comings of agencies – in communication and following procedures for the identification and management of risk.*

The adults involved in Caleb's care had problems in relation to substance use and the key professional involvement with the parents was from criminal justice social work and brain injury specialists. They failed to recognise the risks to Baby Caleb because they did not see child protection as their remit and they lacked expertise in the very area that might have alerted them to the risks.

continued

There was a tendency among professionals in all agencies to make assumptions about the knowledge, training and actions of others. The doctors assumed that the social workers knew things, which in fact they did not. Some professionals failed to acknowledge their own responsibilities for identifying and responding to child protection concerns. This was particularly evident in the gulf we discovered between Children and Families team social workers and the separately administered Criminal Justice social workers. We found that there was a complete failure by Criminal Justice workers and management to recognise that they did have some responsibility for child protection. Similarly, we saw an incomplete understanding of their role in child protection in the actions of addiction professionals and brain injury specialists, who are accustomed to working with adult patients. The police were handicapped by the paucity of information sent to them by the social work department, and did the best they could do in Caleb's case, but we discovered that they were not routinely passing on as much information as the social workers expected.

(O'Brien, Hammond and McKinnon, 2003, p8)

As a direct consequence of Caleb's death and the damning report that followed, the then Scottish Executive launched what turned out to be the first of a number of far-reaching reviews of law, policy and practice regarding children, young people and their families in Scotland, with the report of the Scottish Child Protection Audit and Review 'It's everyone's job to make sure I'm alright' (Scottish Executive, 2002; 2002a) making a number of recommendations to improve child protection services across Scotland (Daniel, 2004; Daniel, Vincent and Ogilvie-Whyte, 2007) which have been followed by a number of other reforms (see Hothersall, 2008).

The Borders Inquiry In the so-called Borders Inquiry (Mental Welfare Commission and Social Work Inspection Agency, 2004), a vulnerable woman with learning disabilities, called Miss X by the Scottish media (The Sunday Herald, 2004), was discovered in March 2001 to have experienced serious physical and sexual assault over a number of weeks at the hands of three men. The victim was known both to the Scottish Borders Council social work service and to the Borders NHS and while there had been concerns noted by these authorities over many years regarding Miss X, no action had been taken to address these. Following a police investigation, the Mental Welfare Commission for Scotland took up its responsibility to make inquiry into the situation. The report was made available to the Scottish Executive at the time when the law regarding protective guardianship of people with mental disorder was undergoing change with the implementation of the Adults with Incapacity (Scotland) Act 2000. The Mental Welfare Commission's report, in conjunction with the Social Work Inspection Agency found, amongst other things:

- *a failure to investigate appropriately very serious allegations of abuse;*
- *an acceptance of the poor conditions in which the people involved lived and the chaos of their lives;*
- *a lack of comprehensive needs assessments, including carers' assessments, or assessments of very poor quality, despite clear and repeated indications of need from the earliest point of agency contact;*

continued

- *a lack of information-sharing and co-ordination within and between key agencies (social work, health, education, housing, police).*

This was also a time of major change in mental health law and the inquiry identified a gap in legal and policy provision in that the victim of this case demonstrated in sharp focus that vulnerable adults required the same protections as were available to children through child protection law and procedure. The result was the Adult Support and Protection (Scotland) Act 2007 and related codes of practice and other supporting policy.

From this, local authorities are now required to implement frameworks which co-ordinate work with partners such as the police, health services and voluntary providers, to provide support and protection to adults who are at risk of abuse, neglect and exploitation. The range of people who might be at such risk is very wide indeed. It includes people who use or are addicted to alcohol or other drugs, people with mental disorder, older and infirm people, people with physical disabilities, people who have committed criminal offences themselves and are at risk in some way and those who work within the sex industry (Scottish Government, 2007). Risk assessment and management are central to the law, policy and practice in this new area, because it is the determination of risk factors that leads to intervention in the form of multidisciplinary packages of support and protection. The Borders Inquiry was therefore a major step in the chain of policy which led to Scotland having two groups of people for whom authorities now have major responsibilities in assessing and managing risk: children under the age of 16 and adults over the age of 16.

The reader might note from the above how the need for protection becomes a consideration in policy making and that we are in fact discussing two strands of dealing with risk: *risk assessment* (the quantification of risks in any given situation) and *risk management* (plans for how to deal with those risks now that they have been identified and how to implement *protective measures*). The link between assessment and management is self-evident; there would be little point in quantifying risk if one was not going to put in place a plan to manage it.

Risk assessment and management: Structures and tools

We have repeatedly asserted that life is both risky and unpredictable. This means that there are too many variables for *risk assessment* to ever be an exact science. However, as Titterton indicates (2005), two strands combine to give it a scientific veneer: actuarial elements drawn from statistical data and approaches developed in the insurance industry on one hand, and refined professional or clinical judgement on the other. However, statistics and the correlation of statistics can be a dangerous and misleading thing if it is not mediated by a degree of specialised professional knowledge. Therefore, the use of both actuarial methods *and* professional judgements is recommended. Taken together, these are referred to as *consensual approaches* to risk assessment and may incorporate the use of other frameworks to guide thinking; for example, those generic frameworks like the Integrated Assessment Framework (Aldgate and Rose, 2007) and the 'My World' framework (Scottish Executive, 2005a; 2005b) available for working with children and their families.

HCR20 (Webster et al., 1997; Webster and Hucker, 2007) is a good example of a risk assessment tool that blends actuarial elements with professional and clinical judgement. The 'H' stands for *historical*, the 'C' stands for *clinical* and the 'R', for *risk,* in a twenty-item inventory, which asks questions about the subject's history (such as history of violence related to substance misuse), clinical elements (such as ability to co-operate with services) and resulting risks. Tools like HCR20 are validated, which means that they hold up to empirical research which supports their effectiveness. However, this does not mean that they are anything less than a means by which to attempt prediction in a complex and uncertain future of innumerable variables. The common usage of the term *tools* might suggest something more scientifically accurate (Scottish Executive, 2002b). Nevertheless, they do serve to standardise the risk judgements made by professionals trained in their use as personal experience inevitably influences professional judgements to some degree (Jeffrey, 1992). This suggests that some regulatory and guiding framework is needed to help us quantify the basis upon which judgements on the degree of risk are made.

CHAPTER SUMMARY

This chapter has ranged widely across a number of different issues. We have considered how the issue of *protection* is intimately connected to need, *vulnerability* and *risk* that were the prime subjects of Chapters 1 and 2. We have also considered how the issue of protection has increasingly become the business of everyone, from governments to professionals to private individuals and illustrated how this has generated a range of measures and mechanisms at the wider societal/group level and at the individual level. We have also shown how there is an increasing use of *fundamental principles* to underpin law and policy and that these are supported by increasing amounts of policy in the form of Codes of Practice that aim to assist practitioners in working in these difficult areas. The chapter has also highlighted that while protection, as commonly understood, has a focus upon protecting individuals from harm, there is another level at which such protective measures are increasingly operating and that is in the area of *public protection*, and we have looked at some of the arrangements that exist across the four countries of the UK to manage this issue.

FURTHER READING

Patrick, H (2006) *Mental health, incapacity and the law in Scotland*, Edinburgh: Tottel.
An in-depth look at many of the issues referred to above as they relate to Scotland.

Mandelstam, M (2008) *Safeguarding vulnerable adults and the law*. London: Jessica Kingsley.
As above, but with the focus on England and Wales.

Pritchard, J (ed) (2008) *Good practice in safeguarding adults: Working effectively in adult protection*. London: Jessica Kingsley.
A text which takes a broad look at a range of practice-based issues in the area of adult support and protection.

Chapter 4
Capacity and incapacity

Mike Maas-Lowit

Achieving A Social Work Degree continued

Key Role 5: Manage and be accountable, with supervision and support, for your own social work practice within your organisation.
- Carry out duties using accountable professional judgement and knowledge-based social work practice.
- Maintain accurate, complete, accessible, and up-to-date records and reports.
- Provide evidence for judgements and decisions.
- Implement legal and policy frameworks for access to records and reports.
- Share records with individuals, families, carers.

Key Role 6: Demonstrate professional competence in social work practice.
- Use professional and organisational supervision and support to research, critically analyse, and review knowledge-based practice.
- Implement knowledge-based social work models and methods to develop and improve your own practice.

Scottish Standards in Social Work Education
Key Role 1: Prepare for, and work with, individuals, families, carers, groups and communities to assess their needs and circumstances.
- Preparing for social work contact and involvement.
- Working with individuals, families, carers, groups and communities so they can make informed decisions.
- Assessing needs and options in order to recommend a course of action.

Key Role 2: Plan, carry out, review and evaluate social work practice with individuals, families, carers, groups, communities and other professionals.
- Identifying and responding to crisis situations.
- Working with individuals, families, carers, groups and communities to achieve change, promote dignity, realise potential and improve life opportunities.
- Producing, implementing and evaluating plans with individuals, families, carers, groups, communities and colleagues.
- Developing networks to meet assessed needs and planned outcomes.
- Working with groups to promote choice and independent living.
- Tackling behaviour which presents a risk to individuals, families, carers, groups, communities and the wider public.

Key Role 3: Assess and manage risk to individuals, families, carers, groups, communities, self and colleagues.
- Assessing and managing risks to individuals, families, carers, groups and communities.
- Assessing and managing risk to self and colleagues.

Key Role 4: Demonstrate professional competence in social work practice.
- Working within agreed standards of social work practice.
- Understanding and managing complex ethical issues, dilemmas and conflicts.

Key Role 5: Manage and be accountable, with supervision and support, for your own social work practice within your organisation.
- Managing one's own work in an accountable way.
- Contributing to the management of resources and services.
- Working effectively with professionals within integrated, multi-disciplinary and other service settings.

Key Role 6: Support individuals to represent and manage their needs, views and circumstances.
- Representing, in partnership with, and on behalf of, individuals, families, carers, groups and communities to help them achieve and maintain greater independence.

Introduction

This chapter focuses on issues of capacity and incapacity in relation to our core themes of need, risk and vulnerability. Do not be discouraged if you are unfamiliar with the terms *capacity* and *incapacity*, as they tend to become complicated and multifaceted concepts when encountered in practice, so we will take time to discuss them in context, with the use of a case study. We will also make reference to the very different law and policy positions in England and Wales, Northern Ireland and Scotland and refer to relevant European Human Rights case law that impacts upon all laws governing capacity in the UK.

What is incapacity?

Capacity and incapacity are vital concepts whenever any decisions are being made by, with, about or on behalf of a person. Capacity is, roughly speaking, a person's ability to make reasoned decisions. The difficulty in defining capacity is that none of us make wise, safe, well-thought through or even responsible decisions *all of the time*. Therefore, any law that seeks to define the point at which a person ought to be protected from the decisions they might make has to carefully build in our right to make decisions that no other person would agree with. The importance of this, in the context of the theme of our book is as follows: if a person is in need and/or at risk, the entire approach to the situation will need to shift if he or she is unable to make reasoned decisions (see Figure 4.1 below).

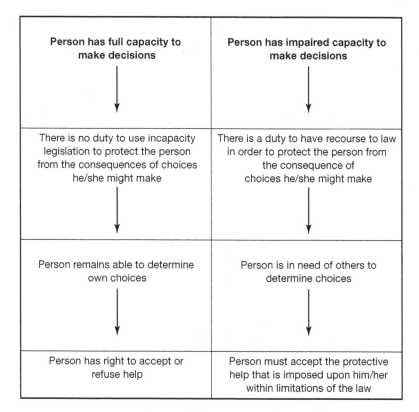

Figure 4.1 Summary of full and impaired capacity

We will ask you to return to this figure later, but for the moment, note that the downward arrows suggest that a person with incapacity requires protection by recourse to laws which allow others to make decisions for them. This places the person in a different relationship to the support that is being offered, *in that the person may not be able to refuse such help.*

> *Capacity refers to our ability to make competent decisions determining our life choices. It is based on the assumption that the State does not seek to intervene unnecessarily in the life of its citizens and will therefore not interfere with the choices anyone makes, provided that they are lawful choices. In other words, by and large, provided you do not choose to break any laws, the State will not assume any authority to take control of the decisions you make, no matter how unwise they may seem to others.*

> (Hothersall, Maas-Lowit and Golighley, 2008, p59)

This, in itself, could be the subject of an entire book because it contains a number of assumptions worth exploring. For example, while modern liberal democracies like the UK are not entirely free from accusation of flaws in their human rights track records, not every state will have a body of laws around which to promote a liberal policy of non-interference in the basic freedoms of its citizens. If you wish to obtain a clearer picture of countries where the state is sometimes brutally intrusive of the freedoms of its citizens, visit the website of Amnesty International UK.

The UK, as a modern liberal democracy, is signatory to the European Convention on Human Rights, which affords its citizens a relatively wide degree of freedom to determine their own actions. We have now arrived at a good start point from which to explore issues of how incapacity might be managed in the UK: that it is rooted in the basic freedoms which citizens enjoy and it exists in very close proximity to the body of law which protects human rights.

This leads us to an interesting point: From our wide experience of explaining capacity and incapacity to many students, we have noted that a surprisingly large number of people have lived their lives freely making a wide range of large and small choices and decisions, while never stopping to ponder that the authority to make such choices is loosely underpinned by law.

We could say that *capacity* is a term closely related to the law and that it refers to the wide range of choices that we are able to exercise as far as the law allows. In Hothersall, Maas-Lowit and Golightley (2008), readers are asked to consider the scope of their freedom to make lawful choices by reflecting on the potentially infinite range of things we can decide to do, from choosing what socks to wear to deciding to make a will; from going food-shopping to buying a home; from getting married to choosing one's friends. Capacity underpins the authority to make all of these choices.

Note that we are using the word *authority*. Our experience of enabling students to understand about capacity has led us to note that many people confuse *authority* with *ability*. For example, many of us may have the *ability* to commit armed robbery: we may have the nerve to do it, the ability to set aside moral qualms, the planning skills and the requisite knowledge of weaponry. However, because armed robbery is a crime, none of us has the *authority* to commit it. On the other hand, there will be many things that we have *authority* to do, but which we lack the *ability* to do. For example, this author may have the authority to juggle while tap-dancing, but he certainly lacks the ability to do it!

ACTIVITY *4.1*

The above discussion on ability and the authority to make decisions and exercise choice begs the following questions. Read them and take a minute to reflect upon them, taking a note of your answers.

- *What ought to happen when a person lacks or loses the capacity to make choices?*

- *In other words, what ought to happen when, through loss of critical faculties, such as loss of memory through dementia or brain injury, we lose the ability to safely make choices?*

- *Or, to reword the question yet again, this time in terms of the above discussion, should people who seriously lack the ability to make critical decisions about their lives still retain the authority to make them?*

- *What ought to happen when, through lasting conditions like severe learning disability, a person would make such poorly reasoned decisions as to be placed at risk?*

Comment

This situation is what we refer to as incapacity. Did you think that, in such circumstances, is it fair and responsible for the rest of society to stand back and say that, regardless of ability, the person should retain the same authority to make decisions no matter what the consequences? If so, there would be extreme financial and welfare risks in allowing the person in the case study below to make free choice on this basis.

Limitations upon definition of incapacity

One last issue before we move on to examine a case study relating to incapacity: we would be storing up complicated legal difficulties for ourselves if we did not draw strict parameters around who can be legitimately considered as having incapacity. Consider the following two examples.

- In the Soviet Union, psychiatry was sometimes infamously used to control political dissidents by declaring them to be mentally ill (Bloch and Reddaway, 1977). This is an example of the political dangers of having ill-defined boundaries set around incapacity.

- We would create great problems if we allowed temporary and self-willed conditions like drunkenness to fall under the definition of incapacity. Imagine how it would open the door to using *temporary incapacity* as a defence for drunk-driving: 'I'm so sorry your honour, but I could not help myself. I was so drunk when I got into the car that I had incapacity.'

Therefore, incapacity is limited in law to areas where the person is unable to make a decision by reason of mental illness, learning disability or cognitive impairment and sometimes personality disorder and inability to communicate because of physical disability (Department of Health, 2005 and Scottish Executive, 2000). This latter point may seem odd, when you consider that inside his or her mind, a person may have full capacity. However, if that capacity to make decisions is 'locked-in' by a physical disability such as a deteriorating neurological disorder, the person will be unable to communicate these wishes to anyone in the outside world. Therefore, the person with such complete physical disability *would* require the same protections as a person who cannot make decisions because of *mental* incapacity (Scottish Executive, 2006). We will return to the issue of physical disability later on (and see Chapter 9), after we have discussed some general issues and then closely examined the concept in relation to mental incapacity.

Issues of incapacity in practice

At this point it may be appropriate to reflect upon issues of free-will and self determination. Best professional practice in social, nursing and medical care now generally recognises that the individual service user is an autonomous agent. Based on this, it is better to provide support, information and guidance rather than to disempower by taking control of the person's circumstances. By this token, if the person chooses to ignore whatever advice is given, they must accept the consequences, but may also be provided with the opportunity to learn and grow from their mistakes (Eastman in Heller et al., 1996; Scottish Executive, 2001b). More than this, notions of inclusion and partnership suggest that service users bring great expertise in their own situations and that it is at best arrogant for *service providers* to set themselves up as experts in the experience of others. The Scottish Recovery Network (2007) use a simple diagram to show the progression from a paternalistic model of intervention, where the expert professional does things to the service user, through an enabling approach of doing things with the person, to an approach of working alongside the person in partnership of equals.

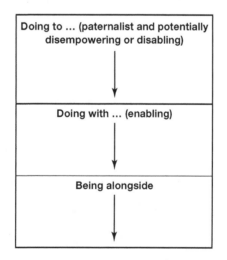

Figure 4.2 From 'doing to ...' to 'being with ...'

The implication of the shift from expert who knows what is best for the person to the orientation of *being with* ... is that skills and experience are shared and that the professional takes a more restrained and passive approach, moving from *doing* to *being*.

We would not wish to suggest anything as crude as the notion that someone with incapacity needs total protection by having all choice removed and given to someone else. However, we do suggest that the existence of incapacity places some service users in a different position relative to service providers from that self-determined partnership suggested above. If a person truly lacks capacity to understand or act upon the range of choices at his or her disposal, and if that person would not have the ability to learn from any mistakes made in the pursuit of decision making, it suggests that such a person ought not to be allowed the freedom to undertake potentially harmful courses of action. Indeed, *freedom* is a misplaced word in this context.

While the transfer of authority to manage the person's decision-making must to be done with proper recourse to the appropriate laws, and while it ought to be hedged with care only to exercise such powers in areas of decision-making and at times when the person truly lacks capacity, it does suggest a different approach to practice from what is generally thought of as empowering (Bennett et al., 1997).

The suggestion that *taking control* of aspects of a person's decision-making might be disempowering can be answered in the following ways: what of the following is more disempowering:

- to stand back and allow the person to make sometimes potentially dangerous choices without realising it; or

- to intervene and take control over those necessary decisions which might avoid serious harm?

Furthermore, if you examine both the principles embedded in UK incapacity laws and the Codes of Practice surrounding them, you will see that they direct the practitioner towards ways of managing such powers in ways which minimise scope for disempowerment (Scottish Executive 2006, and Department of Health, 2007).

CASE STUDY

Edith Lawson is a strong and independently minded woman in her late seventies. She has lived alone since her husband died eight years ago. Edith describes herself as 'a fighter' who has brought up her three children in poverty, worked in a variety of menial jobs and gone to college at the age of forty to get the education she missed in her childhood. In the last year, Edith has become increasingly forgetful and, being aware of what was happening to herself, she devised a strategy of writing everything down, using her notebooks to replace her dwindling short-term memory. Sadly, this strategy only worked for so long and as she becomes confused with increased memory loss, she forgets about the system of notebooks. Eventually, her two surviving sons cannot continue to respect her wishes to be left to get on with her life. It seems that Edith has lost five thousand pounds of life savings to a fraudulent builder who advised her that the guttering on her roof needed replacing. She is also unable to budget, she frequently forgets to shop adequately and she recently started a small fire by placing the electric kettle on the gas hob.

Comment

Progressive and sustained memory loss over such a long period at Edith's age is almost bound to be some form of dementia. This would fall within the legally accepted causes of incapacity in the confines of the UK's incapacity laws. With medical help it can sometimes be slowed down but, so far as current medical technology goes, it is unlikely to be reversible. In the following exercise, you should take account of the theme in the above case study that Edith has a strong and independent personality that will not diminish with her growing incapacity. You may take it as read that she will not accept any intervention from outsiders, including her sons.

ACTIVITY 4.2

Take a moment to reflect upon the following sequence of questions and jot down your thoughts. Then compare your thoughts with our deliberations below.

What risks can you discern from reading the above case study?

To what extent are these risks caused or amplified by Edith's diminishing capacity to make safe and reasoned decisions?

Do you think that Edith's wish to be left to manage her deteriorating situation ought to be absolutely respected?

Comment

In such a brief case study, there is much room for interpretation, so do not worry if your answers deviate from our own. However, it is clear that, however well Edith's strategy of managing memory loss by use of notebooks might have been, it has crossed a tipping point where it will increasingly fail as she forgets the purpose of the notebooks. Therefore she is at increasing risk from fraudulent callers, from inability to care for herself on a basic level and, specifically, from fire resulting from use of the kettle. Anyone who knows a little about the prognosis of dementia will know that this will get worse. Therefore it is fair to say that the risks are entirely caused by the mental deterioration of a once highly competent person. It could therefore be argued that her long-held wish to be left alone to manage her life is also now a manifestation of her growing incapacity and it is possible or even likely that Edith will not realise that she is at risk and therefore her wish for continuing independence is not realistic. Furthermore, to leave her alone could have dire consequences, possibly amounting to serious accident or even loss of life (Department of Health, 2000). This poses the difficult question of what protection ought to be available to a person who can no longer manage the freedom to make independent decisions.

Return to Figure 4.1 above and consider Edith while reading it. You might now note that the existence of law on incapacity imposes a *duty* to use the law to replace the decision-making powers of a person in Edith's situation with powers given to another party. The idea behind such law is that this other party may then make reasoned decisions in Edith's best interest, where she has lost the ability to do so. This will then minimise risks arising from her lack of capacity. It will also allow for her welfare and financial needs to be met.

Incapacity caused by physical disability

We have suggested above that, for a minority of people with certain extreme forms of disability, communication with the outside world may be so impaired that it is in their interests to consider them as lacking capacity. Before we move on to discuss the contents of the law, let us examine this situation.

As suggested above, physical disability would only ever become a cause of incapacity were there a total inability to communicate one's wishes to the outside world. We will examine the precise set of needs that this imposes and the risks arising out of them. To limit the discussion it may firstly be important to clarify that it is difficult to envisage how sensory impairments alone might constitute incapacity, because there are ways of maintaining communication even in the most extreme cases of people who are totally deaf, mute and blind.

Where the cause of incapacity is not mental disorder, it must be due to an inability to communicate. We already referred to this above. We stated that, in the case of a person who is locked inside themselves because of physical disability, the outside world cannot consider him or her to have capacity, even if he or she is able to consider making rational decisions. The reason for this is that the only purpose of being able to think rationally about the decisions one might wish to make, is that one can turn them into action by communicating them.

The case of Jean-Dominique Bauby (2007), illustrates this well. Bauby was the successful editor of a prestigious French magazine when he suffered a stroke which left him with 'locked-in syndrome', a condition of muscular paralysis, which leaves the person almost unable to move, while remaining in full possession of all mental faculties. Bauby learned to communicate by means of his only remaining physical ability: blinking one of his eyelids. Remarkably, in this manner he narrated his best-selling account of the experience, *The Diving Bell and the Butterfly* (2007). The point of telling you this is that Bauby clearly did not have incapacity. Had he been unable to blink with one eyelid, he would have had incapacity and his beautifully related story of his experience would have remained locked inside his head until he died. If this moves you to read his book, you will begin to imagine what an awful experience it must be to be so locked inside oneself. By taking the step beyond Bauby's book, we can approach the unimaginable experience of what it might be like to think clearly but not be able to externalise our thoughts.

In such a case, the needs of the person would be absolute. They would require someone to be appointed to preside over every decision that might be required in all spheres of life. However, incapacity through physical disability is not just limited to the rare cases of locked-in syndrome, or people in comas, with head injuries which render them paralysed or with other such conditions. It also extends to people who have physical conditions which make speech indecipherable and make it impossible to write or use hand signs. For example, Parkinson's disease is a progressive and terminal illness of the brain, which makes fine movement more and more difficult to perform. Ultimately, the sufferer cannot co-ordinate coherent speech, and cannot control movement of the limbs, so that writing or even pointing to things may not be possible.

To make sure that incapacity is present, the law sets out limitations upon when it may be deduced: the inability to communicate must be such that it cannot be overcome by any sort of aid to communication. There is a wide variety of aids to communication from machines which turn the user's typed words on a key-board into electronic speech, to simple picture boards on which the user indicates needs by pointing to a picture, for example, of a plate of food, or a bed, or a toilet.

The Scottish Adults with Incapacity Act (Scottish Executive, 2006) uses the words *whether of an interpretive nature, or otherwise*. This refers to aids to communication such as the various sign languages that exist. It further refers to the sort of interpretive communication that Bauby used in blinking his eyelid. It may even refer to a unique communication that a person has set up with one carer. As long as it can be demonstrated to be a means of communication, it will limit incapacity to the extent to which it communicates complex need.

Before passing on to discuss the law, we said we would discuss risk in relation to physical disability: The risks are two-fold. On the one hand, there is risk that any powers to take control of a person's decision making could be wrongly asserted. If a person is able to communicate wishes but is disempowered by control being taken away, it is potentially destructive to well-being on many levels. This is why the law takes such care to spell out that every means to communicate must be exhausted before incapacity is deduced.

On the other hand, allowing someone to languish in a disability which debars them from communicating their wishes is neglectful and allows scope for abuse to take place.

The legal position on mental incapacity in the four countries of the UK

It is impossible to convey in any depth the widely diverging positions that the Scottish, Northern Irish and English & Welsh legal systems take on the issue of incapacity. What follows is therefore rather superficial. Should you require a more in-depth discussion, you are directed to the further reading at the end of this chapter and, in particular, MacKay (2008).

The common ground

Any law regulating personal autonomy and capacity is going to be complicated in its links to wide-ranging aspects of the legal system within which it sits. It will have to dovetail with laws in relation to banking, inheritance, housing, medical treatment and personal welfare to name but a few. Therefore it is not only the cultural, political and demographic differences across the land that make these three legislative endeavours so very different, it is also the other laws they have to relate to. While the three legal systems of the UK do differ hugely in terms of court structures, legislative processes, etc., there are underpinning commonalities based on a regard for managing incapacity coherently and consistently within these differences in structure.

The European Court of Human Rights judgment in HL *v* United Kingdom (commonly referred to simply as *Bournewood*, because HL's initial complaint was against Bournewood Health Authority) is a piece of European law which impacts massively upon the area of incapacity law in the UK legal systems (European Court of Human Rights, 2004). Briefly,

HL is a man with a high level of autism that seriously affects his ability to communicate his wishes. He lives with a couple in a private care arrangement. When he was 49 years old, in 1997, he was upset one day on the bus on his way to his day care centre and he ended up being restrained in the local hospital, where he remained for three months. His carers objected on his behalf that there was not only no reason to keep him in hospital, but there was no legal ground to do so, since he was never detained under any mental health law. Bournewood Health Authority argued that HL's passive compliance with his incarceration in hospital represented sufficient grounds to presume that he wished to be there.

To cut a long story short, after the case was determined locally, appealed against, over-turned and remitted to the House of Lords, it was finally determined in the European Court that HL's detention breached his human rights. It follows that, where any person lacks capacity to communicate his or her wishes, passivity can no longer be taken as agreement. This effectively meant that potentially thousands of people with a range of conditions from learning disability to dementia were effectively being wrongly deprived of their freedom in a wide range of care settings across Europe. The *Bournewood gap*, as this position became called, influenced the drafting of the English and Welsh Mental Capacity Act 2005 and the the drafting of a discussion paper in Northern Ireland.

It is significant from the above discussion that Scotland has had an Incapacity Act since 2000 and that that legislation was over ten years in the making (Scottish Law Commission, 1995). This means that it pre-dated the final Bournewood decision and that subsequent amendments have had to be put in place to accommodate the Bournewood gap. However, the broad significance of Bournewood for all three countries is that it underpins a broader legal assumption, that it is not lawful to simply supplant the wishes of a person who lacks capacity with decisions made by another person who has no legal basis for making these decisions. In other words, where a person such as Edith, in the case study above, lacks capacity to make a decision, there needs to be a legislative process which gives shape to who ought to make that decision, how they ought to make it and who will scrutinise the process. As we will discuss in conclusion of this chapter, this has serious implications for the protection of vulnerable adults because it very roughly divides those at risk into two groups.

First, there are those who place themselves at risk because they engage in activities with full capacity to understand the consequences; for example, a person who engages in high risk sexual activities and has no existing condition which might underpin incapacity (no mental illness, dementia, learning disability, etc.) which might cloud their judgement. While support, advice and guidance may be offered to this group of people, there is no legal means by which to remove their authority to make these risky decisions.

Second, there is the group of people discussed above, who lack capacity as determined by law. For this group of people, there is a legal duty to intervene and remove the authority to make such decisions.

Scotland and England & Wales

In brief summary, the legal positions in Scotland and England & Wales, while widely different in detail, have broad similarities.

Because children are loosely under the authority of their parents, or those with parental authority, both the Adults with Incapacity (Scotland) Act 2000 and the Mental Capacity Act 2005 only have effect on those aged 16 and over. They both have sets of principles that govern how any person will use the Acts and the common ground between them may be summarised as follows.

- It is wrong to ever assume that a person totally lacks capacity. The adult must be assumed to have capacity until a situation arises which challenges the assumption. Only then may powers be used.

- Practicable help must be given to overcome difficulties before anyone treats the adult as not being able to make decisions.

- Unwise decisions are not, in themselves, reason to assume a lack of capacity.

- Anything done on behalf of a person who lacks capacity must be done in their best interests.

- Anything done on behalf of a person who lacks capacity should be the least restrictive of their basic rights and freedoms. The person's wishes and feelings and the views of significant others must be taken into account.

Note from the above list the principle that *capacity must be assumed unless proven otherwise*. While this is more clearly expressed in the principles of the 2005 Act than the 2000 Act, it is a feature which runs throughout the Scottish and English legislation alike. What this implies is that we must never regard any person as entirely incapable of making decisions, no matter what level of disability they may have. We must take each instance on its merit and only use the law to take authority away from the person when justified to do so. In other words, even the most incapacitated person must be assumed to be able to manage their lives until the next event arises to challenge that assumption.

In detail the two Acts' principles differ and the above general statement is not to be taken as the law. Anyone involved in using the law must go to the specific source to read the exact principles. This is because, no matter how well intentioned your intervention may be, it is almost guaranteed to be unlawful if you cannot demonstrate how you have invoked the specific principles in relation to your actions.

Both Acts make provision for Powers of Attorney. These are powers that anyone may draft for themselves, provided that they have full capacity to do so. The person drafting powers of attorney (called *a granter* in Scotland and *a donor* in England) identifies a person or persons who will have authority to exercise these powers should the granter/donor ever acquire incapacity. At such a point, the powers become effective and the attorney (called a *donee* in England) assumes authority to make any decision that is listed in the powers of attorney which the granter/donor is unable to manage. To draw an example from our case study above, suppose that, before she became too incapacitated with dementia, Edith had drawn up powers of attorney identifying one of her sons as attorney/donee. Provided she had done this in the proper legal format and provided it had been done while she was capable of understanding what she was doing, her son could now use that power to make necessary decisions for Edith. The scope of these powers would depend upon what Edith had listed in her power of attorney document. If, for example, she had granted the power to make decisions about where she resided and the type of care she could receive, her son could resolve the issue of her outstanding needs and the risks attendant upon her now. It goes without saying that he would have to do so with recourse to the principles.

This raises the question, What ought to happen if someone acquires incapacity before they have the opportunity to draft a power of attorney?

Under both Acts, there is provision for the Court to grant powers identifying a person (called a *guardian* in Scotland and a *deputy* in England) and authorising that person with specific powers. In appointing a guardian or making a declaration appointing a deputy, the Court is effectively setting up a power of attorney when it is too late for the person to do so for him/herself. The process of doing this under the 2000 Act is very different from the process under the 2005 Act. For example, the Scottish law usually requires the involvement of a specialised social worker called a *mental health officer*, while the English Act only requires the Court to consider appointing a specialised advocate to represent the interests of the subject. Both Acts require specialist medical assessment to verify incapacity to the Court.

To continue the example, at the point in Edith's life indicated in the case study, were there no power of attorney, she would almost certainly require a guardianship order/declaration of a deputy. Otherwise there would be no way of making decisions about where she should live to protect her safety, without contravening the Bournewood judgment (European Court of Human Rights, 2004).

ACTIVITY 4.3

Look back upon the case study and make a note of Edith's needs arising out of the risks posed by her dementia. Assume that a court has identified you as her guardian or deputy.

- *How would you wish to meet her needs by making decisions on her behalf?*
- *Would the principles impact on how you did this and would they affect the decisions you made?*

Comment
There might be a wide range of possibilities for intervention here. They would depend upon the powers that the Court gave you to intervene, the specific nature of Edith's difficulties (which, in reality, would require very full assessment) and the resources available. They might range from the slightly premature assumption that Edith must be removed into some form of sheltered or residential setting, to the intervention of home care/support. The reason we suggest that the option of removal into residential care is premature is because it does not exactly sit with the principles. Have a look back at the broad outline of principles above and see if you can see why we say this.

Northern Ireland

The position in Northern Ireland is as yet less clear. The current law, the Mental Health (Northern Ireland) Order 1986 is subject to review (the Bamford Review, August 2007). A response from the government following from Bamford (in June 2008) will result in a draft Mental Health and Mental Disability (Northern Ireland) Order. If you read the substance of Bamford and the subsequent government response, you will see similarities with the 2000 and 2005 Acts. You will also see the impact of the Bournewood judgement.

Conclusion

The significance of incapacity in the assessment of needs, risk and vulnerability cannot be underestimated. Where it exists, incapacity represents a watershed in the way that any issues of need ought to be approached: It flags up a duty to protect by using the law to make any decision where incapacity challenges the individual's own ability to determine choice. It represents the dividing line between allowing the person to determine his or her own actions and taking control to provide necessary protection regardless of the person's lack of compliance (please refer back to Figure 4.1 above).

In the subject population of this book, there is a high instance of mental illness, learning disability, personality disorder and physical disability which might impair communication of wishes. For these reasons, consideration of issues in relation to incapacity ought to be the first philtre through which the practitioner assesses any person who seems at risk.

C H A P T E R   S U M M A R Y

In this chapter we have considered the related notions of capacity and incapacity, thinking about their relevance and applicability in relation to people's day-to-day lives and on practice. We have noted that it is important for practitioners to be very clear about the myriad issues involved in decision-making regarding capacity or the lack of it and how reference to a rights-based approach helps us to appreciate how such complex notions can be utilised for the benefit of those affected by this issue, emphasising the potential for empowerment within situations where the opposite is in fact the issue to be dealt with. We have also considered some of the limitations inherent within this area and the role of the law and Codes of Practice in providing a framework within which decisions concerning capacity and incapacity can take place.

FURTHER READING

Beauchamp, TL and Childress, JF (2009) *Principles of biomedical ethics* (6th edn). Oxford. Oxford University Press.
Regarded by many as the definitive work on this subject. Detailed coverage of the many ethical issues bound up in the issues referred to above.

Mackay, K (2008) The Scottish adult support and protection legal framework. *The Journal of Adult Protection* 10(4) pp25–36.
This is an excellent review of Scottish Incapacity law in the context of Adult Support and Protection.

Pritchard, J (ed) (2008) *Good practice in safeguarding adults: Working effectively in adult protection.* London. Jessica Kingsley.
A text which takes a broad look at a range of practice-based issues in the area of adult support and protection.

Part Two

Chapter 5

Need, risk and protection in work with children, young people and their families

Steve J Hothersall

A C H I E V I N G   A   S O C I A L   W O R K   D E G R E E

National Occupational Standards
Key Role 1: Prepare for, and work with, individuals, families, carers, groups and communities to assess their needs and circumstances.
- Work with individuals, families, carers, groups and communities to identify, gather, analyse and understand information.
- Assess needs, risks and options taking into account legal and other requirements.

Key Role 2: Plan, carry out, review and evaluate social work practice, with individuals, families, carers, groups, communities and other professionals.
- Identify the need for legal and procedural intervention.
- Plan and implement action to meet the immediate needs and circumstances.
- Develop and maintain relationships with individuals, families, carers, groups, communities and others.
- Work with individuals, families, carers, groups, communities and others to avoid crisis situations and address problems and conflict.
- Apply and justify social work methods and models used to achieve change and development, and improve life opportunities.
- Take immediate action to deal with the behaviour that presents a risk.
- Work with individuals, families, carers, groups, communities and others to identify and evaluate situations and circumstances that may trigger the behaviour.
- Work with individuals, families, carers, groups and communities on strategies and support that could positively change the behaviour.

Key Role 3: Support individuals to represent their needs, views and circumstances.
- Present evidence to, and help individuals, families, carers, groups and communities to understand the procedures of and the outcomes from, decision-making forums.
- Enable individuals, families, carers, groups and communities to be involved in decision-making forums.

continued

Achieving A Social Work Degree continued

Key Role 4: Manage risk to individuals, families, carers, groups, communities, self and colleagues.
- Identify and assess the nature of the risk.
- Balance the rights and responsibilities of individuals, families, carers, groups and communities with associated risk.
- Regularly monitor, re-assess, and manage risk to individuals, families, carers, groups and communities.
- Assess potential risk to self and colleagues.
- Work within the risk assessment and management procedures of your own and other relevant organisations and professions.
- Plan, monitor and review outcomes and actions to minimise stress and risk.

Key Role 5: Manage and be accountable, with supervision and support, for your own social work practice within your organisation.
- Manage and prioritise your workload within organisational policies and priorities.
- Carry out duties using accountable professional judgement and knowledge-based social work practice.
- Maintain accurate, complete, accessible, and up-to-date records and reports.
- Provide evidence for judgements and decisions.
- Implement legal and policy frameworks for access to records and reports.

Key Role 6: Demonstrate professional competence in social work practice.
- Exercise and justify professional judgements.
- Use professional assertiveness to justify decisions and uphold professional social work practice, values and ethics.
- Work within the principles and values underpinning social work practice.

Scottish Standards in Social Work Education
Key Role 1: Prepare for, and work with, individuals, families, carers, groups and communities to assess their needs and circumstances.
- Assessing needs and options in order to recommend a course of action.

Key Role 2: Plan, carry out, review and evaluate social work practice with individuals, families, carers, groups, communities and other professionals.
- Identifying and responding to crisis situations.
- Working with individuals, families, carers, groups and communities to achieve change, promote dignity, realise potential and improve life opportunities.
- Tackling behaviour which presents a risk to individuals, families, carers, groups, communities and the wider public.

Key Role 3: Assess and manage risk to individuals, families, carers, groups, communities, self and colleagues.
- Assessing and managing risks to individuals, families, carers, groups and communities.
- Assessing and managing risk to self and colleagues.

Key Role 4: Demonstrate professional competence in social work practice.
- Evaluating and using up-to-date knowledge of, and research into, social work practice.
- Working within agreed standards of social work practice.

Key Role 5: Manage and be accountable, with supervision and support, for your own social work practice within your organisation.
- Working effectively with professionals within integrated, multi-disciplinary and other service settings.

Introduction

In this chapter we look at issues of need, risk and protection as they relate to professional practice with children, young people and their families. We shall begin by considering how these issues have been dealt with over time in order to appreciate the current form legal, policy and practice frameworks now take. We then look at a range of themes and issues that can generate particular forms of *need* that may contribute to increased *risk* and a subsequent need for *protection*. As we saw in Chapter 1, it is important to think about those things that are likely to increase a person's *susceptibility* to *vulnerability* (Kottow, 2003), and while childhood *per se* (James and Prout, 2003; Cunningham, 2006), with its associated immaturity and dependence upon adults brings with it the potential for increased vulnerability, there are a number of other factors that may negatively impact upon childhood and compound children's difficulties and disproportionately increase the risk of harm to them *and* their families.

The nature and development of professional practice with children, young people and their families

Of necessity it is important to understand how professional responses to children, young people and their families have developed over time through differing social and political contexts. The current legislative, policy and practice context is one that has *evolved*; where things are now is as a direct result of where we have been, for better or for worse. It is possible to see themes developing as a result of changes in society and shifts in attitudes towards the way we view the nature of childhood, the family and society as a whole (Smith, 2010). Social phenomena such as increases in youth offending are not new; the Ingleby Committee in England and Wales (Home Office, 1960) and the Kilbrandon Committee in Scotland (Scottish Home and Health Department and Scottish Education Department, 1964; Kilbrandon, 1966) debated these issues at length then and provided legal and policy responses which are still evident today, particularly in relation to Kilbrandon which laid the foundations of the Scottish Children's Hearing system (Hothersall, 2008) which is still active today and regarded as a fundamental part of the Scottish child welfare system, much envied by other nations. We can see therefore that the law, policy and practice responses are for the most part evolutionary, pragmatic and to some extent, cyclical.

ACTIVITY 5.1

Talk to your grandparents and your parents or someone you know of their generation. Ask them what sorts of things they typically experienced as a child. What was school like? What did they do in their leisure time? What was home life like? Then think about your childhood and the things you typically experienced. Finally, think about a child you know well and consider these issues from their perspective today. Are there any significant differences in experience? What are these and why do you think things may have changed in the way they have? Perhaps you could try and identify what it is that has contributed to these changes as you read the rest of this chapter.

Comment

It is likely that you identified some significant differences in relation to how things were when grandparents and parents were young. These might have been around differences in the perceived sense of freedom people had when young to roam around, apparently without concerns about being attacked or abused by strangers. You might also have been surprised at the different ways children amused themselves when at home; quite different perhaps from today's 'digital culture'. You may also have spotted some differences between how you remember your childhood and what you see as 'typical' for a younger child today. These differences are important in highlighting how societal changes, either in real terms or as perceived, can affect the way we all think and behave.

The foundations of current practice

The Children Act (UK) of 1908 is generally regarded as the first 'Children's Charter' because of its wide-ranging impact and its concern for the rights of children. This Act abolished the death sentence for children and put restrictions upon why, when and for how long children could be imprisoned. This piece of legislation was the first to refer specifically to the need for the courts and others involved with children to have regard to their *welfare*, even though the dominant philosophy of the time was that of the Poor Laws of 1601 and 1834 (*see* Fraser, 2009). Children who had been abused or neglected were generally removed from home rather than supported to remain there and the care of those children who were in public care became an increasing cause for concern, especially following the death of Denis O'Neil (Home Office, 1945) who died while in 'foster care' in England. This added impetus to the calls for a major review of public childcare provision. These and other developments resulted in the Children Act 1948 (UK), which placed responsibility for services to children with the newly created Children's Departments, and the 'Boarding Out' of children (Foster Care) was promoted. People were now beginning to realise that children had feelings and the significance of loss, change and transitions in children's lives was beginning to be recognised.

It was also the case that child abuse and neglect was not recognised in the way it is today. It took the pioneering work of Henry Kempe and his colleagues (Kempe et al., 1962) to begin the process of consciousness-raising in relation to the physical abuse of children before people began to recognise this for what it was (Lynch, 1985). Since then, other significant events involving the death and significant suffering of many, many children have continued that slow process in relation to other aspects of children's welfare and the extent of harm occasioned upon them in a variety of forms including the impact of child sexual abuse and, more recently, emotional abuse and neglect. Such tragedies have also been the catalyst for changes in how society responds to and manages such things (Hothersall, 2008).

As public awareness of both the physical and emotional needs of children became more acute, the responses began to be more flexible and oriented towards *prevention*. Although by today's standards the preventative approach then was perhaps somewhat limited, it did nonetheless foreshadow what today we refer to as the *ecological approach* (Bronfenbrenner, 1979; 1986; 1989; Jack, 2000) nowadays central to major policy initiatives. Concern was evident as to the need to ask what the child(ren) thought about their situation and also why it was that some families seemed to benefit from assistance, whereas others did not. In relation to these situations, the term 'problem family' was first coined (Philp and Timms, 1962) and Children's Departments in England and Wales, and the Social Work Departments in Scotland began to utilise an ever-increasing range of different partners to assist them in delivering services, indicating a growing awareness that local authority services could not do it all on their own, thereby moving towards what today we know as *professional collaboration* in all its guises.

These *thematic* developments relating to prevention, early identification and practical help took shape in the UK through new legislation in the form of the Children and Young Person's Act 1963 (UK) which for the first time placed a *duty* upon Local Authorities to undertake *preventative* work with children and their families in order to minimise the likelihood of them being received into public care. The practice of *social casework* (Biestek, 1961) began to emerge at this time and was seen as the best way to provide services. This arrangement involved workers undertaking assessments and providing direct assistance designed to help people resolve their difficulties. Central to this approach was the *relationship* that developed between the worker and the family. There was an increased emphasis upon information sharing and cooperation between professionals, at least relative to how things had been done before because people were now beginning to realise that *children in need* and their families often required the services of a number of professionals simultaneously. Interestingly, these themes appear in the very recent reviews of social work across the UK, *Changing Lives* in Scotland (Scottish Executive, 2006a) and *Social Work at its Best* in England and Wales (GSCC, 2008) giving something of the flavour of 'back to the future'.

The growth of child protection

The abuse and neglect of children is something that has always happened. Our formally articulated concern with it nowadays is a relatively recent phenomenon and represents changing attitudes towards children and their changing status within society. The organised and bureaucratised approach to the protection of children we see today really began following the death of Maria Colwell at the hands of her step-father on 6 January 1973. The subsequent public inquiry (DHSS, 1974a) resulted in the issuing of circular LASSL (74) (13) (DHSS, 1974b) that triggered the establishment of what we now refer to as the child protection system. This included the development of Area Review Committees (now Area Child Protection Committees in Scotland (Scottish Executive, 2005c) and Local Safeguarding Children Boards in other parts of the UK (HM Government, 2006)) and through these, child protection conferences (and now 'core groups') and the child protection register. Through a strict access protocol these registers are accessible by other agencies and professionals who, if they have concerns about a child, can check to see whether a child's name is present (Pugh, 2007). This tragic event was seen as a major turning point regarding the relationship between the *state* and the *family*. As Ashenden (2004) notes:

> *Child protection is one set of practices through which relations between families and the state are constituted and regulated. This set of practices enables us to examine the*

negotiation of the relationship between public and private life. Modern management of the legal, social and cultural boundaries between families and the state is effected by the mobilisation of a range of professional forms of knowledge and practice such as law, medicine, psychology and social work, specialising in determining where and when intervention is reasonable and legitimate, all of which are premised on the idea of the 'best interests of the child'. (p10).

Prior to this point, the role of social work was very much seen as being about approaching the problems of individual families in a way that maintained the clear boundary between the *public sphere* of local authorities and the state and the *private sphere* of the family. The Children Act 1975 (UK) followed and the powers of the state regarding children thought to be at risk were increased dramatically and a 'rescue and remove' attitude tended to prevail in terms of practice which was very defensive, underpinned by what today we would refer to as the 'precautionary principle' (Sterling Burnett, 2009; Hood and Jones, 1996).

One issue we need to think about nowadays is how the notion of *need* appears to be being replaced in the parlance of professional practice with that of *risk*. The whole issue of *vulnerability* nestles next to the concept of need, whereas that of *protection* is increasingly tied to issues around risk. We can think about how these ideas are interrelated by looking at the following diagram:

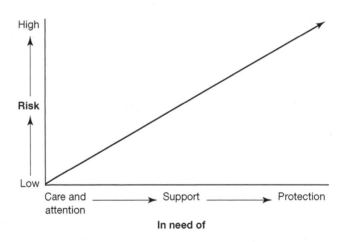

Figure 5.1 A continuum of need and increasing levels of risk

There is a sense in which the lexicon of welfare and well-being is being replaced by one of risk and protection. We appear to be in the 'risk society' having shifted away from the welfare society and the welfare state because of new right ideologies and the associated cult of individualism. Kemshall, citing several writers, suggests that *the universalism of need has been replaced by targeted strategies of risk avoidance, prevention and management* (2007, p154). In a similar vein, France and Utting (2005) refer to the emergence of the *'risk-focused prevention'* paradigm (p78) as the prevailing approach underpinning New Labour's broad-based policies in relation to children and families, a position now firmly established (Frost and Parton, 2009) and evident across the UK as a whole.

The social and professional context for practice

As we have seen, the law and policy acts as the broad framework within which social work practice takes place. We need to appreciate that law and policy are reflections of what society either values or disapproves of at any given time and act as mechanisms for responding to what is happening generally.

As society evolves and social (group) living becomes more complex, the context of and for your practice changes too. For example, recent years have seen an increase in the prevalence of substance misuse, particularly drug misuse (see Chapter 10). As a result, social workers have found themselves increasingly involved in situations where drugs and alcohol are a mediating factor in many instances of family breakdown, child abuse and neglect. Social work and other forms of professional practice have had to take these and other phenomena into account and respond accordingly. Munro (2005) puts it well when she says that:

> *The persistent problems for practitioners, revealed in public inquiries into child deaths and research studies, lie in their skills and knowledge, in their ability to collect, interpret and communicate information accurately. The solutions to these problems involve improving the expertise of the workforce and ensuring that they have the work conditions that allow them to practise to a high level, ensuring, for example, that workers have the skill and the time to interview children and learn their view of what is happening to them (p386).*

Today, we have a much more complex infrastructure with a host of related systems and initiatives in place which, for the most part, have been specifically designed to promote the well-being, welfare and protection of children. Interestingly though, there appears to be a developing assumption in some areas that these *systems* will protect and support children and their families. In isolation, they won't. These are socially constructed entities that should be regarded as *tools*, used to assist professionals in exercising their professional judgements while discharging their duties. People protect people; systems can help to organise, coordinate and provide frameworks for action, but *whether* a response happens and *how* it happens is fundamentally down to *people* (Keenan, 2007). Frost and Parton (2009), referring to Smith (2001) suggest that many of the changes introduced over the past few years across England and Wales, although it is arguable that the same point can be made across the whole of the UK, appear to *have substituted* **confidence** *in systems in place of* **trust** *in individual professional practice* (p161: emphasis in original). This is a somewhat incongruous position to be in when, according to a number of governmental missives, the professional autonomy of social workers is in fact something to be promoted and regarded as fundamental to the promotion of children's well-being (Scottish Executive, 2006a; GSCC, 2008). The various Governments and Assemblies across the UK all have a similar vision for children and these revolve around core themes of safety, health, achievement, nurturance, being active and making positive contributions, respect, responsibility and inclusion (*Getting it Right for Every Child* (Scottish Executive, 2005a; 2005b); *Every Child Matters* (Department for Education and Skills, 2004a; 2004b; 2004c); *Our Children and Young People: Our Pledge* (Office of the First Minister and Deputy First Minister (Northern Ireland) OFMDFM, 2006); *Children and Young People: A*

Framework for Partnership (Welsh Assembly Government, 2002; 2004)) and policy and subsequent practice responses are focused upon addressing these broad objectives.

Other issues, for example changes in technology, present social workers and other professionals with different challenges. Many children who are born with severe genetic, chromosomal or other defects are now more likely to survive into adulthood and are therefore more likely to have a broad range of complex needs and they will as a result require to be supported in new and challenging ways for increasingly longer periods of time (CSCI, 2007). Other technology-related issues appertain to the collection, collation and sharing of information between professionals which is now very much an issue underpinned by reference to information and communication technologies (ICTs). Such developments are clearly evident in Governmental policy initiatives designed to enhance outcomes for children (e-care initiatives – see Hudson, 2002; 2003) although there are a number of ethical issues that have still to be debated before these are utilised routinely and with confidence. Their utility also requires to be evaluated over time and this clearly articulated within the context of the potential changes such technology may impose on professional *social work* practice (Garrett, 2005; Parton, 2008) recently criticised in relation to the case of 'Baby P' (Garrett, 2009) and more generally (White, Hall and Peckover, 2009; Munro, 2008; Ofsted et al., 2008: 7, 14).

As we saw above, social work and its activities have moved between different orientations at different points in time. These shifts can be typified as existing on a continuum (see Figure 5:2 below) with a 'child welfare' orientation at one end and a 'child protection' orientation at the other (Spratt, 2001).

Figure 5.2 *Child care orientations*

All practice can be located on this continuum, although where the generality of practice rests at any given time depends on many of those factors we have referred to above, and today it seems that in some areas, there has been a shift towards the 'child protection' orientation, particularly in the wake of the death of 'Baby P' (Laming, 2009).

Sources of need and risk in relation to children, young people and their families

While there is no definitive statement on which social issue is the most problematic or difficult to deal with, those which follow all have the potential to seriously impact upon the well-being of children and young people and compromise their welfare. Many of these affect families too and it is often the complex interrelationship and the compound nature of these that make many situations very difficult to deal with. The realities of (post-) modern-day life (Giddens, 1990; 1991) have an emphasis upon individualism (Bauman, 2007; 2003; Heywood, 2007) and consumerism and so poverty has arguably taken on new and different forms (Bauman, 2004). A major issue of course is that of child abuse and neglect which, as we shall see, continues to present itself as a challenge and one that appears to evolve into different forms that reflect how society is changing (Hothersall and Bolger, 2010; Parton, 2006).

Child abuse and neglect

There are currently four broad categories of child abuse that are used to locate a child's name on the *Child Protection Register*, with an additional category being used in Scotland, and although there are some variations in operational terminology across the four countries of the UK, they all cover the same range of concerns:

Neglect: this refers to situations where a child's essential needs are not met to such an extent that this is likely to cause impairment to physical health and development. These needs would include food, clothing, cleanliness, shelter and warmth and a lack of appropriate care, including deprivation of access to health care, which may result in persistent or severe exposure, through negligence, to circumstances that endanger the child.

Physical abuse (separated as physical injury and physical neglect in Scotland) refers to the actual or attempted injury to a child which may now also be seen to include the administration of toxic substances and where there is a knowledge, or reasonable suspicion that the injury was inflicted (an act of commission) or knowingly not prevented (an act of omission).

Emotional abuse refers to the persistent emotional ill-treatment of a child such as to cause severe and/or persistent adverse effects on their emotional development.

Sexual abuse: 'Any child below the age of 16 may be deemed to have been sexually abused when any person(s) by design or neglect, exploits the child, directly or indirectly, in any activity intended to lead to the sexual arousal or other forms of gratification of that person or any other person(s) including organised networks. This definition holds whether or not there has been genital contact and whether or not the child is said to have initiated the behaviour' (see Scottish Executive, 2002, pp7-8). There is a slightly different phrasing used in the *Working Together* guidance (DfES, 2006), but the essence of both is much the same.

Non-Organic Failure to Thrive (Scotland) refers to situations where a child significantly fails to reach normal growth and developmental milestones (i.e. physical growth, weight, motor, social and intellectual development) in situations where physical and genetic reasons have been medically eliminated and a diagnosis of 'failure to thrive' has been determined.

As we saw in Chapter 3, there has also been a growth of regulatory legislation and guidance to correspond with changes and developments in legislation around work with children and families that aims to identify those individuals who may pose a risk to children if they were to work with them.

Poverty

Poverty is a major problem for many children today and the Governments of the UK have pledged to eradicate child poverty before the middle of the 21st century (Blair, 1999). There are a number of policy initiatives that exist which have as their stated aim the minimisation and [ultimately] the eradication of [child] poverty. Whether these will work remains to be seen (Mooney and Scott, 2005; Hirsch, 2008) but in terms of social work practice we must recognise the impact such phenomena can have on all aspects of life and respond to this accordingly, ideally adopting more critically aware perspective (Davis, 2007) on the realities and wider structural arrangements (van Wormer et al., 2007; Mullaly, 2007) which maintain this as a pernicious form of disadvantage (Alcock, 2006).

Racism and other forms of discrimination

Racism has been with us for millennia and it is still present throughout society. Its articulation can often be subtle, but it can also be overt. Either way its effects are pernicious and serious. As societies become more diverse in relation to their ethnic and racial compositions, the potential for discrimination, oppression and outright violence and harm increases (see Zimbardo, 2007). Social workers are both morally and professionally bound to challenge and oppose all forms of racism and are often in the front line to help people who are experiencing this at both the individual and institutional level (Dominelli, 2008; Better, 2007; Rattansi, 2009; Swan, 2010). Workers must also be aware of their own attitudes in relation to these matters.

The potential for racism and other forms of discrimination against the person has increased with the shifts in the geo-socio-political landscape and the changes in rates of migration, immigration and asylum seeking (Kohli, 2006; Wade, Mitchell and Graeme, 2006; Kohli and Mitchell, 2009; Swan, 2010) and with the emergence of right-wing extremists as potentially viable political entities.

Social exclusion

Social exclusion is the result of a number of associated and related factors and refers to the experience of people who are unable to engage effectively in and enjoy the benefits of society (Bolger and Morago, 2010). It is a multi-layered concept and in essence is the experience of a *process* that can lead to a number of damaging outcomes (Tisdall et al., 2006) including homelessness (Morago, 2010). Many children and their families with whom you are likely to work will be experiencing some level of social exclusion (Byrne, 2005; Gordon, Levitas and Pantazis, (2006): Sheppard, 2006; Welshman, 2007). The Social Exclusion Unit set up by the New Labour government in 1997 was an attempt to strategically locate within the centre of government a department that had a relationship to all other departments, thus emphasising the interrelatedness of many of the issues deemed to comprise social exclusion (Social Exclusion Unit, 2001).

Crime, disorder and anti-social behaviour

The perception of the general public is that crime and disorder are on the increase. Whether this is *actually* the case and one that could be backed up by clear and unequivocal evidence, statistical or otherwise, relative to population growth is debatable. However, what *is* clear is that this is a hot political issue with governments both north and south of the border issuing law and policy regularly in an attempt to increase the public's sense of 'felt security' (Kraemer and Roberts, 1996; Marris, 1996; Green, 2008). Issues like this are perhaps symptomatic of the 'moral panics' that erupt from time to time (Critcher, 2006) and often force governments and policy makers to act even if the real issues and their consequences are far from clear.

Substance use/misuse

The issues around substance use/misuse in the context of working with children, young people and their families are ones which social workers will often have to deal with on a daily basis (Kroll and Taylor, 2001; Harbin and Murphy, 2000; Straussner and Fewell, 2006; Cleaver et al., 2007 and Chapter 10). The effects upon children and young people should not be underestimated and the difficulties addictions may cause for parents should similarly be recognised as having the potential to do great damage to parenting capacity and therefore have the potential to severely disrupt a child's life.

Mental illness and poor mental health

The impact of poor *parental* mental health and mental illness upon children can be significant and there is a substantial body of research and writing on this issue (Falkov, 1996; Gopfort, Webster and Seeman, 2004; Reder and Lucey, 1995; Reder, McClure and Jolley, 2000; Rutter, 1966; Rutter and Quinton, 1984; Weir and Douglas, 1999). Similarly, poor mental health and mental illness *in children and young people* (including infants) is a situation you are more and more likely to have to deal with (Hothersall, Maas-Lowitt and Golightley, 2008; Heads Up Scotland, 2007; Barnes, 2003) and the effects of both can be quite debilitating.

Domestic violence

Domestic violence and associated forms of intimate-partner abuse are issues that can and do have devastating consequences on both direct and indirect victims. Partners (predominantly but not exclusively female in conventional relationships) who are abused and children who witness this can live in fear for years and have their very sense of 'self' destroyed. Fear, intimidation and secrecy are common ingredients in such situations and must not be ignored. Professionals involved in working with families need to be skilful in identifying and helping people to deal with these issues (Todd, Hothersall and Owen, 2010; Abrahams, 2007; Hester et al., 2006; Humphreys et al., 2006; Radford and Hester, 2006; Calder, Harold and Howarth, 2004) and the same considerations need to be given in relation to same-sex relationships.

Cyberspace and related issues

The advent of the internet, mobile phones and other microchip-based technologies bring huge benefits to many of us and these techno-gadgets are often a source of great delight and even a *necessity* to many young people today. However, as with most things in life, they can be put to uses for which they were not intended and be the source of misery for many. The internet has brought with it the sad reality of child sexual abuse being turned into a marketable commodity through child pornography (Calder, 2004) and the use of e-mail and chat-rooms have their dark sides as well, including cyber-bullying (Mason, 2008). These realities all pose challenges to children, young people and their families and add yet more layers of complexity to social work with this group.

For many of the children and young people you come into contact with, these issues will influence and have an effect on their lives to a greater or lesser extent and have the potential to generate differing forms of need and risk. It is important therefore that social workers are aware of how these factors work and how they can have a cumulative and compound effect.

Responding to need and risk in relation to children, young people and their families

Society in general has become increasingly complex and families too have evolved and now have many accepted variants on the 'traditional', functionalist conceptions of the 1950s. Inevitably therefore, we see that the social work task (Collishaw et al., 2007; Garrod, 2007) has evolved into one where necessary skills are now as much about direct work *with other professionals, their agencies and organisations* as they are about direct work with children, young people and their families. You must be able to make effective use of your communication and interpersonal skills (Moss, 2008; Koprowska, 2008; Thompson, 2009; 2003) in order to work effectively and efficiently with a wide range of other professionals whose own knowledge, skills and values are crucial to achieving the shared task (Horwarth and Shardlow, 2003; Glaister and Glaister, 2005). With ever-changing conceptions of need (see Chapter 1) and risk (see Chapter 2) and increasingly complex demands upon services, achieving this should no longer be seen as the sole preserve of social work, although there are a number of important (reserved) functions which social workers are still best placed to carry out (HM Treasury and DfES, 2007; Scottish Executive, 2005d).

Need

One of the main tasks for social work professionals is to identify those children and families who are in *need*. One of the major activities is to attempt to address (unmet) need in a variety of ways using a range of interventions, including assessments, and these requirements are legislated for in the various Children Acts across the UK. The qualitative nature of the need will of course vary depending upon the particular circumstances and should be specifiable within the context of assessment and this may subsequently manifest itself as a need for *support* or as a need for *protection* (see Figure 5.2 above). The provision of support is something that should be provided within a broader context of prevention and services are increasingly configured along these lines. However, some children find themselves unable to get their basic needs met and are therefore under threat. In the first instance they are likely to turn to their parents or primary caregivers in order to have these needs met or to be protected, and for most they would receive what they require. However, some won't, either because their caregiver can't or won't provide for or protect them, or because that very person may well be the source of the danger itself. In these circumstances, the child would be at risk of harm and would therefore be in need of *protection*. If it is thought that a child is in need of protection, social work and other professionals have both a moral and a *legal* duty to respond to such concerns and the protocols for doing this emanate from the various Children Acts in the UK and the guidance from Area Child Protection Committees in Scotland or Local Children's Safeguarding Boards in England, Wales and Northern Ireland.

Risk

As we have seen in other chapters, within social work generally and social work with children, young people and their families in particular, there is an emphasis on the identification, assessment and management of risk (Calder and Hackett, 2003).

As we know, risk equates with an absence of certainty in any given situation(s) and a formal definition would say that it is the relative variation in possible outcomes (usually negative or harmful) based on measures of probability. A less formal but no less real interpretation would be that risk is something very complex, fluid, subjective, interpretative, interdependent and uncertain; in short, messy. These two definitions complement each other quite well, the first offering us a somewhat technical-rational view whilst the second locates the whole issue in the realm of the subjective experiences of the individual(s) involved.

The likelihood of harm befalling a child in any given situation is something that has to be considered as an integral part to any assessment and within any intervention, particularly in those situations where there already exists a *context for concern*. The assessment of risk and its subsequent management should be seen as a *normative part* of good practice and a consideration of the need for a specific assessment of *risk* should be a part of the overall assessment of any situation (Andrews, 2007; Schlonsky and Wagner, 2005).

In working with children, young people and their families we have to accept that the possibility of a child being harmed by acts of omission and/or commission on the part of their carers and others is a reality, although there are certain circumstances and situations where it would be *more likely* to happen and it is these very circumstances and situations that your assessment is aiming to identify. For example, where there is a history of family violence, a history of abuse and neglect, young parents, mental health problems, disabilities, poor attachment relationships and substance misuse issues then there is a greater likelihood of harm befalling a child in situations like this than in one where none of these factors appears to exist (Cohen, Hien and Batchelder, 2008; Bourassa, 2007; Craig and Sprang, 2007; Connell et al., 2007; Coohey, 2006). This is not to say, however, that harm *will* befall a child; rather that these factors indicate a situation where there are a greater number of potential stressors which may act as triggers to precipitate an abusive act and where abuse has previously been perpetrated, it may have become a 'normative' part of the carers' repertoire. Similarly though, in situations where there were *none* of those factors present, we cannot rule out the possibility of a child being harmed. So we need to take a balanced view of the situation and use our knowledge, values, skills, available tools of various sorts (including actuarial risk assessment tools) as well as the knowledge and experience of our colleagues to collate, analyse and interpret all available information, including that relating to past and present circumstances and behaviours (Moore, 1996; Andrews, 2007), until we can form a judgement on the *likelihood* of certain (usually unpleasant) things happening or not. This is an informed judgement about the probability of a future event happening that could result in (avoidable) harm befalling a child. Do not assume that a risk assessment tool will provide all the answers for you; it won't (Garrett, 2004). Rather, we need to use a blended approach of formalised (actuarial) tools and professional judgements, adopting what is commonly referred to as a *consensual approach* to the assessment and management of risk.

Resilience

The notion of resilience is a theme very current in social work with children, young people and their families. In essence, resilience refers to the capacity to 'bounce back' and overcome adversity (Fonagy et al., 1994). The idea of promoting resilience, which may offset the negative effects of risk and vulnerability and therefore be *protective*, has gained considerable currency (Rutter, 1985, 1995; Gilligan, 1999, 2000), and there exist some useful and very practical guides to resilience and its use in professional practice (see Newman and Blackburn, 2002; Daniel and Wassell, (2002) and Hothersall, 2008, p65).

Having a range of resilience factors present increases the potential to militate against the worst effects of negative experience and toxic environments, however manifest. Social work and other practitioners should see the promotion of such things as integral to their daily work and see these as core activities in their efforts towards helping people build their own sense of capacity and achievement. Too much time is focused on reacting to bad situations and more time and effort should be directed towards the *prevention* of harm and the minimisation and management of risk in such a way as to make it a potentially *creative* force within people's lives. Undoubtedly though there are circumstances that impact upon the lives of some children and their families that are difficult to offset easily; the effects of addictions, poor health, disabling conditions, poverty, differing forms of discrimination and structurally borne and driven inequalities all add to the burdens carried by some people and sometimes with the best will in the world, the effects of these cannot be underestimated nor ignored. Social work services, including its practitioners, need therefore to acknowledge that support at an early stage can be crucial and that this may be required for a long, long time. In today's climate of individualism, economic stringency within public services and short-termism, vulnerable groups are often even more susceptible to harm than ever before and the need for social work is stronger today than it has ever been. Governmental rhetoric around supporting children and their families has to translate into concrete service provision provided by highly trained professionals who care about what they do and know how to do this well.

C H A P T E R   S U M M A R Y

This chapter has looked at how social work with children, young people and their families has evolved, acknowledging some of the wider societal influences that have contributed to the shape and form of current professional practice. We have also looked at some of those factors that are likely to contribute to increases in vulnerability and risk to children and their families as well as a consideration of the broad mechanisms, external and internal (resilience) that exist to support families and to protect children. The chapter emphasises the point that social work with children, young people and their families is a highly political activity and one that reacts and responds to societal changes in a way that constantly brings new challenges to this area of work, and the chapter concludes by re-emphasising the importance of social work and social care practice for this grouping.

FURTHER
READING

Munro, E (2008) *Effective child protection* (2nd edn). London: Sage.
A valuable text that takes a critical view of child protection.

Parton, N (2006) *Safeguarding childhood: Early intervention and surveillance in a late modern society*. Basingstoke: Palgrave Macmillan.
This text offers a valuable commentary on how changes in society are affecting how we perceive and respond to childhood and children.

Reder, P and Duncan, S (2003) Understanding communication in child protection networks. *Child Abuse Review* 12 pp82–100.
These two papers offer useful, pragmatic insights into different but related elements of child care and protection work.

Reder, P and Duncan, S (2004) Making the most of the Victoria Climbié Inquiry Report. *Child Abuse Review* 13 pp95–115.

Chapter 6
Mental health

Mike Maas-Lowit

Achieving A Social Work Degree continued

Key Role 6: Demonstrate professional competence in social work practice.
- Exercise and justify professional judgements.
- Use professional assertiveness to justify decisions and uphold professional social work practice, values and ethics.
- Work within the principles and values underpinning social work practice.
- Critically reflect upon your own practice and performance using supervision and support systems.
- Devise strategies to deal with ethical issues, dilemmas and conflicts.

Scottish Standards in Social Work Education
Key Role 1: Prepare for, and work with, individuals, families, carers, groups and communities to assess their needs and circumstances.
- Preparing for social work contact and involvement.
- Working with individuals, families, carers, groups and communities so they can make informed decisions.
- Assessing needs and options in order to recommend a course of action.

Key Role 2: Plan, carry out, review and evaluate social work practice with individuals, families, carers, groups, communities and other professionals.
- Identifying and responding to crisis situations.
- Working with individuals, families, carers, groups and communities to achieve change, promote dignity, realise potential and improve life opportunities.
- Producing, implementing and evaluating plans with individuals, families, carers, groups, communities and colleagues.
- Developing networks to meet assessed needs and planned outcomes.
- Working with groups to promote choice and independent living.
- Tackling behaviour which presents a risk to individuals, families, carers, groups, communities and the wider public.

Key Role 3: Assess and manage risk to individuals, families, carers, groups, communities, self and colleagues.
- Assessing and managing risks to individuals, families, carers, groups and communities.
- Assessing and managing risk to self and colleagues.

Key Role 4: Demonstrate professional competence in social work practice.
- Evaluating and using up-to-date knowledge of, and research into, social work practice.
- Working within agreed standards of social work practice.
- Understanding and managing complex ethical issues, dilemmas and conflicts.
- Promoting best social work practice, adapting positively to change.

Key Role 6: Support individuals to represent and manage their needs, views and circumstances.
- Representing, in partnership with, and on behalf of, individuals, families, carers, groups and communities to help them achieve and maintain greater independence.

Introduction

A lot of the space in this chapter is taken up with a discussion around the medical/social dichotomy that we see again in Chapter 9. For the purposes of this chapter, it reduces to a discussion of the psychiatric perspective and the social perspective. We have reduced it to these two perspectives so as not to complicate something which, in reality, is endlessly complex, as there are many other overlying perspectives which could also be examined in order to understand situations where people are vulnerable, in need and at risk because of extreme mental distress; a psychological perspective would be one such.

A central theme of this chapter is that the dual strands of policy and practice which flow from these two perspectives, and which offer treatment and protection on the one hand and enhance rights, inclusion and recovery on the other, are *not* incompatible. They are in fact both necessary aspects of meeting people's very varied needs. It is extremely important to articulate this, because there has often been a tension within academic writing on mental health and service delivery between the mainstay medical perspective of psychiatry, with its predominance of drug treatment, and the view of many service users and providers with a more social orientation who see the problem being caused or aggravated by society's lack of acceptance of the ways in which some people express extreme emotional anguish. In order to make sense of these ideas within the context of the chapter, we will need to define the terms *mental health* and *mental illness*, which are often (wrongly) used interchangeably, to great confusion. We will take a brief look at the widely divergent mental health legislation in Scotland, Northern Ireland, England and Wales which attempts to do two seemingly contradictory things: firstly, to improve the working of mental health law to restrict and sometimes restrain people who are adversely affected by mental illness and secondly, to ensure the improvement of rights and control that people in these situations have in their own lives.

This theme, that we need to understand the medical and social perspectives of mental health and mental illness, closely relates to two other themes of this chapter, which are:

- that poor mental health pervades all aspects of society where other forms of disadvantage accrue, creating a special set of needs and risks; and

- that the specific needs and risks attendant upon that section of the population who are vulnerable because of *mental illness* are amplified by the poor *mental health* that they often experience.

If all of this sounds very complicated, it is because the complex mix of individual suffering in body, mind and heart, which is at the core of suffering caused by poor mental health, is indeed a very complicated thing, especially when it meets society's prejudices, rules and regulations. We will unpack these complications and explain them to you.

Defining the terms

Our starting point is that *mental health* and *mental illness* are quite different things: clarity of understanding is the first casualty when we are sometimes encouraged to use the phrase *mental health* either to mean a state of poor mental health, or to mean *mental illness*. This situation is compounded by the *mental health* law of the countries of the UK, which name their laws relating to the care and treatment of mentally ill people the *mental health acts* (or *order,* in Northern Ireland). Furthermore, if you look at the otherwise excellent website of the Mental Health Foundation, you might note that it lists things such as *schizophrenia*, which are arguably *mental illnesses*, as *mental health problems* (www.mentalhealth.org.uk/information/mental-health-a-z/m/). You are therefore excused as a reader for thinking that mental health might refer to mental illness. If you are now feeling very confused, read on:

To start thinking about the above concepts, let us momentarily leave the sphere of mental health and mental illness and examine what we understand by the terms health and illness, in terms of the physical domain of our bodies.

Many people think in misleading terms that illness is the opposite of good health. But we would encourage you to think more deeply about the terms. Address the following questions and take a short note of your answers:

- *Is it possible to be healthy at the same time as being ill?*
- *Can you be unhealthy but not ill?*

Comment

We would agree with you if you answered that it *is* possible to be healthy at the same time as being ill and that it is possible to be unhealthy but not ill. In the first case, think about a champion athlete who has a condition like asthma or diabetes. Any doctor would describe such conditions as illnesses, but one must be very healthy in order to be an athlete.

In the second case, consider someone who takes no exercise, who eats only fried food and who smokes and drinks alcohol excessively. You might say that such a person is more likely to become ill than a more careful person, but it is possible that such a person also has no detectable illness.

From this we may conclude that the relationship between poor health and illness is more complicated than the simple one shown in figure 6.1 below (Tudor, 1996; Scottish Government, 2007b).

However, we would caution you in relation to the following discussion both of health and later, of mental illness, that these concepts are very complicated and that we are simplifying them for the sake of a wider discussion. It is best to approach both health and illness not as tangible entities, but as ideas or ways of looking at human experience (whether physical or mental). The diagrams shown as 6.2 (a) and (b) describe the situation.

Healthy   Ill

Figure 6.1 Continuum from health to illness

(a)   Healthy   Unhealthy

(b)   Not ill   Ill

Figure 6.2 (a) and (b) Dual Continua: Keeping health and illness separate

In this case, there may be a relationship between the *healthy/unhealthy* continuum and the *not ill/ill* continuum, but it is not a simple one. Let us move on to think about the concept of mental health, now that we have freed it from direct association with mental illness.

Mental health

The concept of *mental health* addresses a quality that every one of us has. It is central to our experience of life and it fluctuates between the extremes of good and poor, as illustrated in the diagram. Mental health is also an extremely personal matter, as each individual experiences it uniquely. However, it is possible to identify some general characteristics: The Scottish Government's approach is to coin the term *mental well-being* to describe the experience of being in a state of good mental health:

> [M]ental wellbeing refers to three main dimensions – emotional, social and psychological wellbeing. This includes our ability to cope with life's problems and make the most of life's opportunities, to cope in the face of adversity and to flourish in all our environments; to feel good and function well, both individually and collectively.

(Scottish Government, 2007b, p2)

Mental health has a great deal in common with Maslow's hierarchical structuring of motivation and need (Maslow 1943, and Chapter 1). Generally speaking, Maslow suggested that our needs are structured so that we can only tend to those most immediate to us. Therefore, we will be preoccupied with physiological needs for food, clean water, air to breathe and so on, before we will be concerned with needs for physical safety, such as clothing, shelter and security. Likewise, we will only be concerned with human needs for love and belongingness when we have satisfied our safety needs. After this, being social animals, we will have needs that address our sense of purpose, such as needs for activities that result in others reflecting back to us a sense of worth or esteem. Maslow proposed a final upper stratum of needs which he called self-actualisation. This is a sort of existential 'be-all-you-can-be' to fulfil your potential in whatever you do.

ACTIVITY *6.2*

Take a moment to think and note down how mental health might be adversely affected by lack of access to personal safety in situations in which we are exposed to abuse or danger. Reflect further upon how mental health is challenged by chronic loneliness, lack of love, lack of esteem and self-worth and lack of purpose or meaning in life. To give you a more concrete example to focus upon, consider the challenges to mental health for an asylum-seeker, fleeing abuse and state persecution in her own country, who has lost all her friends and family, has no job, has been up-rooted from one country to another and who feels lost and insecure in a hostile land.

Comment

If you are beginning to grasp the concept of mental health, you may have noted that this asylum seeker would rate poorly against Maslow's hierarchy. From the short description above, she would show outstanding needs at the levels of safety, love and belongingness, esteem and self-actualisation. The impact of this might be to undermine her sense of self-worth, to make her constantly anxious and worried, to make it difficult to relax or sleep and make her instantly suspicious of others, thereby damaging any interaction she has with them. She will therefore feel isolated, lonely and lost. These are all attributes of poor mental health and they all make her more vulnerable to abuse and harm and they all pose risks.

This suggests that health is a quality that we experience in relation to our environment. Much as good physical health is difficult to maintain in a living environment where one is not encouraged to take exercise, where one passively inhales other people's cigarette smoke and where one has only poor quality fast-food to eat, certain environments are more or less conducive to maintaining good mental health. For example, it is more difficult to maintain good mental health in an environment of chronic high stress and insecurity, or in an environment of poverty and exclusion.

If you have read the above paragraph carefully, you will see that more than one reference is made to the word *maintain*. This suggests that at least some of the potential for a person to keep good health (be it mental or physical) lies with the person. Therefore, we may say that the potential to maintain good mental health lies in a dynamic between the individual and their environment. Education, access to choice and the power to exercise self-determination within a safe and secure environment would be attributes that make this task less challenging. Those who live in poverty, lack power and who have outstanding needs because of emotional, physical, sexual or physical abuse and exploitation would all be at risk of suffering poor mental health.

Mental illness

We have said much so far about mental health and well-being as differentiated from mental illness. However, we have rested these arguments upon an assumption that we all know and agree what *mental illness* is. If it was difficult to summarise the discussion on mental health (about which a book could be written) it is harder still to condense the discussion on mental illness, about which a library could be written! The first thing to note is that the concept of illness is a medical term that implies some sort of abnormal functioning.

This notion of abnormal functioning upon which all medical problems are based, assumes an ideal of the perfectly functioning body and mind. It is therefore time to say what the word mental means: mental is an adjective, relating to the mind. *The mind* might be described as the thought processes of the brain: conscious and subconscious thought, emotions and feelings, sensations such as hunger and pain, the process of dreaming, our memories and so on. In short, it is everything we experience and know from birth to death.

The medical concept of *mental illness* is still contested by some people because they feel that it is difficult to generalise the individual working of the mind to a set of common features, so that we can then say that any deviation from these constitutes abnormal functioning and therefore a mental illness (Kendell in Heller, et al., 1996). In a related sense, we tend to shy away from the term *mental illness* because a lot of people who are diagnosed with it do not find it a meaningful way to describe their experiences. However that may be, for the purposes of this book we assume that the concept of mental illness has some validity and the following is a brief summary of the medical approach to mental illness.

The human brain contains approximately one hundred billion (100,000, 000,000,000) neurons or brain cells. These neurons communicate with each other to form thoughts, tell us what we are experiencing of the outside world and store memories by a complex system of electro-chemical impulses and messages. It is extremely difficult to conceive of the fact that your experience of reading these words on the page at this minute is made up of such a mixture of molecular activity in the turnip-sized lump of grey matter situated behind your face. However, assuming that this is the case, the catalogued features of mental illness (experiences such as hearing voices, experiencing depressed mood or excessive elation of mood and so on) are thought to be caused by over- or under-production of these chemicals at times when events in the outside world do not call for it, and by the routing of messages to the wrong parts of the brain (Andreasen, 2004). However, even if you are persuaded that the medical explanation of mental illness is scientific fact, it makes no sense without a good grounding in social explanations: even if we completely accept the medical/scientific rationale for mental illness, it is couched within, and it plays out within social, cultural and behavioural settings (Littlewood and Lipsedge, 2007; Boyle, M in Heller et al., 1996).

The role of culture and society

Roland Littlewood, a psychiatrist and anthropologist, pointed the way to what he and his colleague, Maurice Lipsedge called trans-cultural psychiatry. In this they studied the different ways in which mental illnesses such as schizophrenia, depression and bi-polar affective disorder were manifested in different cultures throughout the world. As psychiatrists, they understood these conditions to be illnesses, caused as described above. However, they also understood that the underlying cause is expressed very differently in speech, action and behaviours depending on the culture of the person who experiences it. Furthermore, they noted that the ways in which different cultures understand and respond to the behaviour of the ill person vary enormously.

Accepting the technological and scientific evidence that such processes lie behind the experience of mental illness (and bearing in mind our caution earlier in the text, that illness and health are ideas and not things), can you see how mental illness differs from poor mental health? There is a complicated dynamic between the workings of the brain and the outside world, even when those workings do not function as they should. However, where illness begins, it is arguable that the dominant factor is the process inside the brain, which might cause undue distress and upset to the person experiencing what, in medical terms are referred to as symptoms. This, in turn, suggests that the person experiencing the symptoms has less control over them than does a person who is only suffering from poor mental health. To extend the analogy to physical illness, a person who struggles to walk up a hill because he is ill with a heart defect is in less control over it than a person who cannot do so because of his poor health, caused by smoking 40 cigarettes a day. This is the key to understanding the difference between health and illness: health speaks to the dynamic factor in which we all engage to maintain our body and mind in good or less-good working order. Illness is the malfunctioning of the body or mind over which we have less control, although that is not to say that we cannot behave responsibly towards our illnesses when we have them and if you visit the website of the Scottish Recovery Network www.scottishrecovery.net), you will see an excellent example of an organisation dedicated to the concept that people can take a large degree of control in their mental illness.

To further complicate the discussion, one of the most significant things that may be deduced from this analysis is that people who live with mental illness, particularly long-term mental illnesses such as schizophrenia, are more likely to live in circumstances where society excludes them, where they are devalued, where they lack choices and therefore, where they experience poor mental health in the form of low self-esteem, loneliness, lack of motivation and lack of sense of purpose in life (Scottish Government, 2007b).

We can now return to the two principle themes of this chapter:

- that poor mental health pervades all aspects of society where other forms of disadvantage accrue, creating a special set of needs and risks and vulnerabilities; and

- that the specific needs and risks attendant upon that section of the population who have mental illness are amplified by the poor mental health that they often experience.

To consolidate what we have discussed so far, the following should be noted.

- Mental health is a different concept from mental illness, in that many people experience poor mental health without being mentally ill and that being mentally ill poses particular challenges to one's mental health.

- There are many different perspectives on mental illness, but it is unhelpful to see the medical/scientific/psychiatric ways of understanding the concept *as being in opposition* to the social orientation, which acknowledges that mainstay society sometimes misunderstands and exercises prejudices against people who display unusual behaviour.

- People with mental illness are best served by approaches that offer them the best available medical intervention **and** the best social support to find their own ways of managing their situations.

- To facilitate this, the best option is a multidisciplinary approach, which should place the service user at the heart of things, encouraging their active involvement.

- From this stance we may see the the needs of people with mental illness are those required to manage the illness and to take positive control of their mental health, working towards a state of mental well-being.

- People remain vulnerable and at risk to the extent to which this process fails.

These latter points are best illustrated by a general discussion of what mental health (sic) law seeks to do across the countries of the UK.

The law

We can most usefully approach this subject by resisting being drawn into the technical details of any one piece of law or any discussion about how the very different pieces of legislation work across the different areas of the UK. This points to the fact that across the UK there are very different sets of laws to regulate important aspects of their very different approaches to mental health service delivery and development: namely the English and Welsh *Mental Health Act 2007* (Department of Health 2007), the Scottish *Mental Health (Care and Treatment) (Scotland) Act 2003* (Scottish Executive, 2003a) and the Northern Irish *Mental Health (Northern Ireland) Order 1987* (Northern Irish Executive, 1987), which is currently undergoing a major review (see www.rmhldni.gov.uk/help.jsp).

As we said in the introduction, the titles of these pieces of law, all of which contain the phrase *Mental Health*, confuses the separation of concepts which we have been at pains to differentiate so far. They all have less to do with *mental health* and more to do with *mental illness*, and they all address the situation for that minority of people who are so severely affected by mental illness that their judgement is impaired in respect of how to best meet their needs, how best to protect themselves from risk and harm and how to manage their vulnerability, all based of course on assumptions that there is such a thing as mental illness and that it can create such a different set of problems from those faced by people who do not experience it.

ACTIVITY 6.3

Consider the case of a man who has been bingeing on alcohol for two weeks, drinking a bottle of whisky a day and topping his alcohol intake up with beer and wine. Jim works in the off-shore oil industry and he has to return to work on an oil rig, thereby stopping dead his binge of alcohol. A sharp and total reduction from this level of drinking can cause a condition called delirium tremens (or DTs), which is often characterised by severe and very upsetting hallucinations both of sight and touch. Often these manifest themselves as a very real sensation that insects such as spiders are crawling all over the person or their surroundings.

By the time Jim disembarks from the helicopter on a remote oil rig surrounded by hundreds of miles of sea, he is shaking uncontrollably. By mid-evening he is frantically upset, convinced by what he sees and feels: that he is covered by small spiders, crawling in his mouth and up his nose.

While DTs is not a typical instance of mental illness, it is a dramatic presentation of some features and that is why we chose it here. It poses the problem in sharp terms. Jim is upset; he is at risk of doing something drastic in a very risky situation, for example jumping into the sea or using some of the powerful machinery of an oil rig to solve his problem. The central trouble is that he sees his problem very differently from how we would view it. Upon the evidence of his sensations, he believes himself to be invaded by spiders. We think that he has a form of temporary mental illness caused by his use of alcohol. The question we want to pose to you is: Given that there would be little chance of calming Jim down and explaining what is really happening, ought there to be some legal means of forcing necessary medical treatment upon him, so that he may be kept safe and have lasting relief from his upset?

Comment

How did you answer the question? We think there are three potential answers:

1 We have no right to intervene at all and Jim ought to be allowed to do whatever he wishes, even if that means placing himself or others at great risk. (We hope that you did not think this answer was a good one.)

2 Why have a law? People should just do whatever is necessary to restrain Jim and make him safe and give him whatever treatment he needs. (We will return to review this position later.)

3 A mental health law that allows enforced care and treatment in such unfortunate circumstances might also set fair and reasonable limitations upon what can be done to Jim. It could also articulate the rights he should have when his freedom is being restricted against his will.

Option 3 is the one favoured by the State in the UK. It mediates between people's basic rights to determine their own actions and to exercise a wide degree of freedom, and the need to protect a person who poses risk to him/herself or others in situations where mental illness clouds one's judgement.

Option 1 would serve no one. Jim might well get hurt. He would be alienated from workmates. He would lose his job and others might get hurt too. Someone might even lose their life.

Option 2 would keep Jim safe in one sense but would not address the loss of liberty and the jeopardy to his rights.

Most cases where mental health law is applied are not quite as dramatic as Jim's. However, the less dramatic the case, the less clear-cut things are and the more important is the need to protect the rights of the individual. Therefore, a good mental health law ought to have clear limitations on how much liberty one can restrict and how much recourse the person has to protection of rights and freedom. For these reasons, the law in all UK countries attempts to give powers to enforce care and treatment in or out of hospital, alongside rights of appeal against this use of force and certain principles which must be upheld to protect the human rights of the service user.

Policy

Policy in all UK countries must be compatible with legislation, although policy development may necessitate subsequent legislative change. Policy sets out what governments hope to achieve and shapes mental health services, being related to both the medicalised aspects. which sit within the NHS and to the social care orientation of services which more broadly address the mental health needs of the population (as opposed to the needs arising out of mental illness itself). The Scottish approach, currently set out in *Towards a Mentally Flourishing Scotland* (Scottish Government, 2007b), is two-fold. On the one hand, it attempts to address the major problems faced by the general population in terms of its mental health needs and on the other it attempts to target services upon those in greatest need because of their mental illness. In this way, the NHS is targeted to reduce the number of psychiatric hospital re-admissions and to improve hospital services for children, adolescents and mothers with babies (Scottish Executive, 2006c). But reading *Towards a Mentally Flourishing Scotland*, it is apparent that the main approach is to change the Scottish public's poor attitude towards maintaining good mental health. In this regard, consumption of drugs and alcohol, reduction of poverty and improvement of emotional intelligence are all targets (Scottish Government, 2007b).

Policy in England is a much larger and more complicated matter than it is in the smaller, less populous countries. There is also a sense that England and Wales are in a position closer to the Scottish one in the years 2003 to 2005, when the government stood so close to the major event of the launch of the mental health act that its energies in relation to policy were taken up by making the new law work (producing regulation, advice and information around the law). In terms of broader policy, the government is reviewing funding of social care for all, in an attempt to improve quality. It is also seeking to personalise social care by making more uniquely packaged care to suit individuals' specific needs (Department of Health, 2009). The mental health campaigning organisation *Mind* is working to ensure that this devolves to the benefit of users of mental health services (www. mind.org.uk).

The question of policy in Northern Ireland cannot be taken out of context of its recent political history. The turbulence of the latter decades of the last century has had a tangible effect upon mental health policy and law. In their large-scale survey O'Reilly and Stevenson (2003) found that political unrest and proximity to violence have had significant measurable effects upon the population's mental health. A consequence of 'The Troubles' has also been that the peace process has slowed down the modernisation of mental health law and policy. For this reason, Northern Ireland is only now moving through its major review of mental health law. Wilson and Daly (2007) suggest that:

> dominant trends in mental health care ... have tended to prioritize the more coercive aspects of the social work role and reinforce existing power inequalities with service users. It is argued that such developments underline the need for a 'refocusing' debate in mental health social work to consider how a more appropriate balance can be achieved between its participatory/empowering and regulatory/coercive functions (p423).

Note the perceived tension between participation/empowerment (goals of a mental health oriented social perspective) and regulation and coercion (functions of the more medicalised preoccupation with the safety, protection and treatment needs of mentally ill people). Daly and Wilson's assessment of the situation in Northern Ireland focuses more sharply on tensions that lie in mental health policy in all of the UK. These tensions, alluded to at the outset of this chapter can only be resolved by getting the proper balance of rights and powers, between focusing on the person's medical and social needs in proper proportion. While Scotland, England & Wales and Northern Ireland are in very different places in relation to these tensions, it would be untrue to say that Daly and Wilson's findings apply solely to Northern Ireland.

Improving the mental health of mentally ill people

We think the statement in the sub-heading is crucially important to our discussions. Mental health is a concept that speaks to people's need for a sense of belongingness and purpose, a need for esteem and meaningful human contact and a need for self-fulfilment or self-actualisation. We have hinted that there are frequent negative social consequences of having a mental illness, as society stigmatises people who exhibit the obvious sorts of difference frequently associated with it. People who come into close contact with the powerful medicalised system of psychiatric services often feel disempowered and it is sadly so easy to lose one's place in society, one's job, one's friends, even one's home and family, when one is struggling with the inner world of mental illness.

All of these aspects of living with mental illness may have an impact upon mental health, resulting in poor self-esteem, lack of motivation and general lack of enjoyment of life. Meeting the person's needs to reclaim some control in their life and to find positive ways of engaging and being included may reverse the trend. From this perspective, read the following case study and consider the questions following it.

CASE STUDY

Duncan is 39 years old. An only child, he was studious and did exceptionally well at school and university, but he abandoned his studies in biochemistry a few months before he was due to graduate with a good degree. Socially, throughout his childhood and early adulthood he was very much the centre of a strong network of friends. He had great interest in reading and listening to music. When he left home to go to university, he kept good contact with his parents, but in his final year of study, he became more distant and his parents were shocked to see how his physical appearance had deteriorated when he left his student flat to return to stay with them. He was painfully thin and dishevelled; his behaviour was odd and markedly changed from the polite and reserved Duncan that his parents had known. Conversation with him was now near-impossible because he seemed to be preoccupied listening to and responding to a voice or voices that only he could hear. He was often very short-tempered and sometimes he slammed doors and broke things in his anger. But he could not, or would not, explain what he was angry about.

Eventually his behaviour led to Duncan being seen by a doctor and then a psychiatric specialist, who finally diagnosed his problem as schizophrenia.

Schizophrenia is a term that applies to a range of conditions, thought to be among the most serious mental illnesses. It is generally a life-long problem and it is characterised by hallucinations (most commonly, hearing voices), delusions (or false beliefs) and confusion of thought, resulting in disorientation and loss of structure and purpose in life (WHO, 2007).

In the following years, Duncan was often in hospital for months at a time. The drugs, which he was sometimes compelled by law to take, subdued his symptoms (of hearing voices and having disturbing thoughts). On the other hand, he seems to have lost his spirit of independence. While he still lives at home, he seems to have no motivation

continued

to do anything, appears to have lost all interest in the things he used to enjoy, and he has now completely withdrawn into his own room. In medical terms, Duncan's mental illness is fairly well regulated as long as he takes the prescribed drugs his psychiatrist offers. However, this leaves his mental health at a low ebb.

ACTIVITY 6.4

We will now pose a series of questions which we would like you to take a moment to reflect upon and jot notes of your answer. We will discuss each one before we proceed to the next.

Can you identify needs arising out of Duncan's challenged mental health?

Comment
Were you able to identify his isolation as a need for social stimulus? If his earlier life at the centre of a close network of friends is a base line, he is now far from meeting those needs. Did you note his lack of motivation and his loss of interest as indicators of need, even if it is difficult to precisely pin down how those needs might be met?

Can you identify needs arising out of Duncan's mental illness?

Comment
This might be a more difficult question to answer. However, we were hoping that you might identify needs for monitoring of Duncan's treatment and the progress of his illness. If you knew more about the subject you might have also identified the need for him to have meaningful explanations of his illness because it might be difficult for him to match his experience of schizophrenia with an awareness that it might be an illness, in much the same way that it would be difficult to persuade Jim that his DTs were not, in reality, an infestation of spiders.

Can you identify risks to Duncan should these needs not be met?

Were you able to identify that the longer his mental health needs go unmet, the more entrenched his life-style of isolation will become? Were you able to discern that such an introverted lifestyle poses increased risks of depression and loss of structure?

Did you also note that, as with any serious illness, if it is not closely monitored and if the person themselves does not participate in its management, there are risks that it will deteriorate? Furthermore, there is an interaction between the risks to Duncan's mental health and the risks of his illness becoming out of control again. The more isolated he is and the less structured his life becomes, the more difficult it will be to engage him in strategies to help manage his illness.

continued

There is a more over-arching risk that Duncan has become a 'passive' patient. This may be because the treatment with long-acting tranquillisers has made it too difficult to be any-thing but compliant. It may also be because he has been forced to comply with treatment under mental health law so often that he sees his position as being futile, or it may be that coping with his illness itself takes all his energy, or it may be a combination of all of these things. Whatever the reason, this passivity will amplify his loss of motivation and interest.

Because of these outstanding needs and the related risks, do you think that Duncan is vulnerable and, as such, that he is in need of particular support?

We would certainly agree with you if you think that Duncan could be described as vulnerable. However, this need not be a lasting position for him. The Scottish Recovery Network characterises an approach to recovery that encourages people to regain control of their lives.

Recovery means different things to different people and no two individuals' journeys of recovery will be the same.

> *We start from the premise that recovery is about much more than an absence of symptoms – it is about having the opportunity to live a satisfying and fulfilling life in the presence or absence of symptoms.*

(Brown and Kandirikirira, 2007, p6)

The approach is one that supports people to find individual pathways towards their own identified definition of what it means to have recovered from their current mental illness and/or period of poor mental health. Coupled with this, Duncan's psychiatrist needs to work in coordination with services that may help him to identify specialist services that may help him to access socially inclusive or non-mental health specific services such as community centres and back-to-work or back-to-study programmes.

C H A P T E R   S U M M A R Y

This chapter may appear to differ from others in the book in that it is much preoccupied with tangential matters in relation to differentiating mental health, mental illness and explaining them. It is not intended that this should detract from the central issues of risk, need and vulnerability. However, the author believes that the art of risk assessment is to understand the concept of risk **and** how to apply it to that which is being assessed. If, for example, you only understood mental illness in terms of some of its popular misconceptions about unpredictability, dangerousness and violence, your assessment would be skewed, no matter how good your general understanding of risk assessment was. Therefore, the chapter has assumed that you will be able to apply the concepts of risk, need and vulnerability, which are explained in earlier chapters.

The final case study is the piecing together of the discussion on mental health, mental illness and the related tensions between empowering and inclusive practice and the need for protection and safety.

FURTHER READING

Andreasen, NC (2004) *Brave new brain: Conquering mental illness in the era of the genome*. New York: Oxford University Press.
Offers a detailed explanation of modern medical understandings of the causation of mental illness.

Heller, T, Reynolds, J, Gomm, R, Muston, R and Pattison, S (eds) (2000) *Mental health matters*. Basingstoke: Palgrave Macmillan.

Tew, J (ed) (2005) *Social perspectives in mental health: Developing social models to understand and work with mental distress*. London: Jessica Kingsley.
These texts offer a social discourse on mental health and mental illness.

Chapter 7
Older people

Amy Clark and Rory Lynch

ACHIEVING A SOCIAL WORK DEGREE

National Occupational Standards
Key Role 1: Prepare for, and work with, individuals, families, carers, groups and communities to assess their needs and circumstances.
- Liaise with others to access additional information that can inform initial contact and involvement.
- Work with individuals, families, carers, groups and communities to enable them to assess and make informed decisions about their needs, circumstances, risks, preferred options and resources.

Key Role 2: Plan, carry out, review and evaluate social work practice, with individuals, families, carers, groups, communities and other professionals.
- Plan and implement action to meet the immediate needs and circumstances.
- Review the outcomes with individuals, families, carers, groups, communities, organisations, professionals and others.
- Work with individuals, families, carers, groups, communities and others to avoid crisis situations and address problems and conflict .

Key Role 3: Support individuals to represent their needs, views and circumstances.
- Assist individuals, families, carers, groups and communities to access independent advocacy.
- Advocate for, and with, individuals, families, carers, groups and communities.

Key Role 4: Manage risk to individuals, families, carers, groups, communities, self and colleagues.
- Balance the rights and responsibilities of individuals, families, carers, groups and communities with associated risk.
- Regularly monitor, re-assess, and manage risk to individuals, families, carers, groups and communities.

Key Role 5: Manage and be accountable, with supervision and support, for your own social work practice within your organisation.
- Contribute to the procedures involved in purchasing and commissioning services.
- Contribute to monitoring the effectiveness of services in meeting need.
- Contribute to monitoring the quality of the services provided.
- Contribute to managing information.

Key Role 6: Demonstrate professional competence in social work practice.
- Exercise and justify professional judgements.
- Use professional assertiveness to justify decisions and uphold professional social work practice, values and ethics.
- Work within the principles and values underpinning social work practice.

continued

Achieving A Social Work Degree continued

Scottish standards in social work education
Key Role 1: Prepare for, and work with, individuals, families, carers, groups and communities to assess their needs and circumstances.
- Preparing for social work contact and involvement.
- Working with individuals, families, carers, groups and communities so they can make informed decisions.
- Assessing needs and options in order to recommend a course of action.

Key Role 2: Plan, carry out, review and evaluate social work practice with individuals, families, carers, groups, communities and other professionals.
- Working with individuals, families, carers, groups and communities to achieve change, promote dignity, realise potential and improve life opportunities.
- Producing, implementing and evaluating plans with individuals, families, carers, groups, communities and colleagues.
- Developing networks to meet assessed needs and planned outcomes.
- Working with groups to promote choice and independent living.

Key Role 3: Assess and manage risk to individuals, families, carers, groups, communities, self and colleagues.
- Assessing and managing risks to individuals, families, carers, groups and communities.

Key Role 4: Demonstrate professional competence in social work practice.
- Working within agreed standards of social work practice.
- Understanding and managing complex ethical issues, dilemmas and conflicts.
- Promoting best social work practice, adapting positively to change.

Key Role 5: Manage and be accountable, with supervision and support, for your own social work practice within your organisation.
- Managing one's own work in an accountable way.
- Contributing to the management of resources and services.
- Working effectively with professionals within integrated, multi-disciplinary and other service settings.

Key Role 6: Support individuals to represent and manage their needs, views and circumstances.
- Representing, in partnership with, and on behalf of, individuals, families, carers, groups and communities to help them achieve and maintain greater independence.

Introduction

This chapter considers aspects of need, risk and vulnerability as they relate to old age, some of the primary causes of which are poverty, mental and/or physical disability, loss of significant others, retirement, antithetical policies and abuse (Victor, 2005) and workers need to be sensitive to the language used in relation to older people and old age to avoid generating negative attitudes that exclude older people from those rights and opportunities the general population take for granted. In a more philosophical sense, ageist attitudes may also make the wider population, particularly the young, fearful of old age, seemingly full of negative connotations and stereotypes (Bond et al., 2007).

How do you view older people and where did your beliefs and values come from? What sorts of things might you do to change ageist practices?

Comment

Our core beliefs are formed during our childhoods and are influenced by family, friends, culture and the media and it would be relatively easy to guess the 'correct' answer to our first question. We have already suggested that detrimental negative attitudes abound in society. You may strongly uphold some of the attitudes which counter this tendency: a belief in the uniqueness of each older person, a belief in the value of the wider experience they have and a belief in the value of the link older people have to the living past. However, were you able to identify any potentially discriminatory attitudes in yourself, attitudes which you may dissociate yourself from, but which are nevertheless present? For example, there is discussion in the media about the drain on public expenses, which the growing numbers of older people 'impose' on social work services and the NHS and whether this can be sustained.

Ageism is the systematic mistreatment of individuals in relation to the role they are accorded within society. This discrimination can be at the personal, cultural and structural level (PCS) (Thompson, 2006). The *personal* may refer to the way that old age is viewed by individuals, particularly the young, where there is a lack of awareness of the individuality of older people and their positive role within society. At a *cultural* level, society may view older people as a generic, homogenised group with similar characteristics, who may be perceived in relation to their vulnerability rather than their strengths and their potential for contributing to society while at a *structural* level older people may live in poverty and lack basic support services related to benefits, pensions and access to community-based services. This structural reinforcement is characterised by a lack of awareness of the real needs of older people, irrespective of their age or abilities. It is therefore essential that social work and social care practice with older people is anti-oppressive and anti-discriminatory (Dalrymple and Burke, 1995; Mullaly 2007).

Old age in context

At the time of writing, we are witnessing the end of the generation that fought in the trenches of WWI. The last of the British soldiers died in 2009. By the time you read these words, there will be no more living memory in the UK of that period, or of the Russian Revolution, or of the sinking of the *Titanic*. It is a luxury to work with people who can give an eyewitness account of history. Here, for example, is a brief account from a man who lived out his last years in a home for older people. It was given to one of the editors of this book by staff at the home and illustrates the remarkable experiences that older people carry. In this case, the anonymous narrator had been present at the Battle of Mons (23 August 1914) and had witnessed the Angel of Mons, alternatively described as the largest mass hallucination or the largest confirmed sighting of an angel ever recorded:

On the evening of the 23rd of August, the position of the 8th Brigade, 2nd Royal Scots ... became very serious. The Germans had outflanked Mons to the East. At the same time, the British were facing the 75th German Infantry... which [made] retreat impossible. There were 70,000 British Troops to 200,000 Germans. Towards midnight, a large angel appeared, dressed in blue, gold and brilliant mauves. At either side were smaller angels, dressed as archers. Soldiers fell to the ground, some in fear of their lives, weeping for salvation. Many prayed. The Germans fled in terror, giving the British Army, under the angels' protection, the chance to retreat in darkness, saving thousands from annihilation.

We should celebrate the fact that 30–40 per cent of western populations can expect to live beyond eighty, compared to only 25 per cent of the population in 1900 who reached their sixty-fifth birthday (Sonnenschein and Brody, 2005), childhood mortality being a significant factor at that time. Women in the UK can now expect to live to approximately eighty years of age and men to seventy-six years. The difference in longevity is attributed to men being more likely to experience acute life-threatening illness resulting in death, whereas women are more likely to experience long-term disabling conditions (Victor, 2005). This tends to exacerbate the sense that mortality is the direct result of old age. This structural approach to the wider health of an older population lacks a needs-led focus and will inevitably result in policies with an increasingly ageist and medicalised approach.

Demographics: The changing shape of society

Demography is that branch of knowledge that studies human populations and analyses the rates of births, deaths, patterns of migration, illness and disease, etc. It provides us with a lot of information that can be used to *predict* how populations may change in the future to allow for strategic planning and other forms of action.

In 2006, the population of the UK was 60,587,600, of whom 16 per cent were sixty-five or over. It is depicted graphically as a 'rectangular society' (see Figure 7.1). The number of people aged sixty-five and over is expected to rise by nearly 60 per cent, from 9.6 million in 2005 to over 15 million in 2031. Of that 15 million, it is projected that 3.8 per cent will be eighty-five and over. The number of people over eighty five in the UK is predicted to double in the next 20 years and treble in the next thirty (National Statistics Online, February 2008). There are more women than men among the very old, and it is likely that this trend will continue. From the point of view of the demographics we can define younger-old in the range 60–75 years of age, as opposed to the older-old adults who fall into the 75 years to 89 years age range (Stuart-Hamilton, 2006).

A good way to conceptualise the variation of age structure between populations is to construct what are termed 'age pyramids'. The bases of the pyramids represent younger people while the middle is comprised of working-age people with older people at the top. As the age structure changes with considerably more of us living longer, the shape of the 'pyramid' changes almost to a rectangle, hence the notion of a 'rectangular society'.

continued

Demographics: the changing of society continued

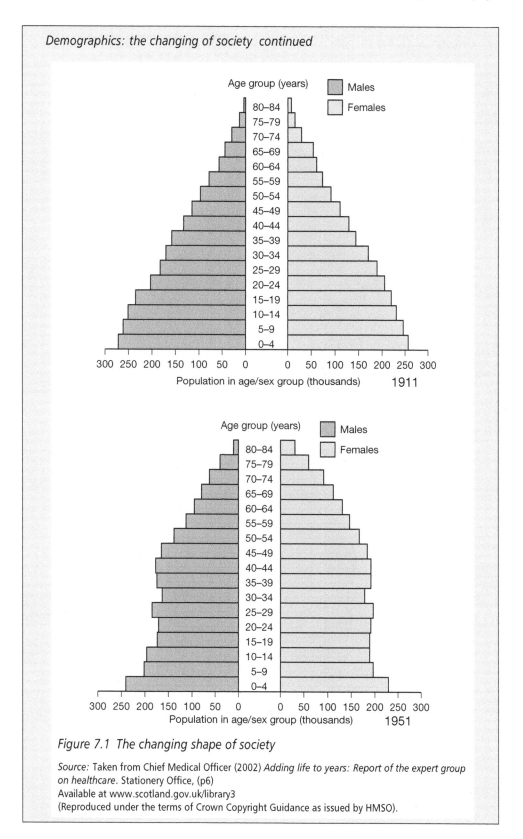

Figure 7.1 The changing shape of society

Source: Taken from Chief Medical Officer (2002) *Adding life to years: Report of the expert group on healthcare*. Stationery Office, (p6)
Available at www.scotland.gov.uk/library3
(Reproduced under the terms of Crown Copyright Guidance as issued by HMSO).

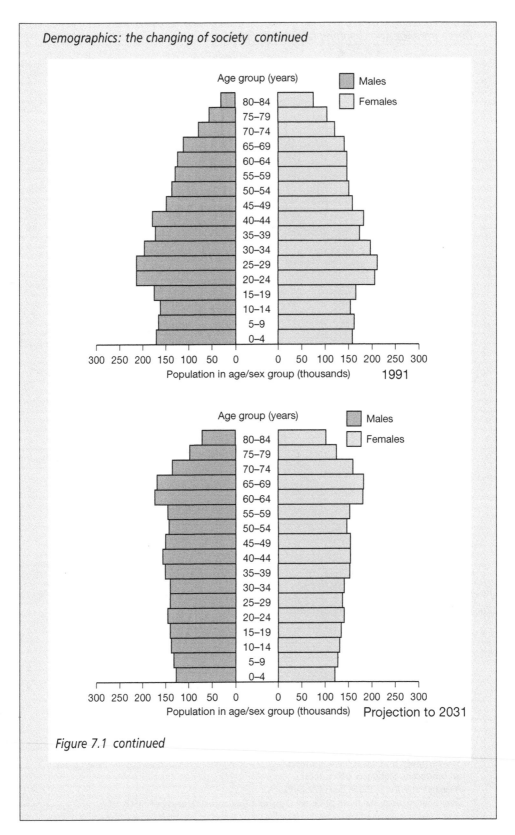

Demographics: the changing of society *continued*

Figure 7.1 *continued*

The tendency for women to live longer than men means that there is the potential for a protracted period of widowhood in old age. This has major implications for the widowed who may perceive a loss of identity and worth (Payne, Horn and Relf, 2000) and for their wider family and friends. There are also more serious implications for poor mental health and mental illness often related to personal and social isolation (see Chapter 6). Older people may lack the resilience and sense of autonomy they had experienced throughout earlier life, which leaves them vulnerable to feelings of worthlessness and hopelessness. These feelings can be exacerbated by the lack of resources (both financial and community based) as well as a deeper sense of social opprobrium that can exist as part of a wider structural oppression in relation to older people (Victor, 2005).

Particular issues for older people

Poverty

Historically, and often because of sexist attitudes in society, many women have been forced to become over-reliant on men for financial support and in their old age this can contribute to poverty and increased vulnerability, particularly if widowed. Having had less opportunity to gain employment or to contribute to an occupational or personal private pension due to them taking on caring roles and raising children, such women are more at risk of economic deprivation and social exclusion.

While some aspects of ageing may not be obvious to the person or his/her acquaintances, the same cannot be said for retirement. This is a socially constructed, somewhat arbitrary event through which people may feel themselves to be *included and productive* one day and *excluded and unproductive* the next (Giddens, 2006; Wilson et al., 2008). A rationalisation of the retirement age to 65 for men and women may refer more to governmental wishes to pay less in pensions – particularly given the increased life expectancy of older people – than to any wider awareness of the inequitable nature of society, dominated as it is by both paternalistic and patriarchal systems. Ironically, it was never intended that the arbitrary ages of 65 for men and 60 for women should define when people retire and now, somewhat paradoxically, such random thinking is being taken to task as there is now regular and increasing discussion among politicians for the need to *extend* the retirement age in the face of economic recession, growing national debt and increasing numbers of older people.

Another issue for many older people at this time is a reduction in returns on investments as a result of significantly reduced interest rates. Those older people fortunate to have savings often rely on the interest paid on these to supplement their state pension, especially if they do not have an occupational entitlement. There is a certain irony in the longer-term promotion by governments of thrift and fiscal prudence that may ultimately result in the impoverishment of greater numbers of older people. While older people may have been brought up to 'make do and mend', they may have seen thrift as a means of supporting themselves through their later years, only to realise now that such prudence has brought them little benefit. Significant socio-economic differences may have very direct implications for older people, as there is evidence to suggest that people from higher socio-economic groups with more disposable assets tend to enjoy a greater life expectancy (Siegrist and Marmot, 2006).

ACTIVITY 7.2

Older people can experience distress and unhappiness through poverty, social exclusion and isolation. What might be the effects of these?

Comment

Older people are more likely to be poorer than the general population. While older men may have an occupational pension supported by their state pension, this may not be the same for women. They may have foregone the capacity for economic independence and the ability to accrue disposable capital while undertaking childcare and the care of other dependents and working, unpaid (un-pensioned) as housewives in middle of the last century. The fact that women have a higher life expectancy may also mean that they experience poverty in old age over a longer period. The *Poverty and Social Exclusion Survey* suggested that between 32 per cent and 62 per cent of pensioner households are in poverty (Patsios, 2006 in Gordon et al, 2006).

Family dynamics and kinship care

Many older people are increasingly called upon to provide kinship care for grandchildren, where the biological parents may struggle with issues of mental health and substance misuse (Hothersall 2008), thereby contributing to a change in the stereotypical image of grandparents over the years. This may also be associated with more psychological and philosophical dimension of generativity i.e. the capacity for negotiating change through the life course, in meeting the challenges of substance misuse and unplanned pregnancy within the family (Bond et al., 2007), because where resources are limited, women are more likely to be burdened with an inequitable share of these tasks in the context of a socially constructed, acquired and gendered perception of function within the family (Roberts, 1996, Dominelli, 1997, Victor, 2005).

Consideration also needs to be given to a family member carrying out personal care for an older relative. The informal carer (relative) may feel embarrassed performing intimate care tasks such as toileting or bathing. They may prefer a formal carer to carry out these roles and the older person themselves may feel that the provision of such care changes the nature of their relationship from one of reciprocity to one of dependence with a consequent loss of esteem and perceived status.

An understanding of the use of direct payments related to the Community Care (Direct Payments) Act 1996 may be of particular help here where the person can purchase their own care package, which would not include the use of relatives as the policy precludes payments to immediate family members. The Carers (Recognition of Services) Act 1995 can however provide an assessment of need and support for carers with shopping, cooking, respite and a range of other services. Ironically, these provisions may actually reinforce negative gender stereotypes in relation to the care of older people as, too often, it is left to female members of the family to subsume their own future ambitions within a caring role.

Changes in family structure and increased geographical mobility have meant that older people may now be more physically and in some respects, psychologically distant from their families which can lead to vulnerability, isolation and less immediate family support. If we assume that commitment and investment in love, affection and wider social support are features of functioning family relationships, we can see how a lessening of contact and therefore reciprocity can result in potential stress and isolation for older people (Victor, 2005). The formation of policy and the development of practice need to respond to such changes to support and promote ongoing contact especially within care home provision.

The abuse of older people

Sadly, we have to acknowledge that older people in society are the victims of a range of different forms of abuse perpetrated against them by a range of people, from family and friends to professional workers.

Abuse may be categorised into the domains of financial, physical, sexual, emotional, psychological and discriminatory. The Select Committee on Abuse (2004) suggested that areas of research on neglect are still too often under-acknowledged and under-explored (Mo, Bernard and Phillips, 2009) and makes the case that older people are perceived in a less equitable fashion than other groups of people in society, which is the essence of discrimination and a precursor for abuse and neglect. However, as we have seen in Chapters 3 and 4 there are now more positive developments in relation to the protection of vulnerable adults, particularly in Scotland.

In England research carried out by Action on Elder Abuse in 2006 identified that 2.6 per cent of people over the age of 66 had experienced mistreatment that involved a family member, a worker in a care setting or a friend in the preceding year. This approximated to a figure of 227,000 older people in the UK and rose to 342,400 older people when neighbours and more casual acquaintances were included within this equation (Ray, Bernard and Phillips, 2009).

Older people who are socially isolated, dependent on others, have poor health or a disability and who are not self-reliant are more likely to experience abuse. The abuse of older people can take place in hospital, nursing or residential care homes, day care, a carer's home and the older person's own home. Kurrle (2001) identifies *abuser psychopathology*, where significant factors include alcoholism, drug abuse, psychiatric illness and cognitive impairment. There can also be a family history of domestic violence, potentially contributing to different forms of abuse. Abusers will undoubtedly wish to exert power and control over vulnerable older people as a feature of their persistent psychopathology, while the older, vulnerable person may be desperate to remain as part of a social and family network, however dysfunctional this may be thereby setting up a particularly complex dynamic that may challenge even the most progressive forms of legislation and policy.

Resilience

One means of offsetting the negative effects of those factors referred to above that are likely to increase an older person's vulnerability to harm is to support and promote their resilience (see also Chapter 5). Misca (in Adams, Dominelli and Payne, 2009) refers to resilience as the capacity that individuals, groups and families have to resist the negative aspects of harm and experience and still develop a positive and generative aspect. In the context of older people, practitioners need to be aware of the accumulation of inequalities that may have impacted on an older person throughout the life course (Davey Smith, 2003). This may be more pronounced where cultural and structural oppression may impact on older people especially at times when they are experiencing a loss of place, role and hopeful expectation for the future. Resilience in old age may be challenged at the time when an older person is experiencing the loss of a spouse, or where their physical and emotional resources may be diminished (Phillipson, 1998). While there is good evidence to support resilience being built up over the life course in relation to attachments (Fonagy et al., 1994), our emotional attachments and engagement with others still needs to be sustained and nurtured in the longer term (Murray-Parkes, Stevenson-Hinde and Marris, 1991). One way to support resilience in older age is to both acknowledge and focus on the previous coping strategies of the older person and support and encourage these in the present through inclusive practice. This means that workers have to engage with the total lived experience of the older person that makes for who they are in the present (McDonald, 2010). If an older person feels that they are being listened to and included in any decision-making that impacts on their future care and provision, they are much more likely to feel engaged with this process.

Domiciliary support and residential services

Domiciliary care services are generally agreed to be the most effective way to meet the needs of older people where this is their choice. This has to take consideration of those more holistic needs of older people in the context of inclusion, role, independence and the ability to make informed choices about their future care needs. Domiciliary care can be provided by a range of statutory, voluntary and private agencies to meet the range of complex and competing needs for an older population (Rothwell-Murray, 2000; Andrews and Phillips, 2004).

CASE STUDY

As you read the following case focus on ways in which you can resource the needs of Jessie Bruce.

Miss Jessica Bruce is aged 82 and is disabled due to a stroke four years ago. The stroke affected her right side and her mobility is very limited. She is unable to walk any distance and her speech is slurred. She also has poor eyesight and chronic pain in her lower back and the medication she takes produces unpleasant side-effects like nausea and vomiting from time to time. As a result, she is often quite low and tearful.

Miss Bruce owns her one-bedroom bungalow but has no income other than a state pension. The house has been equipped with a raised toilet seat with a handle and there is an electric bath seat. Miss Bruce was the youngest child and the only survivor of a family of five. Her best friend Edna died of cancer two years ago and she has no family or friends to speak of. She tends to 'snack' on sweet foods rather than eat proper meals, as she cannot work the cooker in her kitchen.

What arrangements might be put in place for Miss Bruce? Think about some of the factors we have referred to above as arising from the effects of increased longevity and the cumulative effects of poverty and loneliness. What might be the short- and long-term possibilities with regards to her future care?

Comment

As a person grows older, there is increased risk of falling as mobility becomes unstable and eyesight begins to fail. There are numerous medical factors that contribute to this but a basic lack of confidence on one's feet may be a psychological factor. Thinning of bone tissue also makes risk of falling more hazardous and risk of bone breakage carries its own complications in that older people are at risk of hypothermia if they lie unattended in a cold house. Ultimately, a simple fall may be something from which an older person is unable to recover.

To this end, a multi-agency assessment of social, nursing, medical, occupational and physiotherapeutic in-put seems required. It seems very premature to consider that Miss Bruce can no longer continue to live on her own, but support, monitoring and review of medication all seem called for. In all probability, the central aspect lacking in any current package of support for Miss Bruce is the provision of personal care and some form of activity through the day.

In a systematic review and meta-analysis related to 15 studies of home visits carried out by Elkan et al. (2001), there was clear evidence to suggest that effective domiciliary services contributed to a reduction in mortality and admissions to longer-term institutional care.

Admission to a residential care or nursing home can be a traumatic experience for older people. The majority of residents in care homes are women aged over eighty, often with multiple disabilities. There is a clear correlation here between the wider focus on community-based care and ensuring that older people retain the capacity for independent living for as long as possible. Fries (2000) suggests through the 'compression of morbidity' theory that while the range of diseases or conditions people can die from has been reduced or brought under control, which means people are living longer, it may also mean that older people live with disability and discomfort for a much longer period of time.

The national evaluation of partnerships for older people projects

This scheme was funded by the Department of Health to promote services for older people with a remit of promoting health, well-being and independent living skills as well as addressing wider areas of risk aimed at preventing or delaying hospital admission or more long term institutional care.

This scheme, which has been funded from 2006–2008, supported 470 projects in 29 areas, and the evidence shows that there was a net saving of £2,166 for every older person accessing services within the areas assessed through the

continued

> *The national evaluation of partnerships for older people projects*
>
> *continued*
>
> use of preventative risk measures and a wider promotion of independent living skills for those older people living at home. These measures included handyman schemes to address immediate problems of domiciliary care as well as funding to support falls avoidance schemes, fire services, police, housing associations and the local authority and private providers of services.
>
> There was also a clearly evidenced reduction of hospital admissions for those more vulnerable older clients and a net reduction in spending. (www.community care.co.uk/popps).
>
> The partnership focused on a range of services from promoting healthy eating and socially inclusive practice as well as the more formal structures of supported discharge and rapid response schemes for those hospitalised or in danger of hospitalisation. There were over a quarter of a million recipients of these services and the evaluation shows that over the period of the partnership there was a reduction of 29 per cent in the use of Accident and Emergency departments as well as a reduction of 47 per cent in overnight hospital stays.
>
> Significantly all the localised projects involved older people in their management and design. (www.pssru.ac.uk).
>
> Windle, K, Wagland, R, Forder, J, D'Amico, F, Janssen, D and Wistow, G, (2010) The national evaluation of partnerships for older people projects: Executive summary. The personal social services research unit.

Personal care

Significantly, a large proportion of domiciliary care services are still provided by statutory organisations (usually the Local Authority). These are primarily delivered under the duties imposed upon local authorities in all countries of the UK, by the NHS and Community Care Act 1990 and other related legislation and regulations. It makes provision for a range of people in need, including older people to be cared for within their own homes. Significantly, the Community Care and Health (Scotland) Act 2002 made free personal care available to older people. This has impacted significantly on the increased uptake of domiciliary services in Scotland. In England, their strategic policy of *Putting People First* (Department of Health, 2009) has identified that supporting and extending greater control and choice to the people they support should be the main focus of social work intervention. At the time of writing this, before the general election of 2010, there is too much political uncertainty to say how the current government's plans to implement limited free personal care in England and Wales will progress. There is a specific emphasis on *personalisation* in the UK where public services can be adapted to meet the individual needs of clients. While this creates a tension with diminishing resources and the talk of restricted funding of public services in future budgets, it addresses and moves forward the agenda of person-centred and individualised services.

Nutrition

Nutrition does not just sustain life, it also prevents illness. This is particularly the case in regard to older people in relation to such diseases as diabetes type 2 and bone and hip fractures, where calcium deficiency is a risk. At a time when older people may be under increased financial stress, this can result in growing reliance upon cheaper, more readily available but less nutritious food.

Recent media reporting on malnutrition in relation to older people raises the wider question of how an older and ageing population will have these needs met by domiciliary care services. Research by Quereshi and Henwood (2000) and Raynes et al. (2001) identifies reliability, the skills and attitudes of care workers, awareness of support in the area of nutrition and the ability to respond quickly to any emergency as the main focus of older people's need in terms of quality domiciliary support. Most Local Authority areas have dedicated dieticians who will review a person's dietary needs either in their own home or in a care setting although it has recently been identified that large numbers of older people within care and hospital settings are in fact malnourished which is a cause for alarm (Maud and Webster, 2009). Underpinning all of this is the single focus of the services being dedicated to the specific and individual needs of the service user.

ACTIVITY **7.4**

How would you as a worker tackle poor nutrition if you became aware that an older person had stopped eating a healthy diet?

Comment

There is a range of factors that impact on older people's choice of food. These can relate to the physical, medical, environmental and psychological. Poor nutrition may result in a range of health issues related to weight loss or obesity, diabetes, dysphagia (difficulty in swallowing) or poor appetite itself. These concerns may be compounded where there is conflicting information about what constitutes healthy food, particularly if this is at odds with what older people have assumed and been taught is healthy throughout their life. A particular example of this is where there is an over-emphasis on low fat foodstuffs, when older people may actually need more high-energy foods. Dietary management should encourage small but regular protein rich meals, along with food fortification and supplements and snacks between meals. A balance of these not only increases the incidence of good and long-term health but may also be related to concentration, memory and cognitive functioning more generally.

Some further policy and practice considerations

The ratio of retired people to those of working-age is projected to rise over the next two decades. There are now fewer wage earners because of sustained low birth rates that results in less people contributing to the older generation's basic state pensions. This, in turn, will have widespread consequences for fiscal policy, although comparatively recent research speculates that the funding of pensions for older people will still be sustainable at 5 per cent of the Gross Domestic Product until 2050 (Hills, 1993). There is a possibility that the UK Government will raise the official retirement age to sixty-seven while encouraging the younger people of today to save for their own retirement in anticipation of such a shortfall. Successive governments have tried to encourage people to save for their own retirement because of this shortfall and the low level of basic state pension. Unfortunately this will not benefit people from lower socioeconomic groups.

Middle-class women and men, particularly the 'Baby Boomers' with greater socioeconomic status, are likely to fare better than others with less socio-economic status. Gender is enmeshed in the context of class, culture, race, cohort life stage, economy and social policy (Arber and Ginn, 1997; Walker, 1993) and as such, gender needs to be considered as one factor in a wider paradigm of oppression.

This potential for change and loss of role will have emotional and financial consequences. Policies in the past, such as a compulsory retirement age, have encouraged early retirement rather than keeping older workers in the workforce. These arrangements led to some people claiming social assistance or incapacity benefits because of pseudo illness which may be related more to vulnerability and a reduced sense of self in relation to coping. This relates closely to how older people may perceive their sense of identity through their employment and how a commensurate loss of this may result in a diminished sense of self.

While this is an example of personal, cultural and structural oppression (Dalrymple and Burke, 1995) it also focuses in on how older people are perceived in terms of their potential for contributing, with an over-emphasis on their disengagement from the wider community (Stuart-Hamilton, 2006). While older people may choose to withdraw more in old age as a precursor to the inevitability of death, this should not be assessed in the context of passivity, but more in the context of the natural progression through the life stages. It may also be the case that those older people who feel a greater degree of disengagement have *always* felt themselves to be removed from the wider assets of society through unresolved earlier life experiences (Barnes et al., 2004). This should be a particular focus of social work intervention, as this awareness will support clarification of presenting needs that may formerly have been masked by the sense that it is 'normal' for older people to become withdrawn in later life.

Housing has presented a significant challenge for policy makers and older vulnerable people since the 1920s. The need for adequate housing had to be balanced with wider issues of welfare provision which came to a head in 1980 when the Conservative government enacted legislation to ensure that council tenants had a right to buy their properties at a discount. Considerable numbers of older people used this opportunity to buy their properties, which reduced the public housing stock. These new owner-occupiers now had the responsibility of maintaining these properties and this added a considerable financial burden on older people, many of whom were already struggling financially and who had to manage on state pensions and other limited forms of income whilst shouldering the cost of household repairs, etc.

'Life-satisfaction' research has focused on the quality of life: people's aspirations, morale and happiness (Arkoff, Meredith and Dubanoski, 2004; Pavot and Diener, 2008). Generally it is not until people reach that 'fourth age' (eighty and over) that support services are required. Support services should not undermine self-help or family care as this further marginalises older people and denies them their acquired social and political place in society (Wilson et al., 2008). This is why practitioners need to be aware of the language they use in relation to older people, to ensure that they do not demean, patronise and infantilise them. The very term 'older people' refers simply to an accumulation of years, while the more generic term *'the elderly'* is replete with oppressive, ageist and judgemental connotations. The reality is that if older people are perceived in the context of their presenting *disabilities* as opposed to their *abilities*, it is likely that they will become marginalised in a society that values individuals for their productivity and youth as opposed to their life skills and experience.

C H A P T E R   S U M M A R Y

Social work and social care provision for and with older people confronts us in extremely challenging times in which increasing demands on resources conflict with the need for an increasing awareness of, and engagement with, the wider needs of older people. This work has to be addressed in the context of inclusion, empowerment and the personalisation of services. For services and interventions to be effective there must be full engagement in meeting the care needs of older people, underpinned by a more holistic consideration of those aspects of loss, resilience and the lived experience and inner worlds of all older people. The worker needs to understand the past and present experience of the older person, their emotional intelligence as well as attending to the physical task. The national reviews of social work recently undertaken across the UK (GSCC, 2008; Scottish Executive, 2006) present both the actual and aspirational facets of professional social work practice now and in the future, and suggest that a fundamental role of social work is the development of a therapeutic relationship between the service user and the professional to ensure actual defined need is met through an engaged, collaborative and empathic relationship that recognises the importance of ensuring that the older person can retain some sense of control during the processes involved in any form of intervention. We need to ensure that older people are involved in decisions about their future as, too often, they are marginalised and excluded where decision-making is concerned, which can be particularly acute in the area of residential care (see Crawford and Walker, 2008; Pritchard, 2003a).

FURTHER READING

Crawford, K and Walker, J (2008) *Social work with older people* (2nd edn). Exeter: Learning Matters.

McDonald, A (2010) *Social work with older people*. Bristol: The Policy Press.
Both these texts provide thorough discussions of many aspects of working with older people in a range of contexts and settings.

Hudson, A and Moore, L (eds) (2009) *Caring for older people in the community*. Chichester: Wiley Blackwell.
Primarily focused on the nurse within the community setting, but the book has huge relevance for social work and social care practitioners too.

Chapter 8

Need, risk and protection in criminal justice social work and probation

Anne Shirran

National Occupational Standards.
Key Role 1: Prepare for, and work with, individuals, families, carers, groups and communities to assess their needs and circumstances.
- Liaise with others to access additional information that can inform initial contact and involvement.
- Work with individuals, families, carers, groups and communities to identify, gather, analyse and understand information.
- Work with individuals, families, carers, groups and communities to enable them to assess and make informed decisions about their needs, circumstances, risks, preferred options and resources.
- Assess and review the preferred options of individuals, families, carers, groups and communities.
- Assess needs, risks and options taking into account legal and other requirements.
- Assess and recommend an appropriate course of action for individuals, families, carers, groups and communities.

Key Role 2: Plan, carry out, review and evaluate social work practice, with individuals, families, carers, groups, communities and other professionals.
- Identify the need for legal and procedural intervention.
- Develop and maintain relationships with individuals, families, carers, groups, communities and others.
- Apply and justify social work methods and models used to achieve change and development, and improve life opportunities.
- Regularly monitor, review and evaluate changes in needs and circumstances.
- Negotiate the provision to be included in the plans.
- Review the effectiveness of the plans with the people involved.
- Renegotiate and revise plans to meet changing needs and circumstances.
- Work with individuals, families, carers, groups, communities and others to identify and evaluate situations and circumstances that may trigger the behaviour.
- Work with individuals, families, carers, groups and communities on strategies and support that could positively change the behaviour.

Key Role 3: Support individuals to represent their needs, views and circumstances.
- Prepare reports and documents for decision-making forums.

continued

Achieving A Social Work Degree continued

- Present evidence to, and help, individuals, families, carers, groups and communities to understand the procedures of and the outcomes from, decision-making forums.
- Enable individuals, families, carers, groups and communities to be involved in decision-making forums.

Key Role 4: Manage risk to individuals, families, carers, groups, communities, self and colleagues.
- Identify and assess the nature of the risk.
- Balance the rights and responsibilities of individuals, families, carers, groups and communities with associated risk.
- Regularly monitor, re-assess, and manage risk to individuals, families, carers, groups and communities.
- Assess potential risk to self and colleagues.
- Work within the risk assessment and management procedures of your own and other relevant organisations and professions.
- Plan, monitor and review outcomes and actions to minimise stress and risk.

Key Role 5: Manage and be accountable, with supervision and support, for your own social work practice within your organisation.
- Maintain accurate, complete, accessible, and up-to-date records and reports.
- Provide evidence for judgements and decisions.
- Implement legal and policy frameworks for access to records and reports.
- Share records with individuals, families, carers, groups and communities.

Key Role 6: Demonstrate professional competence in social work practice.
- Review and update your own knowledge of legal, policy and procedural frameworks.
- Use professional and organisational supervision and support to research, critically analyse, and review. knowledge-based practice.
- Implement knowledge-based social work models and methods to develop and improve your own practice.

Scottish Standards in Social Work Education
Key Role 1: Prepare for, and work with, individuals, families, carers, groups and communities to assess their needs and circumstances.
- Preparing for social work contact and involvement.
- Working with individuals, families, carers, groups and communities so they can make informed decisions.
- Assessing needs and options in order to recommend a course of action.

Key Role 2: Plan, carry out, review and evaluate social work practice with individuals, families, carers, groups, communities and other professionals.
- Identifying and responding to crisis situations.
- Working with individuals, families, carers, groups and communities to achieve change, promote dignity, realise potential and improve life opportunities.
- Producing, implementing and evaluating plans with individuals, families, carers, groups, communities and colleagues.

Key Role 3: Assess and manage risk to individuals, families, carers, groups, communities, self and colleagues.
- Assessing and managing risks to individuals, families, carers, groups and communities.
- Assessing and managing risk to self and colleagues.

continued

Achieving A Social Work Degree continued

Key Role 4: Demonstrate professional competence in social work practice.
- Evaluating and using up-to-date knowledge of, and research into, social work practice, working within agreed standards of social work practice.
- Understanding and managing complex ethical issues, dilemmas and conflicts.

Key Role 5: Manage and be accountable, with supervision and support, for your own social work practice within your organisation.
- Managing one's own work in an accountable way.
- Managing, presenting and sharing records and reports.
- Preparing for, and taking part in, decision-making forums.
- Working effectively with professionals within integrated, multi-disciplinary and other service settings.

Key Role 6: Support individuals to represent and manage their needs, views and circumstances.
- Representing, in partnership with, and on behalf of, individuals, families, carers, groups and communities to help them achieve and maintain greater independence.

Introduction

This chapter will look at criminal justice social work and the role of the probation services in other parts of the UK, identifying current themes and issues. We will discuss *need* with a focus on criminogenic need and examine *risk* in terms of specific offender groups and the use of risk assessment, together with measures undertaken to increase both public- and offender-protection.

The structure and function of services

In Scotland the Kilbrandon Report 1964 (SHHD/SED, 1964) not only reshaped child care with the introduction of the Children's Hearing system, but also prompted a major change in work with offenders through the introduction of the Social Work Scotland Act 1968 (the '68 Act). This saw the disbanding of Scotland's discrete probation service and the introduction of criminal justice social work as an integral part of generic social work provision under the terms of section 27 of the '68 Act. This departure from the English & Welsh model was a major shift in attitude towards offenders, demonstrating a welfare-based approach that saw the offender as a person *in need* although the apparent lack of focus on offenders and a failure to reduce reoffending rates resulted in the introduction of *National Standards and Objectives for Social Work in the Criminal Justice System* (SWSG, 1991). This led to the development of specialist criminal justice teams heralded in by the the Law Reform (Miscellaneous Provisions) (Scotland) Act 1990, which saw the introduction of 100 per cent direct funding of criminal justice social work services from the Scottish Office (now the Scottish Government).

In England and Wales, the National Probation Service is responsible for providing the statutory Criminal Justice Service, responsible for the supervision of offenders in the community and the provision of reports to the criminal courts to assist them in sentencing. It was established in its current form by the Criminal Justice and Court Services Act

2000. Prior to this, the Probation Service operated as separate services within each county in England and in Wales but the establishment of a unified National Service facilitated the introduction of the *National Offender Management Service (NOMS)* whose first priority is public protection. The Offender Management Act 2007 (E&W) introduced changes to the roles and responsibilities of the Probation Service, a key development of which was the introduction of *Probation Trusts* that took on the role of providing probation services within the public sector generally. Essentially this created a system where the Trusts had contracts, or service level agreements, with the Secretary of State to act as the public sector providers of probation services. They act on behalf of the NOMS in partnership arrangements with other statutory organisations such as local police departments and the Prison Service, working in local *criminal justice boards* towards the central purpose of reducing offending. The NOMS has a key role in public protection, ensuring that the punishment of offenders is appropriate, aiming to reduce crime and the fear of it within the community as a whole.

The Criminal Procedure (Scotland) Act 1995 is the legislative framework for criminal justice services in Scotland, setting out the functions of the police, courts and court disposals, as well as the circumstances whereby it is mandatory for the court to request a *Social Enquiry Report (SER)* under section 201. Within this report there is a requirement to provide an analysis of the individual's offending behaviour and form an assessment of the risk they may pose, both in terms of reoffending and risk of harm. The Probation Service in England and Wales have a similar arrangement to provide a Pre-Sentence Report under section 158 of the Criminal Justice Act 2003 (E&W).

The Criminal Justice (Scotland) Act 2003 established the Risk Management Authority (RMA), whose task it is to promote public protection by developing and supporting professional practice in managing the risk of serious harm presented by violent and sexual offenders. The RMA advises the Scottish Government on policy, identifies and circulates research on best practice regarding interventions with offenders, sets standards for risk assessments and undertakes the accreditation of approved risk-assessors.

The Criminal Justice (Scotland) Act 2003 also introduced the *Order for Lifelong Restriction* (OLR). This was introduced as part of a range of risk management strategies relating to those offenders who present an ongoing high risk of reoffending and of causing significant harm. Where the court is considering the imposition of an OLR a risk assessment must be carried out by an approved assessor.

The Management of Offenders, etc. (Scotland) Act 2005 saw the introduction of eight Community Justice Authorities in Scotland. The intention was to strengthen and review how the Scottish Prison Service, local authorities and other organisations work together to reduce reoffending rates in their areas. Importantly it contains provision regarding arrangements for the sharing of information in relation to assessing and managing the risk posed by serious violent offenders and sex offenders and Health Services are also included as a responsible authority in relation to Mentally Disordered Offenders (see Chapter 3 and (Hothersall, Maas-Lowit and Golightley, 2008).

In addition, the principal authorities of each of the eight Criminal Justice Authorities will act in co-operation with other specified agencies in carrying out their function. The intention was that it would result in a more formalised and structured approach in line with the commitments set out the *Concordat on Information Sharing* introduced in November 2005 and strengthened under the Management of Offenders, etc. (Scotland) Act 2005.

In Scotland we have seen the 'welfarist' approach to offenders diminish with an ever-increasing focus on public protection and offender management similar to that of England and Wales. This can be seen with the introduction of Reducing Reoffending: National Strategy for the Management of Offenders in Scotland in March 2006. Similarities can be found in the language used within this strategy to that of the National Offender Management Strategy in England and Wales introduced in 2005 (NOMS, 2005), where the emphasis is placed on communication, information sharing and reducing reoffending through to improving services to offenders.

Criminal Justice social work in Scotland and the National Probation Service in England and Wales are increasingly preoccupied with the assessment and management of risk. The development of risk assessment tools has evolved from professionals using only their judgement and experience in assessing risk. An increasing need for more structured and less personally idiosyncratic assessments of risk in this field has led to the development of specific risk assessment tools relating to offenders and offender typologies. Initially actuarial risk assessment tools (see Chapter 3) were introduced which looked at particular sorts of data used to predict the future risk of re-offending, such as age at which the first offence was committed, age at first conviction and gender, etc. These *static factors* were then considered alongside more *dynamic factors* that interact together to generate criminogenic need (Bonta and Andrews, 2007).

Criminogenic need

McGuire (1995) identified some important principles in relation to work with offenders. This included the *Need Principle,* which requires practitioners to assess criminogenic needs and target their interventions upon them. The strategy embodied in this requires specific approaches to sentencing. If a practitioner is to work in partnership with the offender, it requires certain sentences to be made by the courts that apply a degree of coercion to enable work to be done, either through a structured deferred sentence, a probation order or a licence, as a fine or a custodial sentence would not enable the professional to engage with the offender.

Criminogenic needs or dynamic factors are those associated with continued offending behaviour. Unlike static factors such as current age, age at first conviction, number of previous convictions, number of custodial sentences, which do not change, criminogenic factors do change over time. These include financial problems, substance misuse, lack of social, educational or work skills, lack of accommodation, negative attitudes to law enforcement, mental health problems or mental illness (see Chapter 6) and negative peer associations. In undertaking a risk assessment, identification of criminogenic needs is very important, as targeting those for intervention can reduce recidivism (Andrews, 1995; Hollin, 1999). In doing so, this encompasses the principles of the *Risk, Need and Responsivity* model (Blanchette and Brown, 2006.) This model draws heavily on social learning theory (Bandura, 1977) and looks at three significant domains involved in the way people learn: family, peers and the media. The model acknowledges that offending behaviour can be learned when children observe parents, family members or friends who are involved in crime, peer pressure exerting a strong influence on the behaviour of young people, although early research into the effects of such vicarious learning through the medium of TV/Video was ambivalent about cause and effect (Browne and Pennell, 1998). However, if we accept that behaviours are learned, we can work with the premise that such behaviours can be *unlearned*, recognising the cognitive element within the processes of *learning* and the *internalisation* of behavioural responses.

The National Treatment Outcome Research Study by Gossop et al. (2003) indicates that substance misuse is prevalent among offenders, particularly in relation to acquisitional crime (primarily shop-lifting to fund substance use). Women offenders dependent on heroin were often involved in prostitution to fund their substance misuse (James et al., 1979 and Chapter 10). The characteristics surrounding female offending differ to a large extent from those of male offenders, in that women often have been, or continue to be, victimised by a male, highlighting issues of power and control. Harper et al. (2005) identified a particular increase in criminogenic need of women with regard to relationships and emotional well-being, whereas male offenders demonstrated an increase in criminogenic need in relation to substance misuse, cognition and attitudes. Given this information, it is important to recognise that programmes of intervention for male offenders are often not appropriate to address the needs of female offenders. Similarly, research by Koons et al. (1997) focused on victimisation and self-esteem in women offenders. They concluded that programmes which addressed previous experiences of victimisation and which targeted self-esteem showed encouraging results. However, they acknowledged that this required further study. It remains unresolved as to whether such issues should be regarded as criminogenic needs, but it does highlight the need for female-specific offending behavioural programmes to be targeted upon their particular needs.

Governments and Assemblies in the UK have highlighted concerns regarding the children of parents with problematic substance misuse. This is demonstrated in the policies such as *Getting Our Priorities Right* (Scottish Executive, 2003) and *Hidden Harm* (Home Office, 2006), which emphasise the need for professionals to identify the impact of parental substance use upon their capacity to care for their children. It is estimated that there are 350,000 children living with parents who are problem drug users and 1.3 million children living with parents who abuse alcohol (Home Office, 2006). Practitioners must consider the implications for children when working with offenders with substance problems and, if necessary, refer the family to children and families social work services.

Offenders who have substance misuse problems often find it difficult to access health services which can cause numerous problems and because of substance misuse, a breakdown in family relationships and other friendships often occurs. The maintenance and re-development of positive relationships with family and friends can assist an offender to move toward desistance by increasing social bonds and promoting conformity to behavioural norms and increasing social inclusion (Maruna, 2000).

Homelessness is a major factor, which often contributes to continued offending behaviour. Young offenders may be asked to leave the family home as a result of their behaviour. In many instances offenders have lost their tenancy as a result of custodial sentences or periods of detention. If release from prison is a critical point in becoming homeless, this contributes to a cycle of offending. This can result in offenders being of no fixed abode, often living a fairly chaotic existence and staying with various friends or acquaintances. The government recognised this issue as a barrier to the rehabilitation and reintegration of offenders into society and the *Rough Sleepers Initiative* was introduced within the United Kingdom in 1990 to provide services to prisoners while in custody to address accommodation issues on release (Social Exclusion Unit, 2001). Funding for this initiative saw the development of through-care service provision, which included housing services to prisoners and young offenders in detention while in custody. The Homelessness Act 2002 in England and Wales and the Homelessness, etc. (Scotland) Act 2003 reflected the need to accommodate vulnerable individuals. This was seen as a positive move, given that a disproportionate number of offenders with mental health problems are identified during assessment as having accommodation needs. The same is true of offenders who have been through the 'care' system as children. As professionals it is important to remember that a basic need for human beings is shelter (Maslow, 1970). If this need is not addressed, it will not be possible to engage an offender by addressing higher-level needs in interventions to reduce reoffending. Similarly, if the offender is of no fixed abode, the Court may be unwilling to impose a community-based sentence. The provision of statutory (local authority-run) probation hostels on both sides of the border can offer stability and support which complements provision by voluntary organisations such as the National Association for Care and Rehabilitation of Offenders in England and Wales and in Scotland, Safeguarding Communities and Reducing Offending (SaCRO).

For a substantial proportion of offenders, low levels of literacy and numeracy are significant issues. Undertaking an assessment of an individual offender's literacy and numeracy skills is important. Lipton (1999) suggests that improving reading skills can reduce reoffending by 6 per cent. Similarly Porporino and Robinson (1992) concluded that those offenders who improved both literacy and numeracy skills were less likely to return to custody. Where it is identified as a need, literacy can be addressed within the education units of prisons or young offenders institutions, as part of sentence planning and management. Such integrated delivery of services is now termed the *Integrated Case Management System* (ICMS). Participation in education can be a precursor to participation in offending-specific programmes.

Often, offenders have little in the way of skills that might be valuable in the pursuit of work. This may be a result of poor educational attainment at school, offending, substance misuse or a combination of all three. Again, one of Governments' priorities in respect of their Law and Order agendas are changes to community sentences. In particular *Community Service Orders* involve the offender undertaking unpaid work for a specified number of hours. These orders have been renamed in England & Wales as *Community Orders* and can include up to 12 ancillary requirements, such as participation in programmes of intervention. A key element is to provide offenders with unpaid work opportunities that will develop their skills and make their entry into the workforce more likely, while addressing the underlying causes of their offending.

ACTIVITY 8.1

Take a minute to consider the following and make a note of your answers: What does the term criminogenic need mean? Identify as many areas of criminogenic need as you can. To get you started, by areas we mean significant aspects of need, such as substance misuse.

Comment

Bonta and Andrews (2007) identify seven major risk/need factors in relation to offenders (see Table 8.1). In addition to these major needs, they also identified four minor needs or risk factors. These were low self-esteem, personal distress, mental disorder (which, you may recall, is mental illness, learning disability or personality disorder) and poor physical health.

Table 8.1 Major need and risk factors (Bonta and Andrews, 2007)

Major risk/need factor	Indicators	Intervention goals
Antisocial personality pattern	Impulsive, adventurous pleasure seeking, restlessly aggressive and irritable	Build self-management skills, teach anger management
Pro-criminal attitudes	Rationalisations for crime, negative attitudes towards the law	Counter rationalisations with pro-social attitudes; build up a pro-social identity
Social supports for crime	Criminal friends, isolation from pro-social others	Replace pro-criminal friends and associates with pro-social friends and associates
Substance abuse	Abuse of alcohol and/or drugs	Reduce substance abuse, enhance alternatives to substance use
Family/marital relationships	Inappropriate parental monitoring and disciplining, poor family relationships	Teaching parenting skills, enhance warmth and caring
School/work	Poor performance, low levels of satisfactions	Enhance work/study skills, nurture interpersonal relationships within the context of work and school
Pro-social recreational activities	Lack of involvement in pro-social recreational/leisure activities	Encourage participation in pro-social recreational activities, teach pro-social hobbies and sports

Risk

Within criminal justice social work and probation services, practitioners must consider and assess four areas of risk. These are the risk of reoffending, the risk of harm to others, the risk of harm to self and the risk of custody.

The use of risk assessment tools combined with the application of professional judgement can aid the practitioner in assessing risk (see Chapter 2). Risk assessment tools have evolved significantly over the last twenty years or so beginning with the application of actuarial methods that superseded the previously rather unfocused approach to risk assessment. Thereafter the development of risk/need instruments that considered both actuarial factors and dynamic factors were introduced. Currently '4th generation' risk assessment tools are used that include both static and dynamic factors and, importantly, they also contain a case risk-management plan. Examples of these are the *Risk Assessment Guidance and Framework 1–4*, (Scottish Executive, 2000) and *LSI/CM1*, currently in use in

Scotland. In England & Wales, the Probation Service and Her Majesty's Prison Service use the Offender Assessment System (OASys).

McGuire (1995) suggests a number of 'what works' principles in relation to interventions with offenders. These included the *risk principle,* where the level of service should be matched to the offender's assessed risk of re-offending and/ or risk of harm. As practitioners, we need to be aware of what we are assessing when it comes to risk.

> *A risk assessment can only identify the probability of harm, assess the impact of it on key individuals, and pose intervention strategies, which may diminish the risk or reduce the harm. Assessment cannot prevent risk.*
>
> (Hope and Sparks, 2000, p137)

There is no clear definition of risk and there is a lack of consistency in definitions of high, medium and low risk across agencies and disciplines, especially in the criminal justice field. This is due in part to the use of professional judgement and the differing contexts in which it is applied (see Chapter 2). In Scotland, the Risk Management Authority (RMA), defines risk as the *nature, likelihood, frequency, duration, seriousness and imminence of an offence* (Scottish Government, 2006, p50), but it argues that the level of risk presented is a matter of *professional judgement* (p27).

There is an increasing tendency to reduce the number of offenders in custody or detention through the imposition of robust community sentences. This highlights the need to provide services for prisoners and their families in preparation for release in order to promote desistance from further offending. This can be done through assisting resettlement and in the maintenance of social bonds (Maruna, 2000).

Young offenders

In the UK as a whole there has been growing concern regarding persistent young offenders, leading to measures being taken to address this such as the imposition of curfew orders and anti-social behaviour orders. Historically we can see where the media has encouraged the fear of crime through sensationalist reporting. This impacts on the work undertaken by practitioners within the criminal justice system. Public concerns regarding levels of youth offending have shaped negative attitudes toward the treatment of young persistent offenders. These have shifted between punitive and rehabilitative perspectives and back again. The influence of media and the political context of the time can be seen in the introduction of the *Crime and Disorder Act 1998* which introduced *Anti-Social Behaviour Orders (ASBOs)*. ASBOs were viewed as a means of preventing or discouraging young people from engaging in criminal activity by addressing the risk factors associated with offending. The main element was that the young person would be held accountable for their behaviour by placing an emphasis on restorative justice. Restorative justice aims to repair the harm caused by criminal behaviour through challenging apparent deficits in their moral reasoning. Hannah-Moffat (1999, p88) suggests a blurring of needs with risks has taken place. Risk becomes focused on the failings of the young offender, often arising from poor parental guidance, such as disruptive behaviour either at school, at home or through their association with an anti-social peer group. To address this, *Parenting Orders* were introduced in the *Crime and Disorder Act 1998*. These have been used in England and Wales but not in Scotland. This, in part, could be due to the measures at the disposal of the Children's Hearing System (see Hothersall, 2008).

The Crime and Disorder Act 1998 also provided the legislative framework for the introduction of Youth Offending Teams in England & Wales. It also provided additional measures to manage youth crime and disorder, setting out the aims and management structures for the Youth Justice Service.

In Scotland, it was recognised that the transition between the Children's Hearing system and the Criminal Justice System was too abrupt. Within Criminal Justice social work the emphasis was placed on adults as opposed to adapting and addressing features of youth offending. In the Children's Hearing system, the focus centred on welfare issues and failed to address offending behaviour. As a consequence it was acknowledged that a greater balance between the justice and welfare models was required. Pratt et al. (2006) identified four areas of concern relating to the welfare model. These were: intervention with a welfare element was ineffective; it risked becoming coercive; it lacked professional expertise and it did not address offending behaviour. In effect the rehabilitative model was called into question in terms of its effectiveness and this paved the way for a more punitive *just deserts* or retribution justice model.

Restorative justice ideology centres on the young person accepting responsibility for their offending, and its consequences making recompense for the harm caused and on reintegration into society by relinquishing their offending behaviour and adopting a pro-social attitude to law breaking. The use of victim–offender mediation schemes, which bring together both the offender and the victim is facilitated by a practitioner. The aim is to discuss the offending behaviour and its effects upon the victim and how the offender can make amends. Such schemes are widely used in the UK and can be delivered by both statutory and voluntary organisations.

In Scotland in 2002 the *Effectiveness of the Youth Justice Group* was tasked to improve the Youth Justice System. This, together with the Audit Scotland Report (2002) *Dealing with Offending by Young People*, led to the introduction of *National Standards for the Youth Justice System in Scotland.* This was in direct response to the concern regarding young persistent offenders aged 16 to 18 years. It led to the development of *Youth Justice Teams* within each local authority area; this structure and design has similarities to the *Youth Offending Teams* in England & Wales. Primarily, the aim was to address offending behaviour through the provision of early intervention programmes specific to identified needs and thus reduce recidivism.

ASSET is an assessment tool that is specifically designed for use with young people involved in offending. This tool was initially used with Youth Offending Teams (YOTs) in England & Wales. This has now been extended for use in Scotland. ASSET identifies the risk factors associated with offending by young people and is used to assist practitioners to identify appropriate interventions and to evaluate changes and risks of re-offending over time. It can also be helpful in determining triggers to reoffending.

The ASSET assessment model collates information from a number of areas of the young person's life. These include offending behaviour, education and employment, issues around emotional/mental health, substance use, attitudes to offending, motivation to change and positive factors. ASSET also includes a self-assessment questionnaire, indicators of vulnerability and indicators of serious harm to others.

Reports prepared for the Children's Reporter or the Courts by the Youth Justice Teams in Scotland or Youth Offending Teams in England & Wales take on one of two formats dependent on the age of the offender. A Social Background Report (SBR), undertaken on offenders younger than 18 focuses on the young person as a *person in need* and, as such, focuses on events within the young person's life that might have contributed to his or her current situation. This is consistent with the primary principle of the *Children Scotland Act 1995* and the *Children Act 1989* where the welfare of the child is paramount. The focus within these reports is on need, as opposed to the deed. If the young offender is aged 18 years, an enhanced Social Enquiry Report (SER), or Pre-Sentence Report (PSR) will be compiled, where the emphasis is upon the offence and offending behaviour. Do you note the shift in accountability for the offence, as reflected in the focus of the two reports? The SBR for younger offenders focuses on the reasons for offending relatively more than the SER or PSR. In the latter reports, the focus is on the offending behaviour. This implies a focus on diverting younger offenders away from the justice system into which they risk becoming entrapped.

In essence the vast majority of adolescent offenders do not go on to become adult offenders; therefore it is appropriate that they are considered vulnerable (SWSI, 2005).

ACTIVITY **8.2**

Take a minute to revise the areas that should be covered when completing an ASSET assessment. Are you able to see a link between these areas and the general direction of Youth Justice Services in viewing the need, as opposed to the deed? Make a note of your answers.

Comment
Did you identify that there is a risk that young people in need or facing complex criminogenic factors may easily become entangled in the system and effectively labelled as criminals? If so, did you further identify the rationale of Youth Justice Services to deflect them from this by early or timely intervention in their young lives?

Mental health

Both young offenders sentenced to detention and adult offenders receiving custodial sentences can be at risk of self-harm or suicide. In September 2005 an analysis of suicide rates between 1978 and 2003 in England & Wales found that young offenders aged 15–17 years old were 18 times more likely to kill themselves than young people of a similar age within the general population. During this period 1,312 males aged 15 to 60+ years committed suicide, of which 28 deaths occurred in the 15–17-year-old age range. Factors deemed as contributing to this were the presence of mental health problems, existence of overcrowding and, in cases of some young offenders, lack of appropriate treatment for drug withdrawal (BBC News-online, 2005).

Fazel (2008) identified that male offenders who were married, employed and white that received a custodial sentence were more likely to commit suicide. She also identified that vulnerable prisoners were more at risk if placed in single cells. The current trend has seen a rise in the number of prisoners committing suicide over the last two decades (Oxford Academy Media News, 2008). Research by Pratt et al. (2006) indicates that following release from prison, men are eight times more likely to commit suicide than those in the general population. Similarly and perhaps more alarmingly, women are 36 times more likely to commit suicide as compared with the general population.

In some instances, mentally disordered offenders commit offences. Provision for prosecution is contained within the *Criminal Procedure (Scotland) Act 1995*, which has been amended by the *Mental Health (Care and Treatment) (Scotland) Act 2003* and its provisions aim to deal with those people who may be acutely or chronically mentally ill, those with neurosis, behavioural and/or personality disorders, those with learning difficulties and some who, as a function of alcohol and/or substance misuse, have a mental health problem and the Mental Health Act 2007 in England & Wales makes simlar provisions. Like its later English counterpart, the amendments to the Criminal Procedure (Scotland) Act 1995, brought about by the Mental Health (Care and Treatment) (Scotland) Act 2003 introduced a flexible set of orders at the disposal of the Court for compulsory assessment, care and treatment of mentally disordered offenders. The law provides the means to divert an offender into a system of secure hospital and community-based provision, rather than into prison. Within this highly specialised area of work, there is a specialist role for social workers in Scotland (Mental Health Officers) and for a wider body of professionals in England & Wales (Approved Mental Health Professionals) both of whom are involved in the assessment and monitoring of the need for secure compulsory care and treatment of mentally disordered offenders.

It is arguable that a majority of offenders have some level of mental health problems. Note the distinction between *mental health problems* and *mental disorder/mental illness,* as discussed in Chapter 6 (and see Hothersall, Maas-Lowit and Golightley, 2008, Chapter 4). Note also the need to avoid making facile and distorted judgements based upon the worst sort of sensationalist nonsense occasionally perpetrated by some elements of the media about the links between dangerousness and mental health (Hothersall, Maas-Lowit and Golightley, 2008). There are lesser levels of provision than those that divert mentally disordered offenders into these services. An example of this lower tariff provision would be probation, containing a requirement for the probationer to attend for medical treatment for mental disorder. Obviously, in situations where a serious offence has been committed or the offender is considered to pose a significant risk to the public, public protection will become the main concern. In such circumstances it would not be appropriate to recommend lower levels of mental health disposal unless there would be some prospect of benefit to the offender and reduction in risk as a consequence of treatment. Where the offence is serious, it is a specialist forensic psychiatrist, rather than a social worker that makes the recommendation for compulsory secure treatment.

Protection

As previously stated the key priority for governments and assemblies across the UK is public protection, as law and order remains a prime concern for the public. Therefore, political parties often seek to be identified as *the party* committed to acting to reduce offending behaviour and to punish offenders appropriately. Often, this has resulted in the introduction of further legislation to counter both offending and anti-social behaviour. This has resulted in more individuals becoming involved in the criminal justice system, often referred to as *net-widening*.

The introduction of the Risk Management Authority through the Criminal Justice (Scotland) Act 2003 was to a large extent informed by reports into the management of serious violent and serious sex offenders including the *McLean Report* (Scottish Executive, *2000*). This report considered measures to deal with high risk offenders, including those offenders with mental disorder, together with sentencing options and creation of a new sentence: the *Order for Lifelong Restriction. Reducing the Risk – Improving the Response to Sex Offending* (2001) looked specifically at risk assessment, housing needs, monitoring of offenders, programmes of intervention and managing information for sex offenders.

The increased emphasis on managerialism within both the probation service and criminal justice social work demonstrates the government's requirement for robust services that provide an effective, efficient and economically viable service to offenders, with the main aim to reduce reoffending rates. The development of accredited programmes of intervention, which include cognitive behavioural and skills elements, linked to McGuire's (1995) 'responsivity principle', requires practitioners to identify the learning style of the offender and match the intervention in order to increase motivation, competence and strengths of the offender. The Probation Service has 11 accredited programmes currently operating and includes *Reasoning and Rehabilitation, Enhanced Thinking Skills, Think First, Aggression Replacement Training, Domestic Violence and Substance Misuse* and *Sex Offender* programmes. In Scotland the *Constructs: Positive Steps to Stop Offending* programme has been accredited and is widely used within Criminal Justice Social Work services.

Ward (2002, cited in Scottish Government, 2008h), suggests the risk management model used in working with offenders can be perceived as limiting on the part of the offender. He suggests a 'Good Lives' model that is goal orientated. This model looks to promote positive aspects and goals within offenders, enabling them to achieve *primary human goods*. In essence these are a healthy lifestyle, self-determination, meaningful relationships and a sense of purpose, all gained from working toward desistance and living within society's behavioural norms.

Criminal justice services should also assist the victims of crime. This can be seen in the development of *Victim Information Liaison* officers, attached to the procurator fiscal office and through the introduction of the *Scottish Strategy for Victims* in 2001. This strategy recognised the importance of victims within the criminal justice system and the need to provide support, explain the process and keep them informed of what was happening, regarding their own cases. It also acknowledged their right to *have a voice throughout all the stages of the criminal justice system.*

Building on a similar strategy in England & Wales, the introduction of the *Vulnerable Witnesses Act 2004* provided special measures to be taken to support and protect vulnerable witnesses and child witnesses when giving evidence to the court.

Domestic violence has a much higher profile nowadays within the criminal justice system. Where in previous decades it was viewed as a private matter, it is now recognised as a criminal act and as such is treated accordingly. In England, Wales and Scotland the development of domestic violence strategies has prompted local authorities to provide specific services for victims of domestic abuse and within local police forces, specially trained officers lead investigations into domestic abuse.

Another measure to help protect victims of domestic violence in England & Wales is the implementation of section 12 of the *Domestic Violence, Crime and Victims Act 2004* in September 2009. This builds on the *Protection from Harassment Act 1997* as it extends restraining orders to all offences. In Scotland the *Protection from Abuse (Scotland) Act 2001* provides for powers of arrest, where an interdict is in place. This is particularly important given that approximately 750,000 children witness domestic abuse each year and in 2006/07 83 women and 27 men were killed by a partner or ex-partner (Howarth, 2008).

Violent offenders

The introduction of Extended Sentences in the *Crime and Disorder Act 1998* recognised the need to reduce the risk of serious offences being committed and a need to protect the public from those at risk of causing harm. To address this issue, longer periods of supervision were imposed post-release, in order to supervise, monitor and assist offenders to reintegrate into the community. This also provided for arrangements to be put in place at the time of sentencing for a named officer, either from the local authority or probation service, to be allocated to the offender. The primary focus was to maintain contact with the prisoner and his/her family throughout sentence and promote rehabilitation and social inclusion through better preparation for resettlement, following from extended sentences. This relates to those prisoners serving four years or more for sexual or violent offences. For those serious offenders where there are particular concerns, the use of Multi-Agency Public Protection Arrangements (MAPPA) may be appropriate (see below and Chapter 3).

Sex offenders

As a result of increasing public concern regarding sex offenders, the UK Government responded with the introduction of the *Sex Offenders Act 1997*. For the first time all sex offenders who were subject to a sentence of the court on or after 1 September 1997, would become subject of a requirement to register with the police and to provide personal identifying information to them. These provisions were strengthened by the *Sexual Offences Act 2003*. A multi-agency risk assessment would be carried out instigated under MAPPA (see Chapter 3).

Table 8.2 Notification periods for registration purposes under Sex Offenders Act 1997

Description of person	Applicable period
A person who, in respect of the offence, is or has been sentenced to imprisonment for life or for a term of 30 months or more	An indefinite period
A person who, in respect of the offence or finding, is or has been admitted to a hospital subject to a restriction order	An indefinite period
A person who, in respect of the offence, is or has been sentenced to imprisonment for a term of more than 6 months but less than 30 months	A period of 10 years beginning with the relevant date
A person who, in respect of the offence, is or has been sentenced to imprisonment for a term of 6 months or less	A period of 7 years beginning with that date
A person who, in respect of the offence or finding, is or has been admitted to a hospital without being subject to a restriction order	A period of 7 years beginning with that date
A person of any other description	A period of 5 years beginning with that date

The Sexual Offences Act 2003 saw the introduction of Sexual Offences Prevention Orders (SOPOs) which replace the Sex Offender Order established in the *Crime and Disorder Act 1998*. SOPOs are civil orders, which were introduced primarily to protect the public from sexual harm by placing restrictions on the offender's activities. A court may impose a Sexual Offence Prevention Order where an offender has received a conviction for an offence as appears in schedule 3 which relates to sexual offences, or schedule 5 for other serious offences, where he or she is assessed as posing a serious risk of harm. In Scotland the *Protection of Children and Prevention of Sexual Offences (Scotland) Act 2005* provided the legislative framework for the introduction of Risk of Sexual Harm Orders. Such an order can be made where an offender is implicated in sexual activity with a child or in his or her presence; exposing a child to pornography, or using sexual language in any communication with a child.

A key development in identifying internet offenders is the establishment of a Child Protection and Online Protection Centre which is part of the UK police and is involved in identifying offenders working in partnership with other agencies and international forces.

The use of risk assessment tools when assessing sex offenders has developed significantly over the last 15 years. This in part is because it was recognised that sex offenders often have differing patterns and contributory factors in their offending. Therefore the use of generic offending risk assessment tools is not appropriate in identifying the level of risk presented by the offender. Currently *Risk Matrix 2000* and *Stable and Acute 2007* risk assessment tools are being used in Scotland.

An important protection element to be considered for sex offenders is appropriate accommodation both to provide for effective monitoring of the offender and to safeguard the community. This should also take into account any risk of vigilantism, which could put the offender at risk of harm from the public. In Scotland the need to ensure stable and safe accommodation for sex offenders was recognised in *Toward a National Accommodation Strategy for Sex Offenders 2005*. Similar strategies were employed in England and Wales. It was recognised that this was required to improve monitoring and supervision of the offender and facilitate engagement with services to address offending behaviour through use of cognitive programmes of intervention and to reduce the risk of vigilantism.

As a means of increasing the supervision and monitoring of sex offenders who received short custodial sentences, short sentence licences were introduced for all sexual offenders sentenced to six months or more but less than four years. Release occurs after completion of half the sentence and the offender then becomes subject to licence conditions for the duration of the sentence.

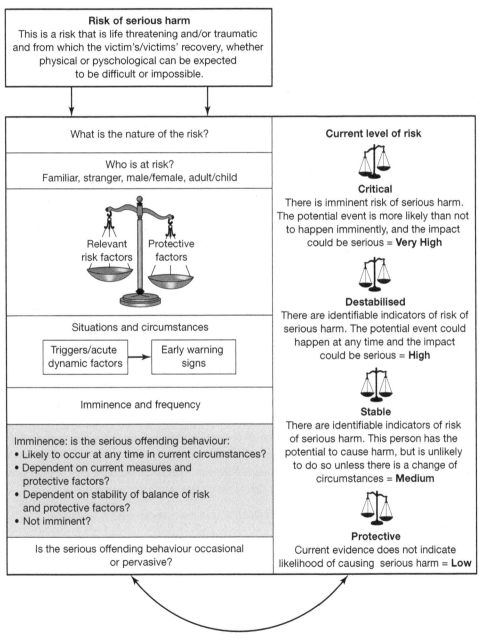

Figure 8.1 Risk assessment and decision-making in MAPPA

Source: Reproduced under the terms of Crown Copyright Policy Guidance Issued by HMSO.

In order for agencies to carry out their functions effectively, a pre-requisite is the effective and efficient sharing of information in order to determine the risk presented by the offender and to develop appropriate risk management strategies with built-in measures for monitoring and review.

ACTIVITY 8.3

John, aged 42 years, has been found guilty of lewd, indecent and libidinous practices against a 10-year-old girl and has been sentenced to three years imprisonment. How long would he require being subject to Registration under the Sex Offenders Act 1997?

Comment

If you refer back to the Notification Periods for Registration purposes under the *Sex Offenders Act 1997*, you will see that as John received a custodial sentence of more than 30 months he will be required to register for an indefinite period. Do you consider this to be overly restrictive or appropriate to the seriousness of the offence? If we consider what registration actually implies monitoring of his activities will in all likelihood be quite limited. Following completion of a risk assessment the level of supervision and monitoring will be determined at a MAPPA meeting and the risk level reviewed as deemed necessary.

A model of the risk assessment process and its link to decision-making in MAPPA is offered in Figure 8.1: from Version 4 of the MAPPA Guidance with Covering Justice and Communities Circular JD/3/2008 and NHS CEL (Scottish Government 2008i).

C H A P T E R   S U M M A R Y

This chapter has looked at aspects of criminal justice and probation services in relation to offending groups associated with the priorities set out in government policy and how this is reflected in the supervision and monitoring of offenders. The main thrust for all agencies involved in the Criminal Justice system is public protection. However there is recognition that offenders can change their behaviour. The use of cognitive behavioural and skills programmes alongside robust monitoring of compliance with supervision requirements within probation orders or parole licences is essential in reducing reoffending. In delivering these evidence-based interventions, skilled practitioners must apply an understanding of the balance required between care and control. Only by this can they hope to reduce recidivism.

FURTHER READING

Sheehan, R, McIvor, G and Trotter, C (2007) *What works with women offenders*. Cullompton: Willan Publishing.
Looks at working with women who offend.

Barry, M and McNeil, F (eds) (2009) *Youth offending and youth justice*. London. Jessica Kingsley.
Offers a thorough account of this area.

McIvor, G and Raynor, P (eds) (2007) *Developments in work with offenders*. London. Jessica Kingsley.
Provides a clear and concise account of current practice with offenders, with lots of relevant theory and research.

Chapter 9
Need, risk and disability

Mike Maas-Lowit

Achieving A Social Work Degree continued

- Critically reflect upon your own practice and performance using supervision and support systems.
- Identify and assess issues, dilemmas and conflicts that might affect your practice.
- Devise strategies to deal with ethical issues, dilemmas and conflicts.

Scottish Standards in Social Work Education

Key Role 1: Prepare for, and work with, individuals, families, carers, groups and communities to assess their needs and circumstances.

- Working with individuals, families, carers, groups and communities so they can make informed decisions.
- Assessing needs and options in order to recommend a course of action.

Key Role 2: Plan, carry out, review and evaluate social work practice with individuals, families, carers, groups, communities and other professionals.

- Working with individuals, families, carers, groups and communities to achieve change, promote dignity, realise potential and improve life opportunities.
- Developing networks to meet assessed needs and planned outcomes.
- Working with groups to promote choice and independent living.

Key Role 3: Assess and manage risk to individuals, families, carers, groups, communities, self and colleagues.

Key Role 4: Demonstrate professional competence in social work practice.

- Evaluating and using up-to-date knowledge of, and research into, social work practice.
- Working within agreed standards of social work practice.
- Understanding and managing complex ethical issues, dilemmas and conflicts.

Key Role 5: Manage and be accountable, with supervision and support, for their own social work practice within their organisation.

- Working effectively with professionals within integrated, multi-disciplinary and other service settings.

Key Role 6: Support individuals to represent and manage their needs, views and circumstances.

- Representing, in partnership with, and on behalf of, individuals, families, carers, groups and communities to help them achieve and maintain greater independence.

Introduction

This chapter will introduce the concept of disability and some key terms in relation to it. It will discuss these concepts as they impose greater levels of need and heighten risk for people affected with disability and you will be able to see how many of these themes are common to a number of chapters within this book.

Setting the scene

In a book of this scope, where we deal with the general areas of need, risk and vulnerability and examine their relationship with different groups, there is a particular problem when it comes to writing about people with disability. The notion of disability is complex. It is the subject of heated debate about which a large number of books have been written. It is difficult to reduce these complicated matters enough for them to fit into a chapter of this size in a way that does them enough justice so that we can address them in relation to our own themes. Therefore the reader ought to be aware that we are synthesising a very complex debate and, if you are in need of a fuller explanation, then you should refer to some of the texts cited within and at the end of the chapter.

Much of the debate is about ownership of the concept of disability. By ownership we mean the following: Disability is a particular concept that is ascribed to certain people because of specific attributes that they are perceived to carry. We will further define these attributes below, when we discuss *impairment* as distinct from *disability*. However, for now let us be content to think of these attributes as things which create barriers for the disabled person, such as poor mobility, or poor eyesight, which may make it difficult to navigate the world on a par with more able-bodied people. These barriers are physical, in that a particular condition may make it difficult for a person to walk, or to see physical obstacles in his or her path. They may also be mental, in the sense of a learning disability, but let us not complicate the scene with too many layers at this stage in the chapter. These barriers are also social, in that the history of disability is the history of ascribing lesser social value to a disabled person than to an able bodied person (Swain et al., 2004; Swain and French, 2008).

Much of the reference to ownership is one in which the debate is about whether disability is essentially a medically owned concept (at the hands of doctors to define), or a socially owned one (at the hands of people with political aspirations to alter the power relationships for people with disability to define). However, it is also broader. For example, some would argue that the term ought to be owned uniquely by each disabled person, so that he or she can define themselves, rather than have others do the defining for them.

The power issues behind the various definitions of *disability* are central to our themes of need, risk and vulnerability, insofar as disabled people have specific needs arising out of the physical or mental impairments they experience. For example a person with mobility needs arising out of cerebral palsy might be at heightened risk of falling and this will increase his or her vulnerability (Kottow, 2003). This need is further overlaid by the additional risk of social disadvantage and exclusion caused by negative connotations being applied to them by society at large.

Disability and impairment

The *Disability Discrimination Act 1995* s1(1) states that a person has a disability if he has 'a physical or mental impairment which has substantial long-term affects on his ability to carry out normal day to day activities' (Department of Health, 1995).

Impairment is a key term within this definition. It refers to loss of, or damage to, a function or faculty. If we divide the human body into its spheres of functioning, these would correspond to areas of the physical and the mental. In order to function, we have developed the faculties of sight, hearing and the other senses, with the most commonly impaired sensory faculties being those of sight and hearing. The range of physical impairment is wide and encompasses impairment of speech, mobility and movement. Mental impairments would include impairment of intellectual capacity or learning disabilities, impairment of memory, such as dementia and the range of mental illnesses

(Hothersall, Maas-Lowit and Golightley, 2008). Some of these matters are explained more fully throughout the book. In particular, Chapter 4 touches on learning disability, dementia and severe physical incapacity in dealing with the concept of incapacity, while Chapter 6 explains need and risk in relation to mental illness.

If impairment speaks to the physical or mental limitations of having a disability, *disablement* is a concept closely related to social exclusion. It refers to physical and social barriers that impose loss or restriction of opportunities for participation in the normal life within communities upon people with some form of disability (Driedger, 1989). The suggestion here is that society is organised in ways which discriminate against and devalue people with disability, and that the issues to be tackled are not those of impairment (the loss or limitation of functioning) but *how society accommodates (or fails to accommodate) impairment*. The rationale behind this argument is that any analysis of our physical environment will show that it is largely constructed to suit the able bodied, the fully sighted, the hearing and those with no mental impairments. Therefore, society does not consider it worth accommodating the difficulties which disabled people may experience in negotiating this world; society has discounted the problems which disabled people have, the conclusion being that they are not worth considering, because disabled people are of lesser value than people without disability (see Wolfensberger, 1972; Russell, 1998).

ACTIVITY 9.1

You may find it difficult to undertake this activity immediately, but make a point, during the next few days, of observing the world around you from the perspective of an awareness of the above contention – that our environment is ill-adjusted to the basic needs of those with disability. You may need to extend this activity beyond the reading of this chapter but we would ask you to complete it nevertheless and to return to this page of the book for some reflection once you have done so. Better still, if you are willing to keep a mini-diary of your observations, it might help you to capture your findings.

Because we conceive of this task as broad and diverse, it may assist you if we give you some guidance on where to look. The more obvious aspects of the physical world would be those of design in the sense of the architecture of buildings and the design of trains, cars, aircraft, lifts, toilets, etc. You may ask yourself how accommodating are they to people with reduced mobility (not just those requiring wheelchair access) and those with limited or no sight? Do not limit your observations to public areas, which may be reasonably well provided for. Think also about private houses. By extension, what parking arrangements are there for people with physical disability, what arrangements are there to help those with poor hearing to cross busy roads and so on? Consider also, the extent to which the world is organised with an assumption of a particular level of what we shall call 'intelligence' (for want of a better short-cut to summarise the problem of learning disability). Consider public notices, newspapers, internet facilities, user instructions for appliances and so on. To what extent are they targeted upon an assumed general level of understanding? Conversely, is there any evidence that they are designed or written with an awareness that a certain section of the population may have a lesser ability to

continued

understand the way concepts are presented? For that matter, considering visual impairment, how wide-spread is the braille labelling of public notices, food-stuffs in supermarkets and so on?

Comment

In setting you the above task, we did not assume that every reader will be free of disability him- or herself. Many of you will be only too aware of the problems of negotiating an imperfectly designed world from the perspective of some form of impairment to functioning or faculty. If you are such a reader, were you still able to develop a wider awareness of other disabilities and the barriers that are present? For example, if you have a mobility or hearing impairment, had you considered the world from the perspective of learning disability?

In terms of general findings, it is true that things have improved in recent years with the imposition of various pieces of UK-wide legislation, most notably the *Disability Discrimination Act 1995*, requiring disabled access to public buildings and requiring services to make *reasonable adjustments* to accommodate to the needs of people with various disabilities. By this token, many public areas and buildings have been redesigned to position wheelchair ramps, hearing induction loops, braille notices, etc. We are guessing that many of you found this to be the case, and it is certainly a triumph of the disability rights movement that such inroads have been made. However, if we look beyond these achievements, is it not still an able-bodied person's world?

The term *reasonable* adjustment resonates across the legislation. For example, section 6 (b) of the *Disability Discrimination Act 1995* states that, where *the disabled person concerned* (is) *at a substantial disadvantage in comparison with persons who are not disabled, it is the duty of the employer to take such steps as it is reasonable, in all the circumstances of the case.* It is a term that speaks to the needs, risks and vulnerabilities specific to people with disabilities. Wherever one reads the word *reasonable* in law, it is a coded reference to the fact that the ultimate decision of what is reasonable or not rests with the Court. For example, in reference to section 6 (b) above, where a person with a hearing impairment is employed as a telephone receptionist, it would be reasonable to provide special adaptations to the telephone system to make it manageable for their level of impairment. Conversely, it would be *unreasonable* to sack the person for not being able to do the job without having provided such equipment. Obviously the Court, in interpreting *reasonable*, will have to take into account matters such as financial cost. For example, if the cost of equipment was such that it was unaffordable by a small company to the point of having to sack two staff to pay for it, this would not be reasonable. It also needs to consider the point at which disability *reasonably* excludes a person from doing a job. For example it would not be reasonable to employ a blind person as a lorry driver because of the dangers to self and others. Therefore, the extent to which the world can be expected to accommodate the needs of disabled people is limited by a range of risks and resource limitations. However, to return to our exercise above, is it accommodating enough, or is there still *unreasonable* failure to meet the needs of disabled people?

We are, in fact, in a process of using law and policy to adjust to accommodating disabled people and so, if you performed the above activity with far greater thoroughness than you have time and resources for, you would find certain areas in which reasonable adjustment is made and certain areas where it is not. Some of these deficient areas will be beyond the current scope of the law. For example, there are numerous disabled actors and many roles in film, play and television, in which able-bodied actors play people with disability. To pick another illustration, we have not yet fully explored the debate of learning difficulty in relation to reasonable adjustment and access to services, in the way that the 1989 Act has forced the issue in terms of physical disability.

Where such *unreasonable* lack of adjustment exists, it is evidence that we still fail to value people with disability enough, leaving them excluded, in need and discriminated against.

Reconciling medical and social perspectives

There is a commonly used twin approach to disability: examining the *personal limitations* that impairment imposes and the *social limitations* that are constructed by potentially disablist assumptions and attitudes in wider society. This brings us to a *medical* and a *social* way of looking at the issue. These approaches should not be seen as competing definitions, as they are often portrayed. For example, on their website, *Disability Equality in Education* have a page which sets out the medical and social models in ways which are adversarial. The medical model is explained using language like *the 'medical model' sees the disabled person as the problem* www.diseed.org.uk/Medical_Social_Model.htm

Many writers on the subject consider more models: Swain and French (2008) cite Priestley's (2003) four models:

- the biological, which relates to physiological aspects of sensory, mental and physical impairment;

- the psychological, which relates to the personal impact that disability makes upon the subject;

- the structural, which relates to formal and informal structures of society including law and policy, which accommodate and fail to accommodate disability; and

- the cultural, which relates to a range of culturally carried perceptions which shape attitudes, some of which perpetuate discrimination.

Some of these conceptions would relate closely to Thompson's (2006) view that discrimination can be analysed with recourse to a PCS model, whereby the P is the personal sphere in which we hold discriminatory ideas and assumptions about an other; the C is the cultural domain in which such ideas are carried; and the S is the structural, as above.

Swain and French (2008) themselves propose four models:

- the individual/medical model;

- the social model;

- the tragedy model (in which disability is viewed as a personal tragedy in the lives of all it touches); and

- the affirmative/non-tragedy model, in which the unique attributes of every person are considered in advance of any impairment or its accompanying disabling factors.

Above, we have synthesised and summarised the main issues in a way that outlines a number of significant themes in relation to the lives of people with a disability. We will now focus on the two main models – the medical and the social, and consider aspects of the debate on power, control and ownership of the term *disability*.

From models to approaches

If some accounts of the medical approaches to defining disability appear to be written with a measure of anger, it is because disabled people themselves have been active in reclaiming ways of defining their own problems after having had them defined by the medical profession throughout its history. As with any political movement of liberation, the case has to be stated forcefully for it to be heard with sufficient clarity for it to break with the oppression of the past. The movement that is claiming rights for disabled people across the world has made much headway in Europe and the UK in particular, in conjunction with the rise of human rights. It has resulted in a series of anti-discrimination and equality laws, some of which are discussed above and in other chapters throughout this book. However, in summary, people with disability still have outstanding needs, reflecting degrees of discrimination which must be overcome before they can feel accepted with true equality in society.

The so called 'Medical Model' is a way of framing the medical needs of the individual arising out of the impairment. As such, it is a definition of one's needs by an expert (usually a doctor), regardless of how the person feels about their needs within him/herself (see Chapter 1 regarding conceptions of need). In a medical formulation, the problem will always be located in the body of the person who has the disability, whereas the social construction of disability will place any problem in a society which does not gear itself up to meet the diverse needs of people with problems outside the mainstay. That social formulations of needs look upon the person holistically in society and place the burden of meeting those needs upon that society, does not negate the reality of, or the potential benefit of, a proper medical assessment of needs.

While the medical way of diagnosing physical causes of impairment may objectify the problem, it also points to the issue which brings about a limitation in functioning in the first place. The medical and the social are overlapping ways of understanding a complicated set of problems. The conditions that may cause some of the impairments listed above very often arise from medical conditions. And while we do not wish to imply an attack upon the importance of the social model, it is not beyond criticism itself (see below) although it does empower the person and agitates for change in the *structures* within society that discriminate against disabled people. It speaks to a social revolution, which is bringing dynamic change to the range of opportunities for people with disability. All we wish to imply is that it is in keeping with modern multidisciplinary practice *not* to discount the role of the medical profession in services.

While speaking of learning disability, Williams could be speaking more broadly of all disability when he says:

> [T]here are different models for conceptualising people with learning difficulties and their needs that are the primary basis of different professions. In particular there is great overlap in the use of the models: for example, psychiatry straddles the medical, psychological/educational models.

(Williams, 2009, p12)

If you are an exceptionally careful reader, you will have noted that we have begun to interchange the phrases *medical model* and *social model* with the phrases medical and social *approaches.* We prefer this way of looking at things for the following reason. A model is a complete way of thinking about how something works. It is therefore difficult to overlay two or more models, because being complete explanations they may be mutually exclusive. There is a certain tendency to try to reduce the complex argument about what disability actually is in its entirety: social, psychological, structural, medical, physiological and cultural manifestations, to the lowest common denominator and to engage in *reductionism.* The author of this chapter has frequently noted students writing in this reduced way, stating that the medical model views the person's disability as the problem and so it is 'bad', while the social model, being holistic in conception, is therefore 'good'. We hope that by encouraging you to see the merits, detriments and limitations of each approach to this multifaceted issue, we will encourage you to develop a multi-layered approach to it.

Criticisms of the social model

Before moving on entirely from the discussion of models, we need to quantify one further element. We mentioned above that the social model (or approach, as we would now prefer to call it) is not itself above criticism.

Much of the above discussion implies progress made by politicising the issue of disability. We made a passing reference to the disability movement. You may find this described in *Disability Politics* (Campbell and Oliver, 1996).

Being a collective movement, the political change that drives the social approach to disability deals with disabled people as a homogenous whole. It does not speak to, or understand the unique experience of each individual person. It is argued that the social model (sic) focuses on disability to the exclusion of other attributes upon which a person may be discriminated – race, gender or sexual orientation, for example. For a passionate rebuff of these criticisms, see Oliver in Swain et al. (2006).

Disability, need, risk and vulnerability

In relation to our theme, there is a tangible sense that people whose lives are directly affected by disability are more vulnerable to risk of harm than are those who live lives free of disability. The heightened vulnerability comes from both risks posed by any given impairment, and also from the exclusion that may result from discrimination (Kottow, 2003). There is a complex dynamic of interaction between these domains: For example, because they may be less able to protect themselves because of their impairment, people with learning difficulties may sometimes be at heightened risk of abuse, neglect and exploitation.

To some degree, the social approach is closer to our purpose in this book than the medical one. For example, Scotland has a law which offers adults protection on a basis not far removed from the duties prescribed in relation to the protection of children (see Chapter 5 and Hothersall 2008 for a full discussion of these issues). Section 3 (1) (c) of the *Adult Support and Protection (Scotland) Act 2007* states that,

> *because they are affected by disability, mental disorder, illness or physical or mental infirmity, (adults) are more vulnerable to being harmed than adults who are not so affected.*

This speaks to a set of outstanding needs and risks which arise out of the social aspects of disability. It is equally true of children with disability. Both the Scottish and English policies for children and young people emphasise the need for more integrated approaches across agencies and the reduction of institutional, cultural and procedural barriers to joint working (Hothersall, 2008). This is because the needs of children with disability are almost bound to be complex and will require multidisciplinary working among social services, education and health professionals. To return to the discussion above on reconciling medical and social approaches, this cannot be achieved if we view the medical and social in opposition to each other.

ACTIVITY 9.2

So far, we have only painted an abstract picture of a person's outstanding needs arising out of disability. In order to begin thinking about what this means in practice, consider the following short scenario.

Rob is 14 years old. He has severe cerebral palsy, resulting from oxygen starvation at birth. This means that he cannot walk or execute fine movements with his hands. He needs help feeding himself and his speech is indistinct to those who are not familiar with and tuned into it. Rob is also lively, bright and exceptionally well read for his age. He has a strong interest in politics and football and he has a wicked sense of humour that sometimes gets him into trouble.

Consider the needs of any 14-year-old boy in the areas of personal and social development, friends and family, education and health. How might Rob's disability impose a more complex set of needs over these?

Comment

The discussion following from this exercise has the potential to fill a book in its own right. Therefore, we will summarise a few key aspects, which is not to say that, if your considerations touched on other areas of life, you are wrong.

Like all boys of his age, Rob will be living in tension between his need for a secure and safe family environment and his need to push the boundaries of freedom as he moves towards adult life. This tension forms much of the turbulent backdrop to adolescence as we view it. He will require physical assistance and will therefore be more dependent upon his adult carers. This will make *the transition* from childhood to adulthood far more complex. Adolescents usually forge their paths through this process in close peer groups but that may be very difficult for Rob to do as he will need such close help from his carers. Adolescents begin to explore and experiment with their sexuality and sexual needs; with Rob's mobility problems, he may not be able to do this in the same way that his peers do. He will need close help with mobility, reading, writing and discussing matters in relation to his education and he will have a greater need of continuing medical attention (physiotherapy and so on) than his peers.

The quotation (above) from the *Adult Support and Protection (Scotland) Act 2007* suggests that the existence of disability may heighten risk for some individuals. We can learn much from some of the inquiries that highlight risks to actual people with disability and deficiencies in their care. In Scotland, the *Report of the Inspection of Scottish Borders Council Social Work Services for People Affected by Learning Disabilities* outlines substantial failings in services designed to protect vulnerable adults (Scottish Executive and Mental Health Commission, 2004). The 'Borders Inquiry' addressed the prolonged financial, emotional, sexual and physical abuse of a woman with learning disabilities over a lengthy period. The woman who was the victim of this abuse was an open case to both health and social work services and the inquiry exposed lack of care in meeting the woman's needs for support and protection. The findings added momentum to the process of creating the above mentioned *Adult Support and Protection (Scotland) Act 2007* (see Chapter 2 and further reading below).

The Mental Welfare Commission for Scotland's inquiry into deficiencies in the care and protection of Ms A, *Justice Denied* (MWC, 2008) recounts significant failings in relation to her care and protection. As in the Borders Inquiry, Ms A is a woman with learning disabilities who suffered sexual abuse at the hands of a number of men in her community. Both the police and the procurator fiscal (the Scottish equivalent of the Crown Prosecution Service) were aware of serious allegations of this abuse. However they took the decision that Ms A would not be a reliable witness because of her learning disability. Therefore they took no action against the perpetrators and she continued to suffer abuse unprotected by the law.

Both these cases suggest that there are heightened risks of various forms of abuse and exploitation where people have any form of impairment that poses barriers against them taking action to protect themselves. It further suggests that disablement factors may impinge to discriminate against the person getting appropriate services and protections. In other words, it sadly appears that there are still areas of service provision where we discriminate and do not meet the person's needs for care, support and protection. Neither does it seem to be a problem of lack of laws to protect people. Both these cases arose in situations where there *were* laws in place precisely to protect them. Therefore practitioners have to carry an awareness of the heightened need of people with disability and the risks of failing to meet those needs.

This is further illustrated by the Mencap report into the deaths of six adults with learning disability in England: *Death by Indifference* (2009), which was produced following the earlier Public Services Ombudsman's report (2009). This points to greater needs for services and the risks attendant when these needs are not met in the very heart of the Health Care system.

C H A P T E R   S U M M A R Y

The issue of disability is wide-ranging and surrounded in complex debate. Both the impairments that generate disability and the resulting social and personal problems raise outstanding need. These are sometimes posed in various risks which render people with disability especially vulnerable in the population at large. All of this requires redress from social work and social services agencies.

FURTHER READING

Kalaga, H and Kingston, P (2007) *A review of literature on effective interventions that prevent and respond to harm against adults.* Edinburgh. Scottish Government. Available at: **www.scotland.gov.uk/ Publications/2007/11/15154941/0**
A useful report that looks specifically to the adult protection agenda in Scotland. Useful reading for all as this issue is one likely to be taken up across other parts of the UK.

Swain, J and French, S (2008) *Disability on equal terms.* London: Sage.
Offers good accounts of the models (sic) of disability and their potential.

Swain, J, French, S, Barnes, C and Thomas, C (2004) *Disabling barriers-enabling environments.* London: Sage.
A classic text which critically discusses a wide range of issues around disability.

Williams, P (2009) *Social work with people with learning difficulties.* Exeter: Learning Matters.
Deals with many aspects of this debate in relation to learning difficulty or learning disability as it is sometimes called in Scotland.

Chapter 10

Substance use: What are the risks?

George Allan

Achieving A Social Work Degree continued

Key Role 5: Manage and be accountable, with supervision and support, for your own social work practice within your organisation.
- Manage and prioritise your workload within organisational policies and priorities.
- Carry out duties using accountable professional judgement and knowledge-based social work practice.
- Monitor and evaluate the effectiveness of your programme of work in meeting the organisational requirements and the needs of individuals, families, carers, groups and communities.
- Use professional and managerial supervision and support to improve your practice.

Key Role 6: Demonstrate professional competence in social work practice.
- Review and update your own knowledge of legal, policy and procedural frameworks.
- Use professional and organisational supervision and support to research, critically analyse, and review knowledge-based practice.
- Implement knowledge-based social work models and methods to develop and improve your own practice.

Scottish Standards in Social Work Education
Key Role 1: Prepare for, and work with, individuals, families, carers, groups and communities to assess their needs and circumstances.
- Preparing for social work contact and involvement.
- Working with individuals, families, carers, groups and communities so they can make informed decisions.
- Assessing needs and options in order to recommend a course of action.

Key Role 2: Plan, carry out, review and evaluate social work practice with individuals, families, carers, groups, communities and other professionals.
- Identifying and responding to crisis situations.
- Tackling behaviour which presents a risk to individuals, families, carers, groups, communities and the wider public.

Key Role 3: Assess and manage risk to individuals, families, carers, groups, communities, self and colleagues.
- Assessing and managing risks to individuals, families, carers, groups and communities.
- Assessing and managing risk to self and colleagues.

Key Role 4: Demonstrate professional competence in social work practice.
- Evaluating and using up-to-date knowledge of, and research into, social work practice.
- Working within agreed standards of social work practice.
- Understanding and managing complex ethical issues, dilemmas and conflicts.
- Promoting best social work practice, adapting positively to change.

Key Role 5: Manage and be accountable, with supervision and support, for your own social work practice within your organisation.
- Managing one's own work in an accountable way.
- Taking responsibility for one's own continuing professional development.
- Working effectively with professionals within integrated, multi-disciplinary and other service settings.

DANOS: National Occupational Standards for Drugs and Alcohol
For the substance problems workforce, a range of competences has been developed within a framework of National Occupational Standards units. DANOS (Drug and Alcohol National Occupational Standards), as they are known, are now part of the broader health care standards, which are the responsibility of Skills for Health (The Skills Sector Council for the UK Health Sector). They form the basis of both ongoing learning and various qualifications. DANOS can be accessed at: **www.skillsforhealth. org.uk/tools/view_framework.php?id=61**

Introduction

I have taken more out of alcohol than alcohol has ever taken out of me

Winston Churchill (1964)

Drugs are a bet with your mind

Jim Morrison (date unknown)

In this chapter we consider the complex relationship, at times enhancing and at times unhappy, between substances and people and the implications of this for social work. The following questions will be explored.

- Do people 'need' substances?

- In what ways do substances themselves present risks?

- What potential problems are related to how we take substances?

- Are some people at greater risk of experiencing difficulties than others?

- What are the implications of problematic use for 'significant others'?

- What are the implications for social work practice of substance use and the risks that this entails?

The parameters of our considerations need to be established from the outset. 'People' covers two distinct groups namely:

- those who are experiencing problems with substances themselves;

- those affected directly by another person's use of drugs. This group includes partners, parents, siblings and children.

It is also essential that we try to clarify what the word 'substance' covers. A simple definition of what constitutes a drug is elusive. McMurran (1994) notes that Gossop considers that the concept of a 'drug' is really a social construct as it used to cover such a wide range of chemicals with very different properties. As Paton, quoted by Edwards, once said: *A drug is any chemical which, when injected into a laboratory animal, will produce a scientific paper* (Edwards, 2005 pxvii). Perhaps the best we can do is to cast our net over substances which Edwards calls 'mind acting' (Edwards, 2005 pxvii). These include:

- alcohol;

- tobacco;

- solvents and other volatile substances;

- drugs, whether or not they are subject to the restrictions imposed by the *Misuse of Drugs Act 1971*.

In this chapter, the generic word 'substance' will be used, except where direct reference is being made to a particular drug. Substances are no respecters of gender, so the pronouns 'he' and 'she' have been used randomly.

Themes and issues

Substances and people's need

The question 'do we need substances?' may seem an odd one. Clearly some people and some cultures hardly use them at all. Over the past fifty years the per capita consumption of pure alcohol has more than doubled in the UK (Scottish Government, 2008k). Does this suggest that we now 'need' to drink more?

ACTIVITY 10.1

Consider these three people.

Mary (30) started to drink at seventeen. She found that she did not enjoy consuming heavily. When out to dinner with friends she only drinks a couple of small glasses of wine. She wonders why her friends demolish up to a bottle each on these occasions but she has no interest in doing so herself.

Billy (20) looks forward to going to clubs on Friday nights when he will drink around twelve units of beer and vodka. For a period he was prescribed medication, which his GP advised him should not be mixed with alcohol. He found he did not enjoy his Friday nights without drinking. He felt nervous approaching girls and a fool whilst dancing. He is pleased now that the course of medication is over.

Janine (23) injects heroin three times a day. When she wakes in the morning she feels shaky and uncomfortable. Her day is centred around trying to obtain money to buy enough of the drug to stave off withdrawals.

Utilising Maslow's hierarchy of human need (Maslow, 1970) and other theoretical perspectives explored in Chapter 1, how might you account for these three people's need for substances?

Comment

Clearly using substances is not a 'universal human need' (see Chapter 1) and for Mary substances appear to hold little attraction. From Maslow's perspective it can be argued that Billy is attempting to meet his needs for 'belonging' and 'self-esteem' and that he has learned that alcohol facilitates his efforts to do so. In addition, there may be a degree to which his feelings are culturally defined by the continuous association of alcohol with dancing and nights out. In contrast, Janine's need for heroin is at the lowest level of a physiological necessity. Her physical dependence on heroin must be satisfied before she can begin to attend to other things in her life.

Substances fulfil a number of disparate functions for people. Their use can:

- act as rite of passage to adulthood for young people;
- allow entry to a group or re-enforce group cohesion;
- facilitate relaxation;

- alter perception;

- engender excitement;

- promote religious experience;

- allow the deliberate courting of risk which can be for some, particularly the young, an attraction in itself;

- reduce psychological or physical pain;

- act as a symbol of rebellion.

Substance use can, therefore, bring benefits and, if it is not a universal need, it is certainly commonplace. The majority of the human race finds value in using substances, whether this entails the morning coffee and cigarette to 'kick-start' the day, the glass of wine to relax after work or the Valium tablets to reduce anxiety. While most people do not experience significant difficulties, with substances there is always a downside and the undoubted benefits are offset by numerous potential harms. It is these that we will now consider.

ACTIVITY **10.2**

Write down the risks which drinking alcohol involves.

Give consideration to how far the risks, which you listed, can be attributed to alcohol, the chemical, and its effects on the body and the nervous system and how far they can be attributed to the ways in which people use it.

Risky business for users

Comment

When people take any substance a complex relationship comes into play (see Figure 10.1).

In the literature, these are often referred to as 'drug', 'set' and 'setting' (Cohen and Kay, 1994). In considering problems, we often fail to explore risk in a logical way. For example, in reporting an Ecstasy death, a newspaper may call for more vigorous action by the police to prevent the drug getting into the hands of young people. The same newspaper, however, will call for better education when reporting the death of a young person following a drinking binge. In the former case, the drug is seen as the problem; in the latter, it is irresponsible use.

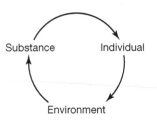

Figure 10.1

Problems with substances

In terms of their effects on the nervous system, substances can be broadly categorised as depressants, stimulants, drugs that reduce pain (analgesics) and drugs that alter perception (hallucinogens) (DrugScope, 2004), although some fall into more than one of these categories. Substances bring short- and long-term risks including the following.

- Depressant drugs, along with drugs which reduce pain, slow the brain's functioning. This can lead to loss of co-ordination and, if taken in quantity, overdose. In simple terms, this involves the brain slowing to the point where it ceases to send the involuntary messages that control heart and lungs. Regular, heavy use leads to tolerance and physical dependence can follow. Alcohol, solvents and the benzodiazepine family are depressant drugs. Opioids are an example of substances that reduce pain.

- Stimulants can cause excitability, increased heart rate and paranoia. The 'come-down' can lead to fatigue and depression. Stimulants include nicotine, cocaine and amphetamine.

- Some substances can cause particular physical problems. Drinking alcohol is associated with various cancers and with heart disease, as is smoking tobacco.

- Altered perception following hallucinogen use can be frightening or convince a person that dangerous activities are safe. LSD, cannabis and some types of mushroom fall into the category of hallucinogens.

- Some drugs loosen inhibitions. While this can be seen as a desirable in certain circumstances, it can lead only too often to behaviour which is unacceptable or regretted.

- Adulterants can cause problems; particuarly when drugs are injected.

RESEARCH SUMMARY

Nutt and colleagues attempted to rank the harmfulness of twenty substances, irrespective of their legal status, by using a nine category matrix covering physical harm, dependence and social harm. A process of scoring and re-scoring by panels of experts, known as a Delphic method, was used. At the time of the project, six of the substances were not subject to the Misuse of Drugs Act 1971. *While it was perhaps unsurprising that heroin and cocaine occupied the first and second places in term of harmfulness, considerable press interest was generated by the ranking of alcohol at fifth and tobacco at ninth. These two substances, both legally available to adults, came in front of nine substances subject to the* Misuse of Drugs Act 1971. *Ecstasy was ranked eighteenth (Nutt et al., 2007).*

The individual

As we have noted, risk involves the individual as much as the substance. Some people are more likely to experience problems than others. While we cannot predict who will develop problems, we do know that certain people who use substances in certain ways and who inhabit certain environments are in heightened jeopardy.

- Different patterns of use bring different problems and these are explored more fully below.

- There is growing evidence that some people may have a genetic vulnerability which increases the possibility of their developing problems with substances. Whether due to learned behaviour or genetic inheritance, substance problems can run in families (Royal College of Psychiatrists and Royal College of Physicians, 2000).

- Gender is an issue. Women are susceptible at an earlier stage than men both to alcohol related liver disease and to vein damage through injection. The implications for the unborn child of the use of a variety of substances during pregnancy are well documented (DrugScope and NHS Lothian, 2005). The need to fund drug use can lead some women, and indeed some young men, into prostitution.

- Mixing drugs brings its own risks. Overdose becomes more likely when depressants are taken together or mixed with drugs which reduce pain.

- How the substance is taken can be more problematic than the potential harms caused by the drug itself. Injecting is the most obvious example of this. It is various compounds in tobacco which cause lung damage. If a non-smoker were to wear a nicotine patch regularly, he would develop physical addiction to nicotine but he would not run the risk of smoking-related lung disease.

- The mood of the user, and what she expects the effects to be, can contribute as much to the experience of using the drug as the chemical effects of the drug itself. It is within this context that withdrawn and aggressive behaviour after use can be viewed.

- There is increasing understanding of the links between mental health problems and substance use. A history of problematic alcohol or drug use increases the risk of suicide (Scottish Government, 2007a).

- The younger an adolescent starts using substances, the greater the likelihood that he will develop problems at a later stage (Grant and Dawson; Robin and Przybeck, both cited in Sullivan and Farrell, 2002).

Implications of the environment

The environment in which a person uses substances or which a person enters after using can also heighten the risk. This has been well described as 'wrong time, wrong place' (Shapiro, 2007, p7).

- A person smoking cannabis occasionally at home may come to little harm but if he does this in a pub, police involvement might follow.

- Taking Valium before driving is likely to lead to impaired reaction times.

- Having a couple of midday beers on holiday has different implications to drinking before the afternoon case conference.

Living in a culture where substances are readily available and tolerated or where particular patterns of use are seen as acceptable is likely to influence the individual. Social groupings, whether these involve smokers huddled in shelters outside offices or heroin users congregating in each other's flats, re-enforce the individual's use. It is not only the immediate environment which is a factor here. In the wider British community, middle-class culture no longer supports smoking; however, binge drinking is widely viewed as a desirable activity by many, a mindset which the authorities are attempting to challenge. There is an association between deprivation and levels of problematic drug use (Scottish Government, 2008k). In addition, environmental influences in a person's past will have contributed to shaping a person's current use.

The law is another factor which fashions the environment. It proscribes the possession of certain substances and it licenses others, attempting to restrict their possession or use to certain categories of people. The law also stipulates that certain behaviours following substance use are not permissible.

Models for making sense of risk

Cohen and Kay (1994) and Thorley (1980) have produced different models which link patterns of use to the problems which may be associated with them. Cohen and Kay (1994), expanded by Cohen (2005), describe four different categories of use.

- Experimental/novice. This phase usually takes place during adolescence but can also occur when anyone tries a new substance. This is a time of learning when the person will not know what to expect from the substance, how much she can take before becoming unwell or her self-control is seriously impaired. As with all learning, experimentation is exciting but fraught with risk. Most people survive this stage and begin to define their relationship with substances by discovering their 'limits' or deciding to abstain.

- Recreational/controlled. This pattern is characterised by the person feeling that he is choosing to use 'as and when' he wants. He feels he is managing his use, not vice versa. Recreational use is not problem-free, however. Drinking a little above recommended weekly limits might be viewed as recreational use but increases the likelihood of health problems. The majority of Ecstasy deaths might well be attributed to recreational use.

- Binge. As a general concept, bingeing is well understood, although what constitutes a binge in terms of amount and time period is subject to some debate. Bingeing brings all the potential problems associated with intoxification such as accidents, overdose, being sick and acting in ways that are later regretted.

- Dependent. With certain drugs, prolonged daily use leads to a person's nervous system adapting in a way which results in withdrawal symptoms if they suddenly stop using. As Cohen and Kay say *These are the ones who are often called 'addicts'* (Cohen and Kay, 1994, p12). However, dependency also covers the 'feeling' that taking a substance is necessary. It can be argued that Billy, in the activity above, has a level of psychological dependence on alcohol.

Over time, a person's pattern may change. Today's novice is likely to be tomorrow's recreational user. A binge user may develop a dependence on her chosen substance. The majority of adults in the United Kingdom can be described as recreational users of alcohol with use declining with age.

Anthony Thorley's model (1980) focuses on alcohol, although it is equally applicable to other substances. Thorley suggests that it can be unhelpful to try to diagnose and label a person. Such an approach can narrow our view of problematic use and can be a barrier to engagement. Better, he argues, to concentrate on the problems the person is experiencing, or might experience, due to his alcohol use. It is these that constitute the risks. He states that people can develop problems related to three different styles of drinking. Problems can occur because a person:

- is intoxicated;

- consumes excessively; drinks very regularly above recommended limits;

- is dependent (physically and/or psychologically).

He says that a person can experience problems in one, two or all three domains. For example, a person who gets drunk on Friday nights might only experience problems related to intoxification although there might be aspects of psychological dependence. Intoxification and psychological dependence are associated with numerous problems but are not necessarily problematic. On the other hand, excessive consumption of alcohol is very likely to lead to health problems and physical dependence always presents difficulties.

This relationship can be represented as shown in Figure 10.2.

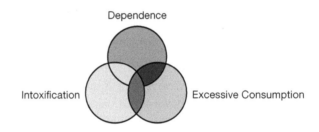

Figure 10.2

Thorley goes on to explore the types of problems which are associated with intoxification, excessive consumption and dependence by listing them under the headings of 'medical', 'legal' and 'social'.

Intoxification
- ***Medical:*** *injury, gastritis, hangover, amnesia, alcohol poisoning.*

- ***Social:*** *neglect of responsibilities, inappropriate behaviour, aggression or passivity, isolation and domestic violence.*

- *An intoxicated person can fall foul of the **law** in numerous ways.*

Excessive consumption
- *Various **medical** problems are associated with excessive consumption of alcohol including liver damage, cancer of the throat, diabetes, epilepsy and alcohol-related brain damage.*

- *The excessive consumer may experience **social** difficulties such as debt, trouble at work and family problems.*

- ***Legal** problems might include theft or fraud to support the cost of consumption.*

Dependence

- *Physical dependence is likely to mean that the person has been a heavy drinker over a long period and so runs the risk of the **medical** problems associated with excessive consumption. Withdrawals bring the risk of seizures and delirium tremens (DTs). A dependent person can experience paranoia and anxiety.*

- ***Social** functioning may be impaired by dependence and stigma may result.*

- *As with excessive consumption, the cost of maintaining the habit may lead to **illegal** behaviour.*

(Adapted from Thorley, 1980)

ACTIVITY 10.3

Applying Thorley's categories, list the problems a person injecting heroin three times a day might experience.

Comment

It is important to remember that the model can be applied to the use of any substance, not just alcohol. You might have noted that the difficulties could be grouped into three categories, intoxification, excessive consumption and dependence. Each of these areas can be considered in terms of potential difficulties in relation to health (medical), falling foul of the law (legal) and a range of problems in terms of relationships, work, etc. (social).

A risky business for others

We will now turn from people taking substances to look at the implications for those close to them.

Significant others – children

There is growing understanding of the implications for children of parent/carer substance problems. Such difficulties are not necessarily synonymous with inadequate parenting and some children do emerge into adulthood unscathed (Tunnard, 2002a; Tunnard, 2002b). However the potential for lasting damage is significant (Kroll and Taylor, 2003).

Use of alcohol, tobacco or drugs during pregnancy can have a variety of implications, some of which are outlined below. However it is acknowledged that it can be difficult disentangling what can be attributed to substances from other factors such as unsatisfactory diet, poor health or general lifestyle (Hepburn as cited by Harbin and Murphy, 2000). The relationship between use and problems is complex and there is much yet to find out but key issues are the amounts taken and over how long a period use continues (Shapiro and Barnes, 2008).

- Smoking is associated with pre-term delivery, low birth weight and miscarriage.

- Alcohol, both regular use and binge drinking, can cause miscarriage and low birth weight. Heavy drinking is associated with intellectual impairment in the child and foetal alcohol syndrome.

- Use of opioids can lead to pre-term delivery and low birth weight.

- Where a mother is physically dependent on a substance, then the new born baby may suffer withdrawals (neonatal abstinence syndrome). This is most commonly found in the U.K. in respect of opioid-dependent mothers.

(DrugScope and N.H.S. Lothian, 2005).

The risks to children shift with age. Young children may experience:

- neglect (physical/emotional – parents not 'available' because of their preoccupation with their substance use);

- lack of safety (fire; needles or drugs left about);

- poor attachment;

- inconsistent supervision;

- exposure to criminal behaviour;

- increased risk of physical abuse.

As children grow older, the following may emerge:

- an increased risk of sexual abuse;

- the possibility that children may blame themselves for the situation;

- some children adopt inappropriate adult roles such as protecting their using parents or caring for their younger siblings;

- educational or behavioural problems;

- some children begin to fear that they, too, will develop problems with substances and, indeed, there is an increased risk of this occurring.

(Cleaver et al., 1999; Scottish Executive, 2003)

Cleaver et al. (1999) and Kroll and Taylor (2003) note that where family relationships are characterised by dissent and aggression then the risks to children increase. The risks may grow where the male carer is not the biological father (Corby, 2006). The impact on individual children in the same household can be very different.

A number of factors have been identified which, while not eliminating the possibility of detriment to children, do potentially provide 'protection'. Ironically, while the substance-using parent entering treatment can be a protective factor, attempts to alter substance use for the better may bring stresses which increase the vulnerability of children (Aldridge cited in Kroll and Taylor, 2003). Conversely relapse, while not necessarily having catastrophic consequences, will always demand a reassessment of the risks for children.

RESEARCH SUMMARY

Cleaver et al. (1999) have explored the implications of parental substance use, mental health problems and domestic violence for the well-being of children. In respect of substance problems, they highlight the following as factors which may reduce the risks:

- *sufficient income and good standards in the home;*
- *one consistent, caring adult in the child's life;*
- *maintenance of family rituals and activities;*
- *substance-using parent in treatment;*
- *regular monitoring by, or help from, health, social work or other professionals (including opportunities for respite);*
- *safe residence for the mother and child if subject to violence;*
- *regular attendance at nursery or school;*
- *sympathetic and vigilant teachers;*
- *participation in out-of-school activities.*

(Cleaver et al., 1999)

Significant others – adults

Parents, partners and siblings of young users can experience a range of difficulties. Siblings, in particular, continue to be a neglected group. Often parents can become so preoccupied with trying to cope with their substance-using child that brothers and sisters can feel disregarded. This can lead to anger, stress and the risk that the siblings will start using too (Dorn et al., 1994). Parents or partners may experience fear, anger, health problems and financial difficulties. In addition, guilt, the belief that they are somehow to blame for the problem, can plague family members (Dorn et al., 1994; Velleman, 1992). Kroll and Taylor (2003) noted that there is a heightened risk of domestic violence, although the relationship between this and use of substances is more complex than is somtimes assumed.

Family dynamics can become skewed with roles altering to cope with the overwhelming problem which has become the central preoccupation of all concerned. Friends may be shed and social lives abandoned through embarrassment. All sorts of strategies, often ineffective, may be used to try to cajole or force the user into changing. Some approaches that relatives adopt may, inadvertently, reinforce the very behaviour they are hoping will change. From a family systems perspective, one member's substance use may come to serve other functions within the complex dynamics of a family (Orford, 1987).

CASE STUDY

Substances and the family

Megan (16) has lived all her life with her mother's drinking. She has cleaned up her vomit, helped her mother to bed and ensured that her younger brother was ready for school. Having stopped drinking, her mother is now trying to take back her maternal role by encouraging Megan to apply herself to her homework and complaining if she stays out late. Megan has started to rebel against this saying 'It's me who has looked after you, so mind your own business'.

Karen and Harry are trying to cope with their son John's heroin use. They have stopped going out together and spend much of their time talking about the latest crisis. They have threatened to put John out of the house if he does not seek help but they have never followed this through. Time and again they have told him that they will not pay his drug debts but, whenever he says that he is being threatened, they have relented. John has called their bluff and knows that, whatever he does, home is a cushion he can rely on.

Significant others – practitioners

In a study by Rowett (cited by Norris, 1990), 15 per cent of social workers who had been assaulted by service users had been attacked by a person under the influence of drugs, alcohol or solvents. There may be little point in trying to engage people who are significantly intoxicated in programmatic work, however practitioners are often involved in their management. A field worker may have to encourage a person to leave the office and return when in a more receptive state or a residential worker may have to ensure that a person under the influence of substances does not cause difficulties for others. Successful management of such situations requires training. Care is needed to avoid needle stick injury. Agencies should have procedures in place regarding the action to be taken if illicit substances or drug paraphernalia are found and as a guide to handling aggressive behaviour. Readily available management support is essential.

The legal context and policy perspectives

In addition to the consequences of problematic use for the individual and his immediate circle, the costs to health and welfare services and the distress caused by crime and anti-social behaviour mean that governments give high priority to trying to control use and limit the detrimental consequences.

Legislation

First, the law is used to control the harms by restricting or prohibiting access to particular substances or proscribing certain behaviours linked to substance use. Such laws are directed at the population as a whole.

Core drug law is not devolved and remains the responsibility of the Westminster Parliament. The key piece of legislation is the *Misuse of Drugs Act 1971*, the purpose of which is to prohibit the use of certain substances completely and to restrict the use of others to specific medical purposes. The Act specifies, in three classes, the penalties which can be imposed for illicit possession for a person's own use or for supply. Regulations under the Act categorise drugs into five schedules which determine who can legally possess them. Schedule 1 drugs are restricted to people with a special Home Office licence whereas those in schedule 5 can be bought without prescription, but only from a pharmacy.

Unlike the *Misuse of Drugs Act*, alcohol-licensing law, for which there is different legislation in England and Wales, Scotland and Northern Ireland, allows the availability of alcohol to adults within a framework aimed at limiting harm. It does this primarily through the granting of licences for the selling of alcohol and specifying conditions regarding its sale. The *Licensing Act 2003* in England and Wales and the *Licensing (Scotland) Act 2005* contain the following objectives which the licensing authorities are obliged to promote:

- the prevention of crime;

- the securing of public safety;

- the prevention of nuisance;

- the protection of children from harm.

Scottish law includes a fifth objective of 'protecting and improving public health'. Attempts to reduce harm can be seen, therefore, as central to the aim of these two Acts.

The health problems associated with tobacco are now so widely understood that recent legislation introduced in all jurisdictions in the U.K. banning smoking in enclosed public spaces and raising the age of sale to eighteen has met with widespread public acceptance.

In addition to laws aimed at control at a population level, there is also legislation geared to dealing with specific issues related to those experiencing problems or causing difficulties due to substance use. The following are some examples.

- The *National Health Service and Community Care Act 1990* (in respect of England, Wales and Scotland) and the *Health and Personal Social Service (Northern Ireland) Order 1972* as amended allow local authorities or, in Northern Ireland, Health and Social Care Trusts, to supplement the funding required to obtain particular non-medical services. This allows individuals with drug or alcohol problems, who cannot afford to pay themselves, to access residential rehabilitation and certain other treatment programmes.

- The *Road Traffic Act 1988* makes it an offence to be in charge of a vehicle while under the influence of alcohol or drugs in England, Wales and Scotland. The relevant legislation in Northern Ireland is the *Road Traffic (Northern Ireland) Order 1995*.

- Drug Treatment and Testing Orders were introduced in England and Wales and in Scotland under the *Crime and Disorder Act 1998*. For offenders aged over eighteen in England and Wales, *the Criminal Justice Act 2003* replaced, over time, the DTTO with the Drug Rehabilitation Requirement as part of a Community Order. The purpose of these orders/requirements is to reduce criminal behaviour among offenders whose drug use has directly contributed to their acquiring a more serious criminal record.

- In Scotland, sections 52(2) (j) and (k) of the Children Scotland (Act) 1995 allow consideration of compulsory measures of supervision on the grounds that a child has misused alcohol, drugs or a volatile substance.

Policy developments

Efforts to reduce the harms are not restricted to legislation. In recent years, the four countries making up the United Kingdom have, separately, drawn the disparate strands of social control into strategic plans. In England and Scotland, there are separate plans in respect of alcohol and drugs but in Northern Ireland and in Wales these are addressed in single plans. Tobacco control plans have also been developed. These plans are updated from time to time. The objective of the tobacco control plans is to eliminate smoking completely while the approach to alcohol is to encourage those who chose to drink to do so in a harm-free way. The drug strategies take the twin track approach of promoting measures to reduce harm, even in circumstances where it is acknowledged that drug use will continue, but within a prohibitionist framework. Exploration of these plans demands a chapter on its own; suffice to say that the strategies tend to address the issues within the broad themes of young people, treatment, supply reduction and law enforcement and the protection of communities. Within the strategies there are the topics which are of particular relevance to social workers involved with people with substance problems, although these may be given different weight in the different countries of the United Kingdom. These include:

- increasing the numbers in treatment;
- improving the protection of children affected by parental problems;
- enhancing support for kinship carers (relatives who care for the children of parents with problems);
- building a range of services to enable people to move beyond core treatment towards fuller integration into society;
- further development of interventions within the criminal justice system for people whose offences are linked to their own substance use;
- a strong emphasis on inter-agency working.

It is not necessary for social workers to know the technicalities of all legislation or to study all aspects of the alcohol, smoking and drug strategies. However, it is important to understand what the law is trying to achieve, not only because some clients may have been charged with offences but also because legislation both reflects and helps to shape what is acceptable and unacceptable behaviour in a given society. The same is true for the different strategies. Detailed knowledge of the law is, of course, needed in circumstances such as working with an offender subject to a Drug Rehabilitation Requirement/Drug Treatment and Testing Order or assessing a kinship carer for financial support.

Alcohol and drug strategies across the UK

Changing political priorities can lead to rapid policy shifts. As of 2009, the following documents shaped the strategic direction regarding control and treatment:

England

Drugs – Home Office, 2008. Drugs: protecting families and communities. The 2008 drug strategy.
Available at: www.drugs.homeoffice.gov.uk/drug-strategy/overview

Alcohol – HM Government, 2007. Safe. Sensible. Social: the next steps in the national alcohol strategy. *Available at:*
www.dh.gov.uk/en/Publicationsandstatistics/Publications/PublicationsPolicyandGuidance/DH_075218

Northern Ireland

Department of Health, Social Services and Public Safety, 2006. New strategic direction for alcohol and drugs 2006–2011.

Wales

Welsh Assembly Government, 2008. Working together to reduce the harm: the substance misuse strategy for Wales 2008–2018.
www.wales.gov.uk/topics/housingandcommunity/safety/publications/strategy0818/?lang=en

Scotland

Drugs – Scottish Government, 2008l. The road to recovery: a new approach to tackling Scotland's drug problem.
www.scotland.gov.uk/Publications/2008/05/22161610/0

Alcohol – Scottish Government, 2009c. Changing Scotland's relationship with alcohol: a framework for action.
www.scotland.gov.uk/Publications/2009/02/27151352/0.

Practice issues – reducing the risks

It is beyond the scope of this chapter to explore in depth the application of effective interventions with people with substance problems. Suffice to say that the best form of risk minimisation is a well-delivered package of interventions appropriate to the individual and his circumstances. In this section we will consider particular points of risk which may present during the process of working with people with substance problems.

RESEARCH SUMMARY

Research findings can be ambiguous and difficult to interpret. However, studies using meta-analysis have shown that a number of interventions are effective with people with substance problems but no one intervention has been shown to be superior to all others. Those which are effective are not effective with everyone. In addition, a range of interventions is more likely to lead to a positive outcome for an individual than one on its own. Research suggests that the following can be effective:

- *pharmacotherapy (the use of different drugs for a variety of purposes including the management of withdrawals, the reduction of craving and substitute prescribing);*
- *motivational enhancement;*
- *cognitive behavioural therapy;*
- *contingency management (the use of rewards or reinforcements to support treatment compliance);*
- *relapse prevention;*
- *twelve step programmes.*

Retention in treatment, particularly in respect of people who are dependent on substances, has been shown to be important. The attitudes and abilities of the practitioner can also affect outcomes.

(Raistrick et al., 2006; Gossop, 2006)

Engagement

Social workers play a variety of roles with people with substance problems and it is these which shape the challenges of initial engagement.

CASE STUDY

Winston (22) has been referred by the Court to the Probation Service for a pre-sentence report following a finding of guilt for possession of amphetamines and cannabis. He says he was keeping the drugs safe for a friend and, although he admits to using drugs occasionally, he says that he has not done so for a while. He is very vague about his past use of drugs and alcohol.

Lennie (49) has been referred to a care manager by his GP who is prepared to detoxify him from alcohol if a place is immediately available in a residential rehab. Lennie is keen on this course of action saying that 'drink will be the death of me if I don't stop'.

What these clients are displaying and how they view their practitioners are very different and will dictate how the latter proceed.

Confronting people directly about their substance use is as likely to elicit denial as it is to lead to admission (Jarvis et al., 2005). Once the drawbridge is up, the probability of it being lowered is reduced. When the client is not directly presenting his relationship with substances as an issue, stealth may be the best tactic. Anthony Thorley makes the telling statement *for the patient to come to the doctor's surgery shows he is motivated about something* (Thorley, 1980, p1816). Addressing what is concerning the person as the starting point, along with carefully framed leading questions which allow the person to describe aspects of his life, can open up the discussion in non-threatening ways. At some point, the person will almost certainly begin to allude to his drinking or drug taking.

ACTIVITY 10.4

Darren (15) is a very good footballer but he has been missing training. He has also been truanting. It is known that he regularly drinks and uses volatile substances with some older boys in the woods. He plays this down saying that his main problem is that the police are always picking on him.

How would you go about engaging with Darren?

Comment

People with substance problems are often ambivalent about change. They are usually aware of the damage that they are causing themselves but may be frightened of the consequences of giving up something that still has benefits for them. In some circumstances, the person may well interpret the risks involved in very different ways from those around them (Griffiths and Waterson, 1996). Motivation regarding change fluctuates, sometimes within very short time periods. A heroin user who is beginning to suffer withdrawals may say she is keen to start treatment but, on obtaining the drug and reducing the physical discomfort, may quickly forget her previous resolve. In addition, an inability by the client to stick to agreed plans may lead him, through a sense of failure, to be reluctant to return. Agencies should have in place strategies to actively keep people involved. For example, sending a supportive letter immediately after non-attendance offering another appointment can work wonders for retention (Ashton and Witton, 2005).

Assessment

Assessment and intervention with people with substance problems will often be a collaborative exercise involving a number of practitioners. A social worker or probation officer working with a young man who uses cocaine and amphetamines on his nights out may consider that there is no need to involve other agencies. However a statutory supervisor, a child care social worker, a health visitor and the staff at the local prescribing service might all be involved with a heroin-dependent mother who is on a Community Order. Case management requires that all services are aware of their respective roles and that liaison is a continuous activity. The days should be long past where a social worker discovers from her client, rather than from the clinic, that he has been taken off a methadone programme for continuing to use street drugs. In respect of the Drugs Interventions Programme for offenders in England, the National Treatment Agency stresses the importance of 'seamless case management' and the value of the Drugs Interventions Record which reduces duplication of assessment and stays with the person as he moves through different services, including the transition from custody to the community (*National Treatment Agency for Substance Misuse, 2006*). Recent years have seen the development, at the local level, of integrated care pathways and the introduction of single shared assessments (Scottish Executive, 2005).

The first priority in assessment is to identify whether there are serious risks which demand immediate action. Does the person's own health, behaviour or circumstances, including such things as risk of self-harm, neglect or overdose, require that something is done straight away? Is anyone else in danger? Are there child protection issues? Government agencies are supporting a stepped approach to assessment starting with screening by generic professionals to identify whether onward referral is indicated through to in-depth specialist assessment (Scottish Executive, 2005). In England and Wales, the National Treatment Agency for Substance Misuse (2006) has promoted the use of a triage approach when a person is first involved with specialist treatment services to ascertain the seriousness of the situation, its urgency and whether referral to another agency is appropriate. A variety of assessment tools are in use. The majority of these address areas of risk within the wider framework of obtaining a clear picture of all issues related to a person's substance use. There are some tools which consider specific behaviours such as injecting practices. Screening for mental health problems should be undertaken routinely. Good assessment will identify and build on a person's strengths as well as addressing the risks.

Assessment must also identify whether there are others involved in the user's life who are either at risk of harm or who need support for themselves. This includes children and partners or the parents and siblings of a young person with a drug or alcohol problem.

The well-being of children is now centre stage. Addressing this presents a challenge to agencies providing for adults with substance problems. Sensitivity and timing are critical. The boundaries of confidentiality need to be made explicit to the client. Information provided by the parents should always be verified with third parties such as health visitors, GPs or reliable family members. As previously noted, parental or carer substance problems may have different implications for different children in the same family. National guidance has ensured that all areas have developed systems and interagency protocols regarding children affected by parental problems. All services for adults have procedures in place regarding both initial and ongoing screening and how to facilitate a full child care assessment if this is indicated. Child protection concerns should be acted on immediately. Ongoing liaison between child care and substance problems workers is essential.

Protocols include arrangements to identify and support women with drug or alcohol problems who are pregnant. A first step in every case will be an assessment of need which will lead to decisions as to what level of service is called for and whether formal child protection proceedings are necessary (Advisory Council for the Misuse of Drugs, 2003; Scottish Executive, 2003). Good practice indicates that similar arrangements should be in place where the partner of a pregnant woman has a significant problem with drugs or alcohol, even if the woman does not have such difficulties.

In political terms, a higher profile has been given to the implications for children of drug users but the principles of screening, assessment and interventions are exactly the same for problematic parental alcohol use.

> **CASE STUDY**
>
> *Davy (33) is a binge drinker and the spur to his seeking help is the threats that his wife, Kathy, has made to leave taking their three-year-old son, Tom, with her. His worker is aware that he must ascertain whether Tom faces any risks and whether his needs are being met. He gives careful thought to when and how he will undertake this task as insensitive handling could lead to Davy not attending again. If this happened, then an opportunity to both help Davy and ensure the well-being of Tom would be lost. Once he has gained Davy's trust and agreed a plan regarding his drinking, his worker suggests that Kathy might attend the next session. This brings the opportunity to widen the discussion to family issues. The worker says that contact between the agency and the health visitor is routine in such circumstances, particularly as the agency does not normally undertake home visits. With trust established, the parents do not object. The health visitor has not seen Tom recently but carries out a home visit. No particular concerns are identified and the health visitor gives Kathy advice about applying for a nursery place. The health visitor and the substance worker agree that the former will visit on a more regular basis and that they will keep each other updated.*
>
> *This case study illustrates the general principles. In practice, Davy's worker would be following specific local procedure.*

Care planning

Care planning involves the practitioner, the service user and, where appropriate, other family members in setting a series of goals aimed at addressing the concerns identified in the assessment. The plan will include the interventions to be used to achieve those goals. The National Treatment Agency suggests that care plans be structured to address four domains in a person's life:

- drug and alcohol use;
- health (physical and psychological);
- offending;
- social functioning (including housing, employment and relationships).

(National Treatment Agency for Substance Misuse, 2006)

Utilising these domains can provide a logical structure for considering goals and for ongoing evaluation of the effectiveness of interventions. The following are some of the key issues regarding care planning for people with substance problems.

- For many service users, it may be best to devise an initial care plan with a small number of short-term, achievable goals. In the early stages of contact, people are often unsettled and ambivalent about change. Encouraging them to consider long-term goals, such as whether to commit to lifelong abstinence or what employment they should consider in six months' time, may be counter-productive.
- Harm reduction begins at the point of initial engagement. It is applicable to alcohol as well as to drugs and it is multi-faceted. Harm reduction includes such action as: giving

advice regarding risk of overdose, especially where polydrug use is an issue; ensuring safer injecting practices; encouraging a heavy drinker to eat one good meal a day; helping a rough sleeper gain accommodation; supporting a person onto a substitute prescribing programme. Harm reduction has sometimes been presented as being incompatible with the longer-term goal of abstinence but this is not the case. Immediate action can lessen risks and even save lives as well as encouraging engagement with services.

- After the initial care plan has helped stabilise the situation, an holistic approach can be taken encompassing the four domains outlined above. To these need to be added interventions to support relatives or to reduce the risks to children.

- If a person is physically dependent on substances, then the full care plan will explore options as to how this will be addressed. Some substances (in particular alcohol, benzodiazepines and barbiturates) present risk of seizures, and even death, in withdrawal. Clients should be advised of this and detoxification should always be under medical supervision. For opioids, the choice of substitute prescribing or detoxification is available. Proceeding at the client's own pace is essential. A completely drug free life may seem like the most attractive option for practitioner and client alike but if detoxification takes place when the client is not prepared or supported for this major change, relapse and a sense of failure may follow.

- For those with less serious problems with alcohol and no associated physical damage, controlled drinking may be a possible goal but some people find this harder to maintain than abstinence. Such programmes involve the client altering both consumption and how and where drinking takes place so that previously experienced problems are eliminated. The GP should always be consulted regarding whether there are any health issues which make controlled drinking an inadvisable goal.

- Involving partners, or the parents of young users, in treatment can improve outcomes for the user (McWhirter and Mir, 2008; Orford, 1987) but this, on its own, does not meet the needs of other family members. Where they are experiencing difficulties, a discrete care plan and a separate practitioner of their own is desirable. Such care plans should aim to help relatives stand back from the day-to-day turmoil and develop consistent strategies regarding how to handle problematic situations and reduce the stress. Where children are affected, the needs of each child must be addressed individually. How relatives are supported is not a once and for all decision. The wife of a drinker might need individual help initially but, when the situation has improved, marital therapy or involvement in the counselling sessions with her husband might become desirable.

- The care plan should also address risks in the environment which militate against rehabilitation. The progress achieved by a person during a spell in residential rehabilitation may well be undone if he returns to the same cold, unfurnished flat near his old drug-using friends.

- Regular review of care plans and a willingness by all parties to respond flexibly to changing circumstances is essential.

Reducing the risks through effective interventions

If a person can use a well delivered package of interventions to his advantage, then many of the risks he and his family face should reduce. Risks, however, do not cease because a person is involved in treatment. For many, a number of attempts to change are made before sustained alteration to behaviour is achieved.

Relapse, whether it is using on top of prescribed drugs or returning to use after a period of abstinence, brings the danger of overdose. Release after a period in custody is a time of concern in this regard. Relapse prevention work, along with advice about the risks, is an integral part of any treatment plan. Relapse has implications for other family members, especially children. Parental relapse may have serious consequences for a child but this may not necessarily be the case. Each relapse needs to be considered on its own merits.

Heavy alcohol use may continue despite a reduction in the use of illicit drugs (Gossop et al., 2003) and services for people with drug problems should also regularly assess their service users' drinking.

Ironically, positive progress by the client may bring problems within the family. We have noted how a teenager might react to her, now alcohol free, mother trying to reassume her maternal role. Similar problems of adjustment can occur between partners and sometimes relationships, which have stayed intact while one person was using, fall apart when there is no longer a focus on the substance problem and readjustments in roles cause new strains. Orford (1987) notes that sometimes family members of people with alcohol problems can actually be resistant to the drinker making positive progress. It is important to consider whether family or marital therapy is advisable. Practitioners should be aware that efforts by parents to deal with their substance problems may not necessarily improve the circumstances of the children. A mother struggling to adapt to a methadone maintenance regime may find that she is less able to respond to the demands of young children than when she was managing to maintain some sort of a routine while using street heroin. Any changes in the adults' circumstances, whether it is relapse, improvements due to treatment or alterations in the composition of the household, should trigger a re-evaluation of the risks to the children.

Finally, there is growing understanding of the need to help people to move towards a constructive and fulfilling life beyond 'treatment'. Providing 'wraparound services', such as housing, financial advice and access to training or employment, is part of a far-reaching process of supporting a person to develop a new identity as someone who no longer has a problem. This fundamental shift to achieving a new sense of self, repairing a 'spoiled identity' in the words of Goffman (cited in Mcintosh and McKeganey, 2002), may be fundamental. This is echoed by what has long been Alcoholics Anonymous' view, namely that abstinence is only a small part of the bigger concept of 'sobriety' – a constructive and fulfilling life beyond the use of alcohol (Maxwell, 1984). This fuller notion of rehabilitation can been seen as somewhat at odds with the current cost driven, target orientated culture; however, its value is beginning to be understood by policy makers. The current English Drug Strategy stresses the importance of the personalisation of treatment and re-integration into society (Home Office, 2008). The current Scottish Drug Strategy goes further than this by borrowing the concept of 'recovery', the idea of individualised, sustained progress towards a new way of living, from the mental health field (Scottish Government, 2008l). Adapting services to meet this aspiration, while improving initial responses to substances users at the earliest stages of engagement in treatment, is becoming the new challenge for social workers and other disciplines involved in helping substance users.

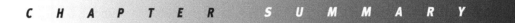

C H A P T E R   S U M M A R Y

Many individuals, social groupings and cultures find positive benefits through using substances in various ways and for diverse purposes. However, substance taking is never a risk-free activity. Harms come in a number of dimensions – the physical and psychological effects of short- and long-term use; the dangers associated with intoxification; the problems involved in particular ways of ingestion; the risks involved in using in certain environments. Inappropriate use has implications for those close to the person and also for the wider community. While attitudes towards substances differ between cultures and change over time, understanding of the potential problems has led societies to try to control, by formal and informal methods, the availability of many substances and how they are used.

Intervention with people with substance problems often involves a number of agencies which makes the co-ordination of care plans, clarity of roles and ongoing liaison essential. The risks to, and needs of, significant others need to be addressed separately from those of the person with the substance problem. In recent years, children affected by parental substance problems have become a priority. A range of interventions, applied by well trained and supported practitioners, are known to be effective with substance users and there is a growing realisation that fuller recovery can be achieved by helping people move beyond treatment towards a different style of life and an altered sense of self.

FURTHER READING

Advisory Council on the Misuse of Drugs (2003): *Hidden harm: Responding to the needs of children of problem drug users.* London: Home Office. Available online: **www.drugs.homeoffice.gov.uk/ publication-search/acmd/hidden-harm**
This is a key document regarding children affected by parental drug problems which has led to the development of both policies and practice initiatives.

Barber, J (2002) *Social work with addictions.* Basingstoke: Macmillan.
This text covers theories regarding the causes of substance problems and how to intervene effectively. Barber places the latter within the wider social context.

Shapiro, H (ed) (2008) *The essential student reader on drugs.* London: DrugScope.
This is a comprehensive introductory text which, among other issues, addresses types of drugs, statistics, drugs and criminal behaviour and arguments regarding social control.

Jarvis, T, Tebutt, J, Mattick, R, and Shand, F (2005) *Treatment approaches for alcohol and drug dependence – an introductory guide.* Chichester: John Wiley.
This is an excellent introduction to working with people with substance problems. The practical application of the main interventions is described in detail.

Scottish Executive (2003) *Getting our priorities right.* Edinburgh: Scottish Executive. **www.scotland. gov.uk/library5/education/gopr-00.asp**
This document describes good practice with regard to children whose parents/carers have alcohol or drug problems. The importance of effective interagency communication is stressed. Its relevance is not confined to the Scottish context.

WEBSITES

www.nta.nhs.uk

The National Treatment Agency for Substance Misuse is a special health authority within the NHS in England. The publications section of the NTA website is a rich source of evidence-based papers on effective treatment and best practice documents. Documents are all available online.

www.drugscope.org.uk

DrugScope is a voluntary organisation which provides expertise and information regarding drugs. Up-to-date information about substances and the UK drugs laws are available on the website.

www.alcoholconcern.org.uk

Alcohol Concern is a voluntary body which provides information about, and campaigns on, all aspects of alcohol misuse.

www.adfam.org.uk

Working with and for families affected by drugs and alcohol is the remit of Adfam, which is another voluntary organisation.

Conclusion

This book has ranged widely both conceptually and practically in an attempt to provide the reader with an overview of a range of issues in present day social work and social care that are becoming ever more pertinent and their management ever more critical.

Need remains a central and underpinning concept in the lexicon of social welfare. Defining, assessing and addressing need is the very *raison d'être* of social work and social care practice; it is why these practices exist in the first place, all of which is predicated upon a now somewhat contested belief that the state has a central and pivotal role in meeting some of the welfare needs of the collective. In particular, we have seen how the institutions of the state have a central and legally mandated role to meet the needs of the most vulnerable people in society as well as an increasingly visible and politicised role in meeting the need for protection of the general public from serious and violent offenders.

Our discussions of need opened the concept up and allowed us to think about how certain ways of looking at need can bring into play a consideration of other, related concepts which have clear relevance to social work and social care practice: risk, capacity and incapacity and protection. All of these issues are closely related and arguably all arising from the human condition of having certain needs which, if not met, leave us vulnerable to harm. The issue then becomes one of how best to deal with this, and the subsequent chapters, with their focus on particular areas of social work practice and service user groupings, have provided you with information to help you address some of these issues within the context of your practice.

The book as a whole could have been twice or three times as long again; each of the chapters has provided a wealth of information but in reality there are many more themes and issues to include and unpick, as well as many debates to be had. We therefore recommend that you use the many citations and references, etc. contained within these pages to further your study of these particular issues.

As a society, we will always have to deal with need. The questions of central importance are *who* is best placed to do this and *how* might this be done in a way that is purposeful, supportive, enabling, empowering and ultimately beneficial to those to whom it applies: all of us. Social work and social care practice is generally regarded as the 'business' of the state, although with the advent of new right ideologies, we have seen a distinctive shift away from collective, state-sponsored responses to more commercially oriented ventures. Fundamental to any approach, however, is the requirement (one might even say the *need*) to value people with all their infirmities and foibles as people first and 'outcomes' second. Welfare practice (broadly defined) has to be cost-effective and there is no doubt that there is a need for performance to be monitored and appraised, but it is essential that we know *what* is being monitored, *why* and *for whose benefit*. One element that appears to be somewhat lacking at present in relation to the whole-service delivery system is the focus on process; the 'how' of meeting need. These elements are so important; how it feels to be on the receiving end of any kind of service is, to us, the critical element of service delivery and yet today there appears to be such an emphasis on how many? how quickly?

and how costly? These are important variables, but if they become the main focus of our concern for how well our services are meeting people's needs, keeping people safe and contributing to what Aristotle referred to as 'ataraxia' (peace of mind and 'evdaimonia' (happiness and a sense of flourishing), then we are in danger of forgetting what being human is actually all about. The whole basis of a collective response to need is the collective recognition that we all have needs and that we all of us owe a duty to each other to make sure that we are OK. To use a phrase that is now very familiar to professionals in Scotland, we must all remember that 'It's everyone's job to make sure I'm alright'.

References

Abrahams, H (2007) *Supporting women after domestic violence: Loss, trauma and recovery*. London: Jessica Kingsley.

Action on Elder Abuse (2006) **www.elderabuse.org.uk/**

Adams, R, Dominelli, L and Payne, M (2009) *Social work: Themes, issues and critical debates*. Basingstoke: Palgrave Macmillan.

Advisory Council on the Misuse of Drugs (2003) *Hidden harm – responding to the needs of children of problem drug users*. London: The Stationery Office.

Agrawal, M (2003) Voluntariness in clinical research at the end of life in *Pain Symptom Management*, 25, S25–S32 cited by Hurst.

Alcock, P (2006) *Understanding poverty*. 3rd edition. Basingstoke: Palgrave Macmillan.

Aldgate, J and Rose, W (2007) *The developing world of the child*. London: Jessica Kingsley.

Andreasen, NC (2004) *Brave new brain: Conquering mental illness in the era of the genome*. New York: Oxford University Press.

Andrews, AB (2007) *Social history assessment*. London: Sage.

Andrews, DA (1995) The psychology of criminal conduct and effective treatment in McGuire, J (ed) *What works: Reducing reoffending – guidelines for research and practice*. Chichester: John Wiley & Sons.

Andrews, DA, Bonta, J, and Wormith, SJ (2006) The recent past and near future of risk and/or need assessment. *Crime and Delinquency, 52*, pp7–27.

Andrews, GJ and Phillips, DR (2004) *Ageing and place*. London: Routledge.

Arber, S and Ginn, J (eds.) (1997) *Connecting gender and ageing: A sociological approach*. Buckingham: Open University Press.

Arkoff, A, Meredith, GM and Dubanoski, JP (2004) Gains in well-being achieved through retrospective-proactive life review by independent older women. *Journal of Humanistic Psychology, 44,* 204.

Ashenden, S (2004) *Governing child sexual abuse: Negotiating the boundaries of public and private, law and science*. London: Routledge.

Ashton, M and Witton, J (2005) *The power of the welcoming reminder. Manners matter Part 1* [online]. London: Drug and Alcohol Findings. Available at: **www.findings. org.uk/docs/Ashton_M_36.pdf**

Audit Scotland (2002) *Dealing with offending by young people*. Edinburgh: Audit Scotland.

Ayto, J (2005) *Dictionary of word origins. (*2nd revised edition). London: A&C Black.

Bamford, D (2007) *The review of mental health and learning disability (Northern Ireland).* Department of Health, Social Services and Public Safety (Northern Ireland).

Bandura, A (1977) *Social learning theory*. New York: Prentice-Hall.

Barnes, J (2003) Interventions addressing infant mental health problems. *Children & Society*, 17, pp386–95.

Barnes, LL, Mendes de Coen, CF, Bienios, JL and Evans, DA (2004) A longitudinal study of black–white difference in social resources. *The Journals of Gerontology Series B: Psychological Sciences and Social Sciences,* 59, pp146–53.

Barrett, G, Sellman, D and Thomas, J (2005) *Interprofessional working in health and social care*. Basingstoke: Palgrave Macmillan.

Barry, M (2007) *Effective approaches to risk assessment in social work: An international literature review*. Edinburgh: Scottish Executive.

Bauby, J-D (2007) *The Diving Bell and the Butterfly*, London: Harper-Perennial.

Bauman, Z (2003) *Wasted lives: Modernity and its outcasts*. Cambridge: Polity Press.

Bauman, Z (2004) *Work, consumerism and the new poor.* (2nd edition). Buckingham: Open University Press.

Bauman, Z (2007) *Liquid Times: Living in an Age of Uncertainty*. Cambridge: Policy Press.

BBC News (2005) at **news.bbc.co.uk/nolpda/ukfs_news/hi/newsid_4245000/ 4245354.stm**

Beck, AT, Ward, CH, Mendelson, M, Mock, J and Erbaugh, J (1961) An inventory for measuring depression. *Archives of General Psychiatry, 4, 561–71.*

Beck, U (1992) *Risk society: Towards a new modernity*. London: Sage.

Bennett, G, Kingston, P and Penhale, B (1997) *The dimensions of elder abuse and neglect: perspectives for the practitioner*. Basingstoke: Macmillan.

Beresford, P (2007) *The roles and tasks of social workers*. Report of Service User consultation for England Review. Shaping Our Lives.

Berger, P and Luckman, T (1979) *The social construction of reality*. London: Peregrine Press/Penguin.

Bernstein, PL (1997) *Against the Gods.* New York: John Wiley & Sons.

Better, SJ (2007) *Institutional racism: a primer on theory and strategies for social change*. New York: Rowman and Littlefield.

Beveridge, Sir W (1942) *Social insurance and allied services*. Cmnd 6404. London: HMSO.

Bichard, Sir R (2004) *The Bichard Inquiry Report*. London: The Stationery Office.

Biestek, FP (1961) *The casework relationship*. London: Unwin.

Bigby, C and Frawley, P (2009) *Social work practice and intellectual disability*. BASW Practical Social Work Series. Basingstoke: Palgrave Macmillan.

Blackburn, R (2000) Risk assessment and prediction in McGuire, J Mason, T and Okane, A (eds.) *Behaviour, crime and legal processes: a guide for forensic practitioners*. Chichester: John Wiley & Sons.

Blair, T (1999) Beveridge revisited: Welfare state for the 21st century in Walker, R (ed) *Ending child poverty: popular welfare for the 21st century*. Bristol: Policy Press.

Blanchette, K and Brown, SL (2006) *The assessment and treatment of women offenders: An integrative perspective*. Chichester: John Wiley & Sons.

Blewett, J, Lewis, J and Tunstill, J (2007) *The changing roles and tasks of social work. A literature informed discussion paper*. London: GSCC.

Bloch, B and Reddaway, P (1977) *Psychiatric terror: How Soviet psychiatry is used to suppress dissent*. New York: Basic Books.

Bond, J, Peace, S, Dittman-Kohli, F and Westerhof, G (2007) *Ageing in society*. (3rd edition). London: Sage.

Bonta, J and Wormith, SJ (2007) Risk and need assessment in McIvor, G and Raynor, P (eds) *Developments in social work with offenders*. London: Jessica Kingsley.

Bourassa, C (2007) Co-occurrence of Interparental Violence and Child Physical Abuse and Its Effect on the Adolescents' Behavior. *Journal of Family Violence* 22(8), pp691–701.

Boxhill, BR (2000) in *A companion to ethics* Singer, P (ed). Oxford: Blackwell Publishers.

Boyle, M in Heller, T, Reynolds, J, Gomm, R, Muston, R and Pattison, S (eds) (1996) *Mental health matters*. London: Macmillan/The Open University.

Bradshaw, J (1972) The concept of social need. *New Society* 30 March, pp640–3. London: Statesman and Nation Publishing Company.

Brearley, PC (1982) *Risk in social work*. London: Routledge & Kegan Paul.

Bridges, W (2003) *Managing transitions: Making the most of change*. London: Nicolas Brealey.

Broadhurst, K, Grover, C and Jamieson, J (eds) (2009) *Critical perspectives on safeguarding children*. Chichester: WileyBlackwell.

Bronfenbrenner, U (1979) *The ecology of human development*. Cambridge, MA: Harvard University Press.

Bronfenbrenner, U (1986) Ecology of the family as a context for human development: Research perspectives. *Developmental Psychology* 22(6) pp723–42.

Bronfenbrenner, U (1989) Ecological Systems Theory. *Annals of Child Development* 6 pp187–249.

Brown, R (2009) *The approved mental health professional's guide to mental health law*. Exeter: Learning Matters.

Brown, W and Kandirikirira, N (2007) *Recovering mental health in Scotland. Report on narrative investigation of mental health recovery.* Glasgow: Scottish Recovery Network.

Browne, K and Pennell, A (1998) *The effects of video violence on young offenders*. Home Office Research and Statistics Directorate. London: Home Office.

Byrne, D (2005) *Social exclusion*. Buckingham: Open University Press.

Cage, RA (1981) *The Scottish Poor Law 1745–1845*. Edinburgh: Scottish Academic Press.

Calder, M (ed) (2004) *Child sexual abuse and the internet: Tackling the new frontier*. Lyme Regis: Russell House Publishing.

Calder, M and Hackett, S (eds) (2003) *Assessment in child care: Using and developing frameworks for practice*. Lyme Regis: Russell House Publishing.

Calder, M, Harold, GT and Howarth, E (2004) *Children living with domestic violence: Towards a framework for assessment*. Lyme Regis: Russell House Publishing.

Campbell, J and Oliver, M (1996) *Disability politics: Understanding our past, changing our future,* London: Routledge.

Carson, D and Bain, A (2008) *Professional risk and working with people: Decision making in health, social care and criminal justice*. London: Jessica Kingsley.

Castell, D (1991) From dangerousness to risk in Burchell, G, Gordon, C and Miller, P (eds) *The Foucault effect: Studies in governmentality*. London: Harvester/Wheatsheaf.

Chu, WCK, Tsui, M-S and Yan, M-C (2009) Social Work as a moral and political practice. *International Social Work* 523 pp287–98.

Churchill, W (1964). *BrainyQuote*. Available at: **www.brainyquote.com/quotes/authors/w/winston_churchill.html**

Clayton, S (1983) Social need revisited. *Journal of Social Policy* 12(2) pp215–34.

Cleaver, H, Nicholson, D, Tarr, S and Cleaver, D (2007) *Child protection, domestic violence, and parental substance misuse: Family experiences and effective practice*. London: Jessica Kingsley.

Cleaver, H, Unell, I and Aldgate, J (1999) *Children's needs-parenting capacity: the impact of parental mental illness, problem alcohol and drug use and domestic violence on children's development*. London: The Stationery Office.

Cohen, J and Kay, J (1994) *Taking drugs seriously: a parent's guide to young people's drug use*. London: Thorsons.

Cohen, LR, Hien, DA and Batchelder, S (2008) The impact of cumulative maternal trauma and diagnosis on parenting behavior. *Child Maltreatment* 13(1) pp27–38.

Cohen, S (1972) *Folk devils and moral panics*. London: MacGibbon and Kee.

Collishaw, S, Goodman, R, Pickles, A and Maughan, B (2007) Modelling the contribution of changes in family life to time trends in adolescent conduct problems. *Social Science and Medicine* 69(12) pp2576–87.

Commission for Social Care Inspection (CSCI) (2007) *Growing up matters: Better transition planning for young people with complex needs.* London: CSCI.

Connell, CM, Bergeron, N, Katz, KH, Saunders, L, Tebes, L and Kraemer, J (2007) Re-referral to *child* protective services: The influence of *child*, family, and case characteristics on risk status. *Child Abuse & Neglect* 31(5) pp573–88.

Coohey, C (2006) Physically Abusive Fathers and Risk Assessment. *Child Abuse & Neglect* 30(5) pp467–80.

Cooley, CH (1998) *On self and social organisation* (ed H-J Schubert). Chicago, IL: University of Chicago Press.

Cooper, A, Hetherington, R and Katz, I (2003) *The risk factor: Making the child protection system work for children*. London: Demos.

Corby,B (2003) Supporting families and protecting children: Assisting child care professionals in initial decision-making and review of cases. *Journal of Social Work* 3 pp195–210.

Corby, B (2006) *Child abuse: towards a knowledge base*. (3rd edition). Maidenhead: Open University Press/McGraw-Hill.

Craig, CD and Sprang, G (2007) Trauma exposure and child abuse potential: Investigating the cycle of violence. *American Journal of Orthopsychiatry* 77(2) pp296–305.

Crawford, K and Walker, J (2008) *Social work with older people*. (2nd edition). Exeter: Learning Matters.

Critcher, C (ed) (2006) *Critical readings: Moral panics and the media*. Buckingham: Open University Press.

Cunningham, H (2006) *The invention of childhood*. London: BBC Books.

Currer, C (2007) *Loss and social work*. Exeter: Learning Matters.

Daily Mail: (2008) *Binge Britain: Under 21s now face ban on buying alcohol*. Daily Mail: Associated Newspapers. 14 August.

Daily Telegraph (2008) Who is to blame for Britain's knife-crime? Telegraph Media Group. 26 May.

Dalrymple, J and Burke, B (1995) *Anti-oppressive practice: Social care and the law*. Buckingham: Open University Press.

Daniel, B (2004) An overview of the Scottish multidisciplinary child protection review. *Child and Family Social Work* 9 pp247–57.

Daniel, B and Wassell, S (2002) *Assessing and promoting resilience in vulnerable children: Early years: School years: Adolescence*, Vol. 1 – *The early years*. Vol. 2 – *The school years*. Vol. 3 – *Adolescence*. London: Jessica Kingsley.

Daniel, B, Vincent, S and Ogilvie-Whyte, S (2007) *A process review of the child protection reform programme*. Edinburgh: Scottish Executive.

Davey Smith, G (ed) (2003) *Health inequalities: Lifecourse approaches*. Bristol: Policy Press.

Davies, M (ed) (2003) *The Blackwell Companion to social work.* (2nd edition). Oxford: Blackwell Publishing.

Davis, A (1996) Risk work and mental health in Kemshall, H and Pritchard, J (eds) *Good practice in risk assessment and risk management.* London: Jessica Kingsley.

Davis, A (2007) Structural Approaches to Social Work in Lishman, J (ed) *Handbook for practice learning in social work and social care* pp27–38. London: Jessica Kingsley.

Deacon, A (2002) *Perspectives on welfare.* Buckingham: Open University Press.

Department for Constitutional Affairs (2007) *The Mental Capacity Act 2005: Codes of Practice.* London: The Stationery Office.

Department for Education and Skills (DfES) (2004a) *Every child matters: Change for children.* London: DfES.

Department for Education and Skills (DfES) (2004b) *Every child matters: Next steps.* London: DfES.

Department for Education and Skills (DfES) (2004c) *Every child matters: Change for children in social care.* London: DfES.

Department for Education and Skills (DfES) (2006) *Working together to safeguard children: A guide to inter-agency working to safeguard and promote the welfare of children.* London: HMSO.

Department of Health (2000) *'No secrets': Guidance on developing and implementing multi-agency policies and procedures to protect vulnerable adults from abuse.* London: Department of Health.

Department of Health (2002) *Social services performance assessment framework indicators*, London: National Statistics.

Department of Health (2007) *Mental Capacity Act 2005* Code of Practice. London: Department of Health.

Department of Health (2009) *Revised guidance on eligibility criteria for social care.* London: Department of Health.

Department of Health and Social Security (DHSS) (1974a) *Report of the committee of inquiry into the care and supervision provided in relation to Maria Colwell.* London: DHSS.

Department of Health and Social Security (DHSS) (1974b) *Non-Accidental Injury to Children.* LASSL (74) (13). London: DHSS.

Department of Health, Social Services and Public Safety (Northern Ireland) (DHSSPS) (1986) *The Mental Health (Northern Ireland) Order 1986.* Belfast: DHSSPS.

Department of Health, Social Services and Public Safety (Northern Ireland) (DHSSPSNI) (2009) *Legislative framework for mental capacity and mental health legislation in Northern Ireland: A policy consultation document.* Belfast: DHSSPSNI.

Dominelli, L (1997) *Sociology for social work.* London: Macmillan.

Dominelli, L (2008) *Anti-racist social work.* (3rd edition). Basingstoke: Palgrave Macmillan.

Dorn, N, Ribbens, J and South, N (1994) *Coping with a nightmare: family feelings about long-term drug use.* Revised edition. London: Institute for the Study of Drug Dependence.

Dow, J (2008) The Mental Health Act 2007. *Journal of Integrated Care* 16(2) pp33–7.

Doyal, L and Gough, I (1984) A theory of human needs. *Critical Social Policy* 4(1) No.10 pp6–38.

Doyal, L and Gough, I (1991) *A Theory of Human Need.* Basingstoke: The Macmillan Press.

Driedger, D (1989) *The last civil rights movement: Disabled people's international.* London and New York: Hurst and Co. and St. Martin's Press.

DrugScope (2004) *Druglink guide to drugs: a guide to the non-medical use of drugs in the UK.* London: DrugScope.

DrugScope and NHS Lothian (2005) *Substance misuse in pregnancy: a resource book for professionals.* London: DrugScope.

Duncker, K (1945) On Problem Solving. *Psychological Monographs* 58(5) (Whole Number 270).

Eastman, N (1996) in Heller, T, Reynolds, J, Gomm, R, Muston, R and Pattison, S (eds) (1996) *Mental health matters.* London: Macmillan/The Open University.

Edwards, G (2005) *Matters of substance. Drugs: is legislation the right answer – or the wrong question?* London: Penguin.

Elkan, R, Kendrick, D, Dewey, M, Hewitt, M, Robinson, J, Blair, M, Williams, D and Brummell, K (2001) Effectiveness of home-based support for older people: systematic review and meta-analysis. *British Medical Journal* 29 (September) pp323–719.

Falkov, A (1996) *Study of 'Working Together' Part 8 Reports. Fatal child abuse & parental psychiatric disorder.* London: Department of Health.

Fazel, S (2008) Oxford Academy media News 2008 at: **www.ox.ac.uk/media/news_releases_for_journalists/081104.html**

Feilberg, F (2007) Working within the organizational context of dynamic change in Lishman, J (ed) *Handbook for practice learning in social work and social care*. (2nd edition). London: Jessica Kingsley.

Fonagy, P, Steele, M, Steele, H, Higgitt, A and Target, M (1994) The Theory and Practice of Resilience. *Journal of Child Psychology and Psychiatry* 35(2) pp231–55.

France, A and Utting, D (2005) The paradigm of 'risk and protection-focused prevention' and its impact on services for children and families. *Children and Society* 19 pp77–90.

Fraser, D (2003) *The Evolution of the British Welfare State*. (3rd edition). Basingstoke: Palgrave Macmillan.

Freud, S (1917) Mourning and melancholia in Strachey, J (1957) (ed) *The standard edition of the complete psychological works of Sigmund Freud* Vol 14 pp237–60. London: Hogarth Press.

Fries, JF (2000) Compression of morbidity in the elderly. *Vaccne* 18 pp1584–9.

Frost, N and Parton, N (2009) *Understanding children's social care: Policy, politics and practice*. London: Sage.

Furedi, F (2002) *The culture of fear*. London and New York: Continuum.

Garrett, PM (2004) Have you seen my assessment schedule? Proceduralisation, constraint and control in social work with children and families in Dent, M, Chandler, J and Barry, J (eds) *New public management: Dilemmas for public sector managers and professionals*. London: Avebury.

Garrett, PM (2005) Work's electronic turn: notes on the deployment of information and communication technologies in social work with children and families. *Critical Social Policy* 25(4) pp529–54.

Garrett, PM (2009) The case of 'Baby P': Opening up spaces for debate on the 'transformation' of children's services? *Critical Social Policy* 29 pp533–47.

Garrod, J (2007) Child well-being. *Sociology Review* 17(1) pp26–7.

General Social Care Council (GSCC) (2008) *Social work at its best: A statement of social work roles and tasks for the 21st century*. London: GSCC.

Giddens, A (1984) *The constitution of society*. Cambridge: Polity Press.

Giddens, A (1990) *The consequences of modernity*. Cambridge: Polity Press/Blackwell.

Giddens, A (1991) *Modernity and self identity: Self and society in the late modern age*. Cambridge: Polity Press/Blackwell.

Gilligan, R (1999) Working with social networks: Key resources in helping children at risk in Hill, M (ed) *Effective ways of working with children and families*. London: Jessica Kingsley.

Gilligan, R (2000) Promoting resilience in children in foster care in Gilligan, R and Kelly, G (eds) *Issues in foster care*. London: Jessica Kingsley.

Glaister, A and Glaister, B (eds) (2005) *Inter-agency collaboration – providing for children*. Edinburgh: Dunedin Academic Press Ltd.

Glick, PC (1977) Updating the life cycle of the family. *Journal of Marriage and the family* 31, pp5–13.

Göpfert, M, Webster, J and Seeman, MV (eds) (2004) *Parental psychiatric disorder: Distressed parents and their families*. (2nd edition). Cambridge: Cambridge University Press.

Gordon, D, Levitas, R and Pantazis, C (eds) (2006) *Poverty and social exclusion in Britain: The millenium survey*. Bristol: The Policy Press.

Gossop, M (2006) *Treating drug misuse problems: evidence of effectiveness*. London: National Treatment Agency for Substance Misuse.

Gossop, M, Marsden, J, Stewart, D and Kidd, T (2003) The national treatment outcome research study (NTORS): 4–5 year follow-up results. *Addiction* 98 pp291–303.

Gough, I (2002) *Lists and thresholds: Comparing our theory of human need with Nussbaum's capabilities approach. Draft paper for conference on promoting women's capabilities: Examining Nussbaum's capabilities approach*. St Edmund's College: Cambridge.

Gould, N (2009) *Mental health social work in context*. Abingdon: Routledge.

Green, M (ed) (2008) *Risking human security*. London: Karnac Books.

Griffiths, R and Waterson, J (1996) Fact, fantasies and confusion: risks and substance use in Kemshall, H and Pritchard, J (eds) *Good practice in risk assessment and risk management*. London: Jessica Kingsley.

H.L. v the United Kingdom, no. 45508 99 (sect. 4), ECHR 2004-ix

Hales, G (1996) *Beyond disability: towards an enabling society*. London: Sage.

Hannah-Moffat, K (1999) Moral agent or actuarial subject: Risk and Canadian women's imprisonment. *Theoretical Criminology* 3 pp71–94.

Harbin, F and Murphy, M (eds) (2000) *Substance misuse and childcare*. Lyme Regis: Russell House Publishing.

Harper, G, Man, LH, Taylor, S and Niven, S (2005) Factors associated with offending in Harper, G and Chitty, C (eds) *The impact of corrections on re-offending: A review of 'what works'*. Home Office Research Study No. 291. (2nd edition). London: Home Office.

Harris, J (2002) *The social work business*. London: Routledge.

Heads Up Scotland (2007) *Infant mental health: A guide for practitioners*. Edinburgh: Heads Up Scotland.

Healy, LM (2007) Universalism and cultural relativism in social work ethics. *International Social Work* 501 pp11–26.

Hester, M, Pearson, C, Harwin, N and Abrahams, H (2006) *Making an impact: Children and domestic violence: A reader.* (2nd edition). London: Jessica Kingsley.

Heywood, A (2003) *Political ideologies.* (3rd edition). Basingstoke: Palgrave Macmillan.

Heywood, A (2007) *Political ideologies.* (4th edition). Basingstoke: Palgrave Macmillan.

Hills, J (1993) *The Future of welfare: A guide to the debate.* York: Joseph Rowntree Foundation.

Hirsch, D (2008) *Estimating the cost of child poverty in Scotland: Approaches and evidence.* Edinburgh: Scottish Government.

HM Government (2006) *Working together to safeguard children: A guide to inter-agency working to safeguard and promote the welfare of children.* London: The Stationery Office.

HM Government (2009) *The vetting and barring scheme guidance.* London: Home Office.

HM Treasury and Department for Education and Skills (2007) *Aiming high for children: Supporting families.* London: The Stationery Office.

HMSO (1968) *Report of the committee on local authority and allied personal social services* (The Seebohm Report) Cmnd. 3703. London: HMSO.

Hollin, CR (1999) Treatment programmes for offenders: Meta-analysis. 'what works', and beyond. *International Journal of Law and Psychiatry* 22 pp361–72.

Home Office (1945) *The Monkton Report.* London: HMSO.

Home Office (1960) Report of the Committee on Children and Young Persons (The Ingleby Report) Cmnd 1191. London: HMSO.

Home Office (2005) *Strengthening multi-agency public protection arrangements.* London: HMSO.

Home Office (2006) Hidden harm: Responding to the needs of children of problem drug users. London: Advisory Council on the Misuse of Drugs: Available at: **www.drugs.homeoffice.gov.uk/publication-search/acmd/hidden-harm**

Home Office (2008) *Drugs: protecting families and communities. The 2008 drug strategy.* London: HM Government. Available at: **drugs.homeoffice.gov.uk/drug-strategy/overview**

Hood, C and Jones, DKC (eds) (1996) *Accident and design: Contemporary debates on risk management.* London: Routledge.

Hood, C, Rothstein, H and Baldwin, R (2001) *The government of risk: Understanding risk regulation regimes.* Oxford: Oxford University Press.

Hope, T and Sparks, R (2000) *Crime, risk and insecurity: Law and order in everyday life and political discourse*. London: Routledge.

Hope, T and Sparks, R (2000) *Crime, risk and insecurity*. London: Routledge.

Horwarth, J and Shardlow, S (2003) *Making links across specialisms: Understanding modern social work practice*. Lyme Regis: Russell House Publishing.

Hothersall, SJ (2008) *Social work with children, young people and their families in Scotland*. (2nd edition). Exeter: Learning Matters.

Hothersall, SJ (2010) The historical context of social policy in Hothersall, SJ and Bolger, JL (eds) *Social policy for social work and the caring professions in Scotland*. Ch2. Aldershot: Ashgate Publishing.

Hothersall, SJ and Bolger, JL (eds.) (2010) *Social policy for social work and the caring professions: Scottish perspectives*. Aldershot: Ashgate Publishing.

Hothersall, SJ, Maas-Lowit, M and Golightley, M (2008) *Social work and mental health in Scotland*. Exeter: Learning Matters.

Howarth, S (2008) *In figures: Domestic abuse*. **www.assemblywales.org/08-040.pdf** (accessed 14th August 2009).

Howe, D (1992) Child abuse and the bureaucratisation of social work. *The Sociological Review* 14(3) pp1–10.

Howe, D (1996) Surface and depth in social work practice in Parton, N (ed) *Social work theory, social change and social work*. London: Routledge.

Hudson, J (2002) Digitising the structures of government: The UK's information-age government agenda. *Policy and Politics* 30(4) pp515–31.

Hudson, J (2003) E-galitarianism? The information society and New Labour's repositioning of welfare. *Critical Social Policy* 23(2) pp268–90.

Hughes, B (1990) The quality of life in Peace, S (ed) *Researching social gerontology*. London: Sage.

Humphreys, C, Thiara, R, Mullender, A and Skamballis, A (2006) *Talking about domestic abuse: A photo activity workbook to develop communication between mothers and young people*. London: Jessica Kingsley.

Hurst, SA (2008) Vulnerability in research and health care: Describing the elephant in the room? *Bioethics* 22(4) pp191–202.

Jack, G (2000) Ecological influences on parenting and child development. *British Journal of Social Work* 30 pp703–20.

James, A and Prout, A (eds) (2003) *Constructing and reconstructing childhood*. (2nd edition). London: RoutledgeFalmer.

James, J, Gosho, C and Watson Wohl, R. (1979): The relationship between female criminality and drug use: Substance Use & Misuse. *The International Journal of the Addictions* Volume 14 Issue 2 J_4 pp215–29

Jarvis, T, Tebbutt, J, Mattick, R and Shand, F (2005) *Treatment approaches for drug and alcohol dependence.* (2nd edition). Chichester: John Wiley & Sons.

Jeffrey, C (1992) The relation of judgement, personal involvement, and experience in the audit of bank loans. *The Accounting Review,* Volume 67, Number 4 (October), pp802–19.

Johns, R (2007) Critical commentary: Who decides now? Protecting and empowering vulnerable adults who lose the capacity to make decisions for themselves. *British Journal of Social Work* 37(3) pp557–64.

Johnson, I (2008) 'Baby P effect': More children now being removed from families by social workers. *Daily Telegraph* 6 December.

Journal of Epidemiology and Community Health (2003) 57 pp488–92; doi:10.1136/jech.57.7.488Public health policy and practice. *Mental health in Northern Ireland: Have 'the troubles' made it worse?*

Keenan, EK (2007) Patterns of interaction: Conceptualising the cross-roads between social structures, interpersonal actions and psychological well-being in *Smith College Studies in Social Work* 77(1) pp69–88.

Kelly, J (2005) *The great mortality, an intimate history of the black death, the most devastating plague of all time.* New York: Harper Collins.

Kempe, H, Silverman, F, Steele, B, Droegemueller, W and Silver, H (1962) The battered child syndrome. *Journal of the American Medical Association* 181(1) pp17–24.

Kemshall, H (1996) *Good practice in risk assessment and risk management.* London: Jessica Kingsley.

Kemshall, H (1997) *Good practice in risk assessment: Key themes for protection, rights and responsibilities.* London: Jessica Kingsley.

Kemshall, H (2003) The community management of high risk offenders. *Prison Service Journal,* March.

Kemshall, H (2007) Risk assessment and management: An overview in Lishman, J (ed) *Handbook for practice learning in social work and social care.* (2nd edition). London: Jessica Kingsley.

Kendell, RE in Heller, T, Reynolds, J, Gomm, R, Muston, R and Pattison, S (eds) (1996) *Mental health matters.* London: Macmillan/The Open University.

Kilbrandon Report (1964) Cmnd 2306. Edinburgh: Secretary of State for the Home Department/ Scottish Education Department.

Kilbrandon, The Hon. Lord (1966) Children in trouble. *British Journal of Criminology* 6(2) pp112–22.

Kliewer, SP and Saultz, J (2006) *Healthcare and spirituality.* Abingdon: Radcliffe Publishing Ltd.

Kohli, R (2006) *Social work with unaccompanied asylum seeking children*. Basingstoke: Palgrave Macmillan.

Kohli, RKS and Mitchell, F (eds) (2007) *Working with unaccompanied asylum seeking children: Issues for policy and practice*. London: Jessica Kingsley.

Koons, BA, Burrows, JD, Morash, M and Bynum, T (1997) Expert and offender perceptions of program elements linked to successful outcomes for incarcerated women. *Crime and Delinquency* 43 pp512–32

Koprowska, J (2008) *Communication and interpersonal skills in social work*. (2nd edition). Exeter: Learning Matters.

Kottow, MH (2003) The vulnerable and the susceptible. *Bioethics* 17(5–6) pp460–71.

Kraemer, S and Roberts, J (eds) (1996) *The politics of attachment: Towards a secure society*. London: Free Association Books.

Kristiansen, K, Vehmas, S and Shakespeare, T (eds) (2008) *Arguing about disability: Philosophical perspectives 1*. Abingdon: Routledge.

Kroll, B and Taylor, A (2003) *Parental substance misuse and child welfare*. London: Jessica Kingsley.

Kurrle, S (2001) The role of the medical practitioner, in Pritchard, J (ed) *Good practice with vulnerable adults*. London: Jessica Kingsley.

Laming, H (2003) *The Victoria Climbié Inquiry Report. Cm5730*. London: The Stationery Office.

Laming, H (2009) *The protection of children in England: A progress report*. London: The Stationery Office.

Lerner, G (1977) *Why history matters*. New York. Oxford University Press in H. Hendrick (ed) (2005) *Child welfare and social policy: An essential reader*. Bristol: The Policy Press. p11.

Leyland, AH (2004) Increasing Inequalities in premature mortality in Great Britain. *Journal of Epidemol Community Health* 2004 58 pp296–302.

Lipton, DS (1999) at **www.crimereduction.homeoffice.gov.uk/workingoffenders/ workingoffenders1.htm** (accessed 17 October 2009).

Lishman, J (2005) 'The Case for Change'. Unpublished Paper. School of Applied Social Studies. The Robert Gordon University, Aberdeen.

Lishman, J (ed) (2007) *Handbook for practice learning in social work and social care – knowledge and theory*. London: Jessica Kingsley.

Lishman, J (2009) Personal and professional development in Adams, R, Dominelli, L, and Payne, M. *Social work: Themes, issues and critical debates*. (3rd edition). London: Jessica Kingsley.

Littlewood, R and Lipsedge, M (2007) *Aliens and alienists*. London: Kindle.

Lymbery, M (2007) *Social work with older people – context, policy and practice.* London: Sage.

Lynch, MA (1985) Child Abuse before Kempe: An Historical Literature Review. *Child Abuse and Neglect* 9 pp7–15.

Macdonald, K and Macdonald, G (1999) Perceptions of Risk in Parsloe, P (ed) *Risk assessment in social work and social care.* London: Jessica Kingsley.

Marris, P (1996) *The politics of uncertainty: Attachment in private and public life.* London: Routledge.

Marshall, TH (1976) The Right to Welfare in Timms, N and Watson, N (eds) *Talking about welfare.* London: Routledge & Kegan Paul.

Maruna, S (2000) Desistance from crime and offender rehabilitation: A tale of two research literatures. *Offender Programs Report* 4(1) pp1–13.

Maslow, A (1968) *Towards a psychology of being.* New York: John Wiley & Sons.

Maslow, A (1970) *Motivation and personality.* (2nd edition). New York: Harper and Row.

Maslow, AH (1943) A theory of human motivation. *Psychological Review* 50(4) pp370–96.

Mason, KL (2008) Cyber-bullying: A preliminary assessment for school personnel. *Psychology in the Schools* 45(4) pp323–48.

Maud, R and Webster, J (2009) Improving nutrition for older people in hospital by assessing current practice. *Nursing Times.* **www.nursingtimes.net/improving-nutrition-for-older-people-in-hospital-by-assessing-current-practice/1987795. article**

Maxwell, M (1984) *The Alcoholics Anonymous experience: a close-up view for professionals.* New York: McGraw-Hill.

McDonald, A (2010) *Social work with older people.* Bristol: The Policy Press.

McGuire, J (ed) (1995) *What works: Reducing reoffending.* Chichester: John Wiley & Sons.

McIntosh, J and McKeganey, N (2002) *Beating the dragon.* Harlow: Pearson Education.

McLean, T (2007) Interdisciplinary Practice in Lishman, J (ed) *Handbook for practice learning in social work and social care: Knowledge and theory.* pp322–43. (2nd edition). London: Jessica Kingsley.

McMurran, M (1994) *The psychology of addiction.* London: Taylor & Francis.

McWhirter, J and Mir, H (eds) (2008) *The essential guide to working with young people about drugs and alcohol.* London: Drugscope.

Mead, GH (1934/1962) *Mind, self and society.* Chicago, IL: University of Chicago Press.

Mencap (2009) *Death by indifference,* on-line at **www.mencap.org.uk**

Mental Welfare Commission for Scotland (2008) *Justice denied*. Edinburgh: MWC Scotland.

Mental Welfare Commission for Scotland and Social Work Inspection Agency (2004) *Investigations into Scottish Borders Council and NHS Borders Services for People with Learning Disabilities: Joint Statement from the Mental Welfare Commission and the Social Work Services Inspectorate*. Edinburgh: MWCS.

Mirvis, PH (1997) 'Soul Work' in organizations. *Organisational Science* 82 pp193–206.

Mo, R, Bernard, M and Phillips, J (2009) *Critical issues in social work with older people*. Basingstoke: Palgrave Macmillan.

Mooney, G and Scott, G (eds) (2005) *Exploring social policy in the 'new' Scotland*. Bristol: The Policy Press.

Moore, B (1996) *Risk assessment: A practitioner's guide to predicting harmful behaviour*. London: Whiting and Birch Ltd.

Morgan, K (ed) (1992) *Gerontology: Responding to an ageing society*. London: Jessica Kingsley.

Morgan, S (2007) *Working with risk*. Brighton: Pavilion Publishing.

Morrison, J date unknown. *BrainyQuote*. Available at: **www.brainyquote.com/quotes/authors/j/jim_morrison.html**

Moss, B (2008) *Communication skills for health and social care*. London: Sage.

Mullaly, B (2007) *The new structural social work*. (3rd edition). Ontario: Oxford University Press.

Munro, E. (1996) Avoidable and unavoidable mistakes in child protection work. *British Journal of Social Work* 26 pp793–808.

Munro, E (2005) What Tools do we Need to Improve Identification of Child Abuse? *Child Abuse Review* 14 pp374–88.

Munro, E (2008a) Lessons learnt, boxes ticked, families ignored. *Independent on Sunday* 16 November: p45.

Munro, E (2008b) *Effective child protection*. (2nd edition). London: Sage.

Murray-Parkes, C, Stevenson-Hinde, J and Marris, P (eds) (1991) *Attachment across the life-cycle*. London: Routledge.

National Statistics Online, see **www.statistics.gov.uk**

The National Offender Management Service (NOMS) (2005) *Strategy for the management and treatment of problematic drug users within the correctional services*. London: Ministry of Justice.

National Treatment Agency for Substance Misuse, (2006) *Models of care for treatment of adult drug misusers: update 2006*. London: National Treatment Agency for Substance Misuse. Available at: **www.nta.nhs.uk/publications/documents/nta_modelsofcare_update_2006_moc3.pdf**

Nevitt, D (1977) Demand and need in Heisler, H (ed) *Foundations of social administration.* Basingstoke: Macmillan.

Newman, J and Yeats, N (eds.) (2008) *Social justice: Welfare, crime and society.* Maidenhead. Open University Press/McGraw-Hill Education.

Newman, T and Blackburn, S (2002) *Transitions in the lives of children and young people: Resilience factors.* Edinburgh: Scottish Executive Education Department.

Norris, D (1990) *Violence against social workers: implications for practice.* London: Jessica Kingsley.

Northern Ireland Executive (1987) *Mental Health (Northern Ireland) Order 1987.* Belfast: NIE

Northern Ireland Office (NIO) (2008) *Public Protection Arrangements: Northern Ireland (PPANI): Guidance to Agencies.* Belfast: NIO.

Nutt, D, King, L, Saulsbury, W and Blakemore, C (2007) Development of a rational scale to assess the harm of drugs of potential misuse. *The Lancet,* vol. 369, issue 9566 pp1047–53.

O'Brien, S, Hammond, H and McKinnon, M (2003) *Report of the Caleb Ness Inquiry.* Edinburgh: Edinburgh and Lothian's Child Protection Committee.

Office of the First Minister and Deputy First Minister (OFMDFM) (NI) (2006) *Our children and young people – our pledge. A ten-year strategy for children and young people in Northern Ireland.* Belfast. OFMDFM.

Ofsted, Healthcare Commission, HM Inspectorate of Constabulary (2008) *Joint Area Review: Haringey Children's Services Authority Area.* London: Ofsted.

Oliver, M (2009) *Understanding disability: From theory to practice.* (2nd revised edition). Basingstoke: Palgrave Macmillan.

Orchard, H (ed) (2001) *Spirituality in health care contexts.* London: Jessica Kingsley.

O'Reilly, D and Stevenson, M (2003) Mental Health in Northern Ireland: Have 'the Troubles' made it worse? *Journal of Epidemiology and Community Health* 57(7) pp488–92.

Orford, J (1987) Alcohol problems in the family in Heller, T, Gott, M and Jeffrey, C (eds). *Drug use and misuse. A Reader.* Chichester: John Wiley & Sons.

Oxford University Press (2007) *Shorter Oxford English Dictionary.* (6th edition). Oxford. Oxford University Press.

Parker, R (1981) Tending and social policy in Goldberg, E and Hatch, S (eds) *A new look at the personal social services,* London: Policy Studies Institute.

Parton, N (2006) *Safeguarding childhood: Early intervention and surveillance in a late modern society.* Basingstoke: Palgrave Macmillan.

Parton, N (2008) Changes in the form of knowledge in social work: From the 'Social' to the 'Informational'? *British Journal of Social Work* 38 pp253–69.

Pascoe-Watson, G (2008) *Baby P: The Sun marches on Number 10.* The *Sun* Newsgroup. 27 November.

Patrick, H (2006) *Mental health, incapacity and the law in Scotland.* Edinburgh: Tottel.

Patsios, D (2006) Pensioners, poverty and social exclusion in Gordon, D, Levitas, R and Pantazis, C (eds) *Poverty and Social Exclusion in Britain: The Millennium Survey* pp431–58). Bristol: The Policy Press.

Pavot, W and Diener, E (2008) The satisfaction with life scale and the emerging construct of life satisfaction. *The Journal of Positive Psychology*, Column 3, Issue 2 April pp137–52.

Payne, S, Horn, S and Relf, M (2000) *Loss and bereavement.* Health Psychology Book Series. Buckingham: Open University Press.

Peace, SM, Kellaher, L and Holland, C (2005) *Environment and identity in later life.* Buckingham: Open University Press.

Pearson, FS and Lipton, DS (1999) The effectiveness of educational and vocational programs: CDATE meta-analyses. Paper presented at the annual meeting of the *American Society of Criminology*. Toronto, Canada.

Phillips, A and Taylor, B (2009) *On kindness.* London: Hamish Hamilton.

Phillips, J, Ray, M and Marshall, M (2006) *Social work with older people.* Basingstoke: Palgrave Macmillan.

Phillipson, C (1998) *Reconstructing old age – new agendas in social theory and practice*, London: Sage.

Philp, AF and Timms, N (1962) *The problem of the problem family.* London: Family Service Units.

Porporino, FJ and Robinson, D (1992) The correctional benefits of education. *Journal of Correctional Education* 43, no. 2 (June): pp92–98. (EJ 445 423).

Postle, K (2002) Working 'between the idea and the reality: ambiguities and tension in care manager' work. *British Journal of Social Work* 32 pp335–51.

Pratt, D, Piper, M, Appleby, L, Webb, R and Shaw, J (2006) Suicide in recently released prisoners: a population-based cohort study. *The Lancet*, 368 (9530) pp119–23.

Pratt, J (2000) Dangerousness and modern society in Brown, M and Pratt, J (eds) *Dangerous offenders: Punishment and social order.* London: Routledge.

Pritchard, J (2003a) *Training manual for working with older people in residential and day care settings.* London: Jessica Kingsley.

Pritchard, J (2003b) *Support groups for older people who have been abused: beyond existing.* London: Jessica Kingsley.

Public Services Ombudsman (2009) *Six lives: the provision of public services to people with learning disabilities.* London: The Stationery Office.

Pugh, R (2007) Variations in Registration on Child Protection Registers. *British Journal of Social Work* 37(1) pp5–21.

Putting People First (2009) *A shared vision and commitment to the transformation of adult social care.* London: HM Government.

Qureshi, H and Henwood, M (2000) *Older people's definitions of quality services.* York: Joseph Rowntree Foundation.

Radford, L and Hester, M (2006) *Mothering through domestic violence.* London: Jessica Kingsley.

Raistrick, D, Heather, N and Godfrey, C (2006) *Review of the effectiveness of treatment for alcohol problems.* London: National Treatment Agency for Substance Misuse. Available at: **www.nta.nhs.uk/publications/documents/nta_review_of_the_ effectiveness_of_treatment_for_alcohol_problems_fullreport_2006_alcohol2.pdf**

Rattansi, A (2007) *Racism: A very short introduction.* Oxford: Oxford University Press.

Rawls, J (1999) *A theory of justice* (revised edition). Cambridge, MA: Harvard University Press.

Ray, M, Bernard, M and Phillips, J (2009) *Critical issues in social work with older people.* Basingstoke: Palgrave Macmillan.

Raynes, N, Temple, B, Glenister, C and Coulthard, L (2001) *Quality at home for older people: involving service users in defining home care specifications.* Bristol/York: The Policy Press/Joseph Rowntree Foundation.

Reder, P and Duncan, S (1999) *Lost innocents: A follow-up study of fatal child abuse.* London: Routledge.

Reder, P and Duncan, S (2003) Understanding Communication in Child Protection Networks. *Child Abuse Review* 12 pp82–100.

Reder, P and Duncan, S (2004) Making the most of the Victoria Climbié Inquiry Report. *Child Abuse Review* 13 pp95–115.

Reder, P, Duncan, S and Gray, M (1993) *Beyond blame: Child abuse tragedies revisited.* London: Routledge.

Reder, P and Lucey, C (eds) (1995) *Assessment of parenting: Psychiatric and psychological contributions.* London: Routledge.

Reder, P, McClure, M and Jolley, A (eds) (2000) *Family matters: Interfaces between child and adult mental health.* London: Routledge.

Roberts, E (1996) Women and families: an oral history, 1940–1970. Oxford: Blackwell.

Rothwell-Murray, C (2000) *Commissioning domiciliary care: A practical guide to purchasing services.* Abingdon: Radcliffe Publishing.

Royal College of Psychiatrists and The Royal College of Physicians (2000) *Drugs: Dilemmas and choices.* London: Gaskell.

Russell, B (1991) *History of western philosophy*. London: Routledge.

Russell, M (1998) *Beyond ramps: Disability at the end of the social contract*. Monroe: Common Courage Press.

Rutter, M (1966) *Children of sick parents: An environmental and psychiatric study*. Institute of Psychiatry. Maudsley Monographs 16. London: Oxford University Press.

Rutter, M and Quinton, D (1984) Parental Psychiatric Disorder: Effects on Children. *Psychological Medicine* 14 pp853–80.

Rutter, M (1985) Resilience in the Face of Adversity. *British Journal of Psychiatry* 147 pp598–611.

Rutter, M (1995) Psychosocial Adversity: Risk, Resilience and Recovery. *Southern African Journal of Child and Adolescent Psychiatry* 7(2) pp75–88.

Shlonsky, A and Wagner, D (2005) The next step: integrating actuarial risk assessment and clinical judgment into an evidence-based practice framework in CPS case management. *Children and Youth Services Review*, 27(3) pp409–27.

Scottish Executive (2000) *The MacLean Committee: Report of the committee on serious violent and sexual offenders*. Edinburgh: Scottish Executive.

Scottish Executive (2000a) *Risk assessment framework and guidance RA1–4*. Edinburgh: Scottish Executive.

Scottish Executive (2001) *The Scottish strategy for victims*. Edinburgh: Scottish Executive.

Scottish Executive (2001a) *New directions: Review of the Mental Health (Scotland) Act 1984*. Edinburgh: Scottish Executive.

Scottish Executive (2001b) *The same as you? A review of services for people with learning disability in Sotland*. Edinburgh: Scottish Executive.

Scottish Executive (2002a) *It's everyone's job to make sure I'm alright: Literature Review*. Edinburgh: Scottish Executive.

Scottish Executive (2002b) *Serious violent and sexual offenders: the use of risk assessment tools in Scotland*. Edinburgh: Scottish Executive.

Scottish Executive (2002c) *National Care Standards for Scotland's Youth Justice Services*. Edinburgh: Scottish Executive.

Scottish Executive (2003) *Getting our priorities right: good practice guidance for working with children and families affected by substance misuse*. Edinburgh: The Stationery Office.

Scottish Executive (2004) *Investigations into Scottish Borders Council and NHS Borders Services for people with learning disabilities: Joint Statement from the Mental Welfare Commission and the Social Work Services Inspectorate*. Edinburgh: Scottish Executive. Available at: **www.scotland.gov.uk/Publications/2004/05/19333/36718**

Scottish Executive (2004a) *National objectives for social work services in the criminal justice system standards for social enquiry reports and associated court services.* Edinburgh: Scottish Executive.

Scottish Executive (2005) *Effective interventions unit: Integrated care pathways guide 9: single shared assessment for drugs users.* Edinburgh: Scottish Executive. Available at: **www.scotland.gov.uk/Publications/2005/03/20841/54394**

Scottish Executive (2005a) *Getting it right for every child: Proposals for action.* Edinburgh: Scottish Executive.

Scottish Executive (2005b) *Getting it right for every child: Supporting Paper 1: The process and content of an integrated framework and the implications for implementation.* Edinburgh: Scottish Executive. Available at: **www.scotland.gov.uk/ Publications/2005/07/25112327/23305**

Scottish Executive (2005c) *Child protection committees.* Edinburgh: Scottish Executive.

Scottish Executive (2005d) *Reserved functions of the social worker.* Edinburgh: Scottish Executive.

Scottish Executive (2005e) *The need for social work intervention.* Edinburgh: Scottish Executive.

Scottish Executive (2006) *Circular No JD/15/2006: Implementation of the multi agency public protection arrangements (MAPPA) in Scotland.* Edinburgh: Scottish Executive.

Scottish Executive (2006a) *Changing Lives. Report of the 21st century social work review.* Edinburgh: Scottish Executive. Available at: **www.scotland.gov.uk/Resource/ Doc/91931/0021949.pdf**

Scottish Executive (2006) *Mental health delivery plan.* Edinburgh Scottish Government.

Scottish Government (2007) *Adult support and protection (Scotland) Act 2007: A review of literature on effective interventions that prevent and respond to harm against adults.* Edinburgh: Scottish Government.

Scottish Government (2007a) *Mental health in Scotland: closing the gaps – making a difference.* Edinburgh: Scottish Government.

Scottish Government (2007b) *Towards a mentally flourishing Scotland: Discussion paper on mental health improvement 2008–2011.* Edinburgh: Scottish Government.

Scottish Government (2008a) *Adults with incapacity (Scotland) Act 2000: Code of practice for continuing and welfare attorneys.* Edinburgh: Scottish Government.

Scottish Government (2008b) *Adults with incapacity (Scotland) Act 2000 Code of Practice – Access to funds.* Edinburgh: Scottish Government.

Scottish Government (2008c) *Adults with incapacity (Scotland) Act 2000: Code of Practice: For supervisory bodies under part 4 of the Act.* Edinburgh: Scottish Government.

Scottish Government (2008d) *Adults with incapacity (Scotland) Act 2000: Code of Practice: For managers of authorised establishments under part 4 of the Act.* Edinburgh: Scottish Government.

Scottish Government (2008e) *Adults with incapacity (Scotland) Act 2000:Code of Practice: For persons authorised under intervention orders and guardians.* Edinburgh: Scottish Government.

Scottish Government (2008f) *Adults with incapacity (Scotland) Act 2000: Code of Practice: For local authorities exercising functions under the 2000 Act.* Edinburgh: Scottish Government.

Scottish Government (2008g) *MAPPA Guidance.* Available at: **www.scotland.gov.uk/ Publications/2008/04/18144823/45**

Scottish Government (2008h) *National management manual for the effective delivery of accredited offending behaviour programmes in the community.* Edinburgh: Scottish Executive.

Scottish Government (2008i) from Version 4 of the MAPPA *Guidance with covering justice and communities circular JD/3/2008 and NHS CEL (2007).* Edinburgh: Scottish Executive.

Scottish Government (2008j) *Protecting Scotland's communities: Fair, fast and flexible justice.* Edinburgh: Scottish Executive.

Scottish Government (2008k) *Changing Scotland's relationship with alcohol: a discussion paper on our strategic approach.* Edinburgh: Scottish Government.

Scottish Government (2008l) *The road to recovery: a new approach to tackling Scotland's drug problem.* Edinburgh: Scottish Government. Available at: **www. scotland.gov.uk/Publications/2008/05/22161610/0**

Scottish Government (2009a) *Adult support and protection (Scotland) Act 2007: Code of Practice.* Edinburgh: Scottish Government.

Scottish Government (2009b) *Protection of vulnerable groups (Scotland) Act 2007: Draft guidance.* Edinburgh: Scottish Government.

Scottish Home and Health Department and Scottish Education Department (SHHD/SED) (1964) *Report on children and young persons, Scotland (Cmnd 2306) (The Kilbrandon Report).* Edinburgh: SHHD and SED.

Scottish Law Commission (1995) *Report on incapable adults (Scotland Law Com No 151).* Edinburgh: HMSO.

Scottish Recovery Network (2007) *Realising recovery: A national framework for learning and training in recovery focused practice.* Edinburgh: NHS for Scotland

Searle, JR (1995) *The construction of social reality.* London: Allen Lane/Penguin.

Secretary of State for Social Services (SSSS) (1974) *Report of the Inquiry into the care and supervision of Maria Colwell.* London: HMSO.

Secretary of State for Social Services (SSSS) (1988) *Report of the inquiry into child abuse in Cleveland*. Cm413. London: HMSO.

Seligman, MEP (1975) *Helplessness: On depression, development and death*. San Francisco, CA: W.H Freeman & Co.

Shapiro, H (2007) *The essential guide to drugs and alcohol.* London: DrugScope.

Shapiro, H and Barnes, M (2008) How do drugs affect children and the family? in Shapiro, H (ed) *The essential student reader on drugs.* London: DrugScope.

Sheppard, M (2006) *Social work and social exclusion: The idea of practice*. Aldershot: Ashgate.

Siegrist, J and Marmot, M (eds) (2006) *Social inequalities in health: New evidence and policy implications*. Oxford: Oxford University Press.

Simon, HA (1956) Rational choice and the structure of the environment. *Psychological Review* 63 pp129–38.

Smith, C (2001) Trust and confidence: Possibilities for social work in high modernity. *British Journal of Social Work* 31(2) pp287–305.

Smith, R (2010) *A universal child?* Basingstoke: Palgrave Macmillan.

Social Exclusion Unit (2001) *Preventing social exclusion*. London: The Stationery Office.

Social Work Services Group (SWSG) (1991) *National objectives and standards for social work services in the criminal justice system,* Edinburgh: The Scottish Office.

Social Work Services Inspectorate (SWSI) (2005) *Review of the Management Arrangements of Colyn Evans by Fife Constabulary and Fife Council*. Edinburgh: Scottish Executive.

Sonnenschein, E and Brody, JA (2005) Effects of population aging on proportionate mortality from heart disease and cancer, U.S.2000–2050. *The Journal of Gerontology Series B: Psychology Science and Social Science* 60 pp110–12.

Spratt, T (2001) The Influence of Child Protection Orientation on Child Welfare Practice. *British Journal of Social Work* 31 pp933–54.

Stalker, K (2003) Managing risk and uncertainty in social work: A literature review. *Journal of Social Work* 3(2) pp211–33.

Sterling Burnett, H (2009) Understanding the Precautionary Principle and its Threat to Human Welfare. *Social Philosophy and Policy* 26 pp378–410.

Straussner, SLA and Fewell, CH (2006) *Impact of substance abuse on children and families: Research and Practice Implications*. New York: Haworth Press.

Stuart-Hamilton, I (2006) *The psychology of ageing.* (4th edition). London: Jessica Kingsley.

Sullivan, T and Farrell, A (2002). Risk factors in Essau, C (ed) *Substance abuse and dependence in adolescence: epidemiology, risk factors and treatment*. Hove: Brunner-Routledge.

Sunday Herald, The (2004) The Legacy of Miss X: Investigation: The shocking failure to help. *Sunday Herald* 9 May by Stephen. Glasgow: Herald Scotland.

Swain, J and French, S (2008) *Disability on equal terms*. London: Sage.

Swain, J, French, S, Barnes, C and Thomas, C (eds) (2004) *Disabling barriers – enabling environment.* (2nd edition). London: Sage.

Taylor, G (2007) *Ideology and welfare*. Basingstoke: Palgrave Macmillan.

Thompson, N (2002) *People skills.* (2nd edition). Basingstoke: Palgrave Macmillan.

Thompson, N (2003) *Communication and language*. Basingstoke: Palgrave Macmillan.

Thompson, N (2006) *Anti-discriminatory practice.* (4th revised edition). Basingstoke: Palgrave Macmillan.

Thorley, A (1980) Medical responses to problem drinking. *Medicine,* 3rd series, vol 35 pp1816–22.

Tisdall, EKM, David, JM, Hill, M and Prout, A (eds) (2006) *Children, young people and social inclusion: Participation for what?* Bristol: The Policy Press.

Titterton, M (2004) *Risk and risk taking in health and social welfare.* London: Jessica Kingsley.

Todd, M, Hothersall, SJ and Owen, K (*Forthcoming*) in Yuill, C and Gibson, A (*Forthcoming*): *Sociology and social work*. London: Sage.

Townsend, P (1954) Measuring poverty. *British Journal of Sociology* 5(2) pp130–7.

Townsend, P (1979) *Poverty in the United Kingdom: A survey of household resources and standards of living.* London: Penguin.

Tudor, K (1996) *Mental health promotion: Paradigms and practice*. London: Routledge.

Tunnard, J (2002a) *Parental drug misuse – a review of impact and intervention studies.* Totnes: Research into Practice.

Tunnard, J (2002b) *Parental problem drinking and its impact on children*. Totnes: Research into Practice.

Uhlenberg, P 1(978) Changing configurations of the life course in Hareven, TK (ed) *Transitions: The family and the life course in historical perspective* pp65–697. New York: Academic Press.

Velleman, R (1992) *Counselling for alcohol problems*. London: Sage.

Victor, C (2005) *The social context of ageing: A textbook of gerontology*. London: Routledge.

Vygotsky, L (1978) *Mind in society: The development of higher psychological processes.* Cambridge, MA: Harvard University Press.

Wade, J, Mitchell, F and Graeme, B (2006) *Unaccompanied asylum seeking children: The response of social work services.* London: British Association of Adoption and Fostering (BAAF).

Walker, A (1993) Intergenerational relations and welfare restructing: The social construction of an intergenerational problem in Bengtson, Vl and Achenbaum, AW (eds) *The changing contact across generations* pp141–65 New York: Aldine De Gruyter.

Walker, S and Beckett, C (2004) *Social work assessment and intervention.* Lyme Regis: Russell House Publishing.

Ward, A (2008) *Adults with incapacity legislation.* Edinburgh: W. Green.

Weber, M (1947) *The theory of social and economic organization.* London: Collier Macmillan.

Webster, CD, Douglas, KS, Eaves, D and Hart, S. (1997) *HCR-20: Assessing Risk for Violence (Version 2).* Mental Health, Law and Policy Institute. Vancouver: Simon Fraser University.

Webster, C.D and Hucker, S.J (2007) *Violence Risk: Assessment and Management.* Chichester: WileyBlackwell.

Weinberg, A, Williamson, J, Challes, D, Hughes, J (2003) What do Care Managers Do? A study of Working Practice in Older People Service. *British Journal of Social Work* 33 pp901–9.

Weir, A and Douglas, A (1999) *Child Protection and Adult Mental health: Conflict of Interest?* Oxford: Reed.

Welsh Assembly Government (2002) *Children and Young People: A Framework for Partnership.* Cardiff: Welsh Assembly Government.

Welsh Assembly Government (2004) *Children and Young People: Rights to Action.* Cardiff: Welsh Assembly Government.

Welshman, J (2007) *From Transmitted Deprivation to Social Exclusion: Policy, Poverty and Parenting.* Bristol. The Policy Press.

White, S, Hall, C and Peckover, S (2009) The Descriptive Tyranny of the Common Assessment Framework: Technologies of Categorization and Professional Practice in Child Welfare. *British Journal of Social Work* 39 pp1197–1217.

WHO (2007) *International classification of diseases and related health problems,* 10th revision, mental and behavioral disorders (F00-F99). London and New York: WHO.

Williams, P (2009) *Social work with people with learning difficulties.* (2nd edition). Exeter: Learning Matters.

Wilson, G and Daly, M (2007) Shaping the Future of Mental Health Legislation in Northern Ireland: The Impact of Service User and Professional Social Work Discourses. *British Journal of Social Work* 37 pp423–39.

Wilson, K, Ruch, G, Lymbery, M, Cooper, A, with Becker, S, Brammer, A, Clawson, R, Littlechild, B, Paylor, I and Smith, R, (2008), *Social Work – An introduction to contemporary practice*. Harlow: Pearson/Longman.

Wolfensberger, W (1972) *Normalisation*. New York. NIMH.

Worden, JW (1991) *Grief counselling and grief therapy: A handbook for the mental health practitioner.* (2nd edition). New York: Springer.

van Wormer, K, Besthorn, FH and Keefe, T (2007) *Human behaviour and the social environment: Macro level-groups, communities and organizations*. Oxford: Oxford University Press.

Wright, Stephen G (2005), *Reflections on Spirituality and Health*. London: Whurr Publishers

Zimbardo, P (2007) *The Lucifer Effect: How Good People Turn Evil*. London: Ebury/ Random House Publishing.

Index